THE INTERNATIONAL MIGRATION OF WOMEN

THE INTERNATIONAL MIGRATION OF WOMEN

Andrew R. Morrison, Maurice Schiff,
and Mirja Sjöblom, Editors

**A copublication of the World Bank
and Palgrave Macmillan**

© 2008 The International Bank for Reconstruction and Development / The World Bank
1818 H Street, NW
Washington, DC 20433
Telephone: 202-473-1000
Internet: www.worldbank.org
E-mail: feedback@worldbank.org

1 2 3 4 10 09 08 07

A copublication of The World Bank and Palgrave Macmillan.

Printed in the USA.
Palgrave Macmillan
Houndmills, Basingstoke, Hampshire RG21 6XS and
175 Fifth Avenue, New York, NY 10010
Companies and representatives throughout the world
A catalogue record for this book is available from the British Library.

Palgrave Macmillan is the global academic imprint of the Palgrave Macmillan division of St. Martin's
Press, LLC and of Palgrave Macmillan Ltd.

Macmillan® is a registered trademark in the United States, United Kingdom, and other countries. Palgrave® is a
registered trademark in the European Union and other countries.

This volume is a product of the staff of the International Bank for Reconstruction and Development / The World
Bank. The findings, interpretations, and conclusions expressed in this volume do not necessarily reflect the views of
the Executive Directors of The World Bank or the governments they represent.

The World Bank does not guarantee the accuracy of the data included in this work. The boundaries, colors,
denominations, and other information shown on any map in this work do not imply any judgment on the part of
The World Bank concerning the legal status of any territory or the endorsement or acceptance of such boundaries.

Cover design: Tomoko Hirata/World Bank
Cover photo: Jim Jurica/iStockphoto

Softcover:
ISBN: 978-0-8213-7227-2
eISBN: 978-0-8213-7228-9
DOI: 10.1596/978-0-8213-7227-2

Hardcover:
ISBN: 978-0-8213-7257-9
DOI: 10.1596/978-0-8213-7257-9

Library of Congress Cataloging-in-Publication Data

The international migration of women / editors, Andrew R. Morrison, Maurice Schiff and Mirja Sjöblom.
    p. cm.
    Includes bibliographical references and index.
    ISBN 978-0-8213-7227-2 — ISBN 978-0-8213-7228-9 (electronic) 1. Women immigrants. 2. Women alien labor.
3. Women—Economic conditions. 4. Emigration and immigration—Economic aspects. 5. Brain drain. I. Morrison,
Andrew R. II. Schiff, Maurice. III. Sjöblom, Mirja, 1981–
    JV6347.I58 2007
    305.48'96912—dc22

2007036239

CONTENTS

Figures

Tables

FOREWORD

Recent years have seen the rapid growth of international migration and remittances as well as an increase in research and policy discussions on this topic. This dialogue has highlighted the development impact of migration and drawn attention to such economic issues as job creation in sending countries, improvements to temporary work arrangements, and increased facilitation of the flow of remittances.

Several important policy initiatives in recent years have deepened this dialogue. In 2004 the European Union launched the AENEAS program, which provides financial and technical assistance to non-European countries in the area of migration and asylum. In 2005 the United Nations Global Commission on International Migration was established to facilitate policy dialogue on migration. In 2006 the first High Level Dialogue on International Migration was held at the United Nations headquarters. This resulted in the creation of the Global Forum on Migration and Development, an informal, voluntary, state-led forum for the discussion of migration and development issues. The forum first met in Brussels in 2007. Regional development banks have also begun to tackle the issue, as have governments of some source and destination countries and a number of research institutes and individual scholars.

The World Bank has also contributed to the policy dialogue on international migration with several research volumes, including *International Migration, Remittances, and the Brain Drain; Global Economic Prospects 2006: Economic Implications of Remittances and Migration;* and the recently released *International Migration, Economic Development, and Policy.*

However, recent research—with a few notable exceptions—has not paid sufficient attention to gender differences in migration patterns, motivations, and impacts.

This is a major omission. Women now account for nearly half of all international migration. Theoretical and empirical models that omit gendered determinants and impacts of migration are missing key elements of the story. Women's roles in destination labor markets and in remittance flows—to cite just two examples—are crucial to understanding the development impacts of international migration.

This volume, prepared by the World Bank's Gender and Development Unit in collaboration with the Development Research Group, surveys the state of our knowledge and provides new research on the gendered determinants and impacts of migration and remittances as well as on the patterns of labor market participation of women migrants. It also sketches a road map for future research on gender and international migration.

This research on women and international migration illustrates the type of analytical work that can shape policies to economically empower women migrants as well as women left behind by male migration. It is our hope that such analysis will lead to policies that boost productivity, raise incomes, and improve welfare in both sending and receiving countries.

Sincerely,

Danny Leipziger
Vice President
Poverty Reduction and Economic Management (PREM) Network

ACKNOWLEDGMENTS

Many institutions and individuals have contributed to the successful completion of this book. The governments of Norway and Sweden provided funding to the World Bank Gender and Development Unit; some of this funding was used to finance this book. Special thanks are due to the chapter authors for their important contributions to the nascent literature on the international migration of women and development.

We are also grateful to international migration experts Graeme Hugo (University of Adelaide), Susan Martin (Georgetown University), J. Edward Taylor (University of California, Davis), and Michael White (Brown University) for their wise counsel on the topics that should be addressed in this volume; to peer reviewers Katharine Donato (Vanderbilt University), Jan O. Karlsson (former co-chair of the Global Commission on International Migration), Susan Martin (Georgetown University), Pierella Paci (World Bank), and Hania Zlotnik (United Nations Population Division) for their comments on draft chapters; and to two anonymous reviewers for helpful suggestions on improving the quality of the volume.

We are grateful to Jinu Koola for reviewing the volume and to Blanca Moreno-Dodson for her valuable suggestions. We would like to thank Stephen McGroarty, Nora Ridolfi, and Dina Towbin at the World Bank Office of the Publisher for their efficient supervision of the production process. Finally, we appreciate the efforts of Alejandra Viveros to disseminate this work.

CONTRIBUTORS

Peri Fletcher, Institute of Governmental Affairs, University of California, Davis

Juan Carlos Guzmán, Gender and Development Unit, Poverty Reduction and Economic Management Network, World Bank

Andrew R. Morrison, Gender and Development Unit, Poverty Reduction and Economic Management Network, World Bank

Ileana Cristina Neagu, International Trade Unit, Development Research Group, World Bank

Çağlar Özden, International Trade Unit, Development Research Group, World Bank

Lisa Pfeiffer, Department of Agricultural and Resource Economics, University of California, Davis

Susan Richter, Department of Agricultural and Resource Economics, University of California, Davis

Maurice Schiff, International Trade Unit, Development Research Group, World Bank; and Institute for the Study of Labor (IZA)

Mirja Sjöblom, International Trade Unit, Development Research Group, World Bank

J. Edward Taylor, Department of Agricultural and Resource Economics, University of California, Davis

ABBREVIATIONS

CCT	Conditional cash transfers
DESA	Department of Economic and Social Affairs (United Nations)
DID	Difference-in-difference estimation
ENHRUM	Mexico National Rural Household Survey (Encuesta Nacional a Hogares Rurales de México)
FCND	Food Consumption and Nutrition Division
FE	Fixed effect
FSU	Former Soviet Union
GATS	General Agreement on Trade in Services
GDP	Gross domestic product
GHC	Ghanaian cedis
GLSS 4	Ghana Living Standards Survey, round four
IFPRI	International Food Policy Research Institute
INEGI	Mexico's National Census Office (Instituto Nacional de Estadística, Geografía e Información)
IOM	International Organization for Migration
IRCA	Immigration Reform and Control Act (U.S.)
IV	Instrumental variable
IZA	Institute for the Study of Labor (Germany)
MMP	Mexican Migration Project
NAFTA	North American Free Trade Agreement
NELM	New economics of labor migration
OECD	Organisation for Economic Co-operation and Development
OLS	Ordinary least squares

PREM	Poverty Reduction and Economic Management
PSM	Propensity score matching
RE	Random effect
UN	United Nations
UNDP	United Nations Development Programme
UNFPA	United Nations Population Fund
WTO	World Trade Organization

OVERVIEW

Andrew R. Morrison, Maurice Schiff, and Mirja Sjöblom

International migration and its link to poverty and economic development have received increased attention in recent years, in large part due to the surge in international migration. Between 1960 and 2005 the number of international migrants in the world doubled, and in 2005 about 190 million people—roughly 3 percent of the world's population—lived outside their country of birth (United Nations 2006). Another reason for this increased interest has been the rapid growth in remittances, currently amounting to approximately $200 billion a year.[1]

The growing importance of this phenomenon led the World Bank to initiate the Research Program on International Migration and Development in 2004, with the aim of improving the meager data sets available on migration and examining issues such as the determinants and impact of international migration and remittances, the brain drain, temporary migration, and the relationships among migration, trade, and foreign direct investment. To date the research program has created several global databases (on bilateral migration, brain drain, and medical brain drain), designed household surveys with migration modules, and published two volumes—*International Migration, Remittances, and the Brain Drain* (Özden and Schiff 2006) and *International Migration, Economic Development, and Policy* (Özden and Schiff 2007)—as well as a number of articles. This volume is the third in this series of monographs.

The current share of women in the world's population of international migrants is close to half, and available evidence suggests that migration flows and their impacts are strongly gendered. Until recently, however, there has been a striking lack of gender analysis in the economics literature on international migration and development. To fill this lacuna, to improve our understanding of the links among gender, migration, and economic development, and to contribute to an informed policy debate, the World Bank initiated a number of studies on the international migration of women in December 2005. This volume presents key outputs of this analytical research program.

One of the most fundamental questions related to the study of women's migration concerns the extent to which women move across borders. The publication "Trends in Total Migrant Stock: The 2005 Revision" (United Nations 2006) estimates that women represented half of the world's migrant population in 2005—that is, approximately 95 million women. Despite the increased interest in women migrants, data on international migration remain surprisingly gender blind. Recent key additions to migration statistics, such as Docquier and Marfouk (2006) on skilled migration, Bhargava and Docquier (2006) on medical brain drain, and Parsons et al. (2007) on global bilateral migration stocks, are especially useful for analysts and policy makers. These data sets, however, do not contain any sex-disaggregated statistics at this time, although the World Bank is in the process of extending Docquier and Marfouk (2006) and Parsons et al. (2007) along gender dimensions.

Today the standard reference on sex-disaggregated migration statistics is the United Nations (UN) database on the stock of migrants, which covers most countries in the world for the period 1960–2005 (United Nations 2006). Overall, these data show that the percentage of international migrants who are women increased almost 3 percentage points, from 46.7 percent to 49.6 percent, between 1960 and 2005. Figure 1.1 shows the change in the stock of female migrants by region for this period.

The largest increases in the proportion of women during the time period were observed in Oceania (from 44 to 51 percent), Latin America and the Caribbean (from 45 to 50 percent), Africa (from 42 to 47 percent), and the former Soviet Union (FSU, from 48 to 58 percent).[2] The only region registering a drop in the share of female migrants was Asia (from 46 to 43 percent). Of the seven regions in figure 1.1, three (Europe, Oceania, and the FSU) have more female than male migrants, two (Latin America and the Caribbean and North America) have about the same number of female and male migrants, and two (Africa and Asia) have more male than female migrants, with a decline in the share of female migrants in Asia. The region with the lowest proportion of women migrants is Western Asia (the Middle East), where women only represent 38.4 percent of the migrant population (not shown in figure 1.1).[3] It is also interesting that the share of female migrants is substantially higher in developed than in developing countries (not shown in the figure). By 2005 there were more female than male migrants in developed countries, while the share of female migrants was 46 percent in developing countries (United Nations 2006). Overall, the UN data show that the proportion of women in the world's stock of migrants has increased steadily during

Figure 1.1. Proportion of Women in Migrant Stocks, by Region, 1960 and 2005

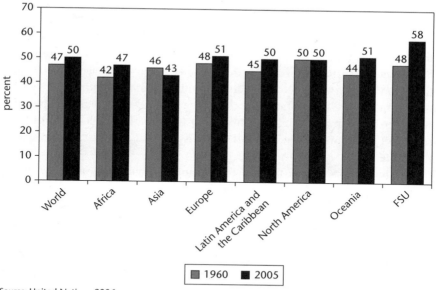

Source: United Nations 2006.

the past 45 years, but that their overall increase in share has been modest (about 6.6 percent over the 45-year period).

The problem with the UN data is that they do not tell us whether a change in the stock of migrants in any particular country is due to inflows, outflows, or mortality of migrants. Guzmán (2006) presents sex-disaggregated data on migration flows to major destination countries and shows a much more modest feminization than emerges from the UN data.[4] As this book goes to press, two new data sources are becoming available: Docquier et al. (2007) and Dumont et al. (2007). These sources show a substantial increase in the share of female migrants in OECD countries in the past decades.

As the chapters in this volume show, men and women exhibit important differences in the determinants of their decision to migrate, the amount of remittances they send back to their family in their country of origin, and the allocation of these remittances across various expenditure categories. The studies included in the volume are based on household data, although aggregate data on female migration will prove essential to improving our understanding of cross-country differences in aspects of women's migration.

This volume addresses several issues. The second chapter reviews the existing research on gender and international migration and can be considered a starting point for the remaining chapters. The third chapter focuses on the gendered determinants of migration and remittances in rural Mexico, an important sending country. The following two chapters (chapters 4 and 5) address the impact of migration and remittances on sending countries and provide analysis of household-level data from Ghana and Mexico. Chapter 6 turns to the labor market participation and performance of female migrants in a major destination country, the United States. The volume concludes with a forward-looking chapter that summarizes the major findings, links those to migration policy, and outlines some of the important research and policy issues that need to be addressed in the future.

The remainder of this introductory chapter provides an overview of the volume; it includes a description of methodology, data, main results, and conclusions from the six remaining chapters.

Previous Research: Where Do We Stand?

The second chapter, by Pfeiffer, Richter, Fletcher, and Taylor, contains a critical review of economic research on gender and migration. The chapter outlines the current state of social science thinking about the role of gender in international migration.

The authors systematically survey the most important studies on international migration and gender and outline a simple theoretical framework that serves as a starting point for thinking about women's role in shaping international migration and its impacts. They then present a critique of the treatment of gender in economics research based on models of individual migration. The remaining parts of the chapter discuss other models of gender and migration, including joint models of migration, gender in "split" household models of migration (migration of some household members), and models that emphasize the role of international migration networks. Finally, some priorities for incorporating gender into future economic research on international migration are presented.

The chapter shows that when gender is introduced into empirical models, it is generally found to be an important variable shaping migration and its outcomes. Furthermore, the authors argue that much of the treatment of gender to date—as a control variable in empirical models—is unsatisfactory and that the focus must turn to gender as a central issue for understanding international migration and for which hypotheses can be tested. They also note that critical pieces of the gender-and-international-migration puzzle have been largely ignored. These oversights include differences between the genders with regard to the opportunity costs of migration; the impact of migration and remittances on household investments and expenditures, production, and technology choices; and the community characteristics both at home and abroad that determine the patterns and effects of migration. Finally, the review points to the importance of bringing a gender focus into household surveys and other instruments used in data collection in order to support future research in this field. Several of the important research gaps identified in this chapter are addressed in other chapters in this volume. Additional considerations on directions for future research on gender and migration are presented at the end of the second chapter.

Gendered Determinants of International Migration

The third chapter focuses on the determinants of migration in rural Mexico. Richter and Taylor investigate how the determinants of international migration differ between men and women. The authors use a unique panel data set with retrospective migration histories that is representative of the rural population of Mexico and apply it in random-effect and fixed-effect models. Their results indicate that international migration selects men and women differently. Overall, women are less likely than men to migrate abroad. Schooling is positively associated with international migration of females (to nonagricultural jobs), but not of males. Age deters international migration slightly more for men than for women. One reason might be that men are typically engaged in highly demanding physical work overseas, including in construction and agriculture.

The authors show that networks—that is, contact with family members who are already abroad—play a more important role in the determination of migration than macroeconomic and policy variables and that these networks are both sector and gender specific. Male migration networks are not more influential than female migration networks, but they nevertheless are highly significant in explaining both male and female international migration. Female networks are significant in explaining male migration, and in some cases they are more significant than own-gender male networks. The latter supports the hypothesis that females are deeply committed to their family and community back home; therefore, their networks are deeper than those of male migrants and may provide services that male networks cannot. The results also show that agricultural own-gender migrant networks are not significant in explaining the number of migrants engaged in nonagricultural jobs for either males or females in the United States; this suggests that networks are also sector specific.

Most policy and macroeconomic variables are insignificant in explaining either female or male international migration. The exception is increased border expenditures in the United States, which significantly deter migration by women but do not seem to have a significant impact on migration by men. The authors speculate that women may be less willing than men to play a "cat and mouse" game, in which border officials catch migrants and release them back into Mexico, whereupon they try to cross the border again and often eventually succeed. A possible reason is that repeated migration attempts are likely to be more risky for women than for men. Overall the authors unambiguously reject the assumption that the determinants of migration from Mexico to the United States and their changes over time are gender neutral.

Impacts of the Migration of Women in Origin Countries

The two following chapters turn to the impact of migration and remittances in origin countries and include two studies focusing on Mexico and Ghana.

Chapter 4, by Pfeiffer and Taylor, explores the hypothesis that the impact of international migration and remittances on economic activities of members left behind differs according to the gender of the migrant. More specifically, they investigate the impact of migration and remittances on households' crop production, staple production, nonstaple crop production, livestock production, and local wage work. They also study the impact of female and male migration on household investments in education and health. The authors use a probit model, employing the same data used in chapter 3; they control for potential endogeneity by using historical migration rates by gender as instrumental variables.

Their findings reveal strikingly different impacts of male and female migration on production activities. Overwhelmingly, the impact of male migration on household production is negative, while that of female migration is positive or insignificant. In more detail, the authors find that neither female nor male migration has any effect on the propensity to produce staple crops, whereas nonstaple crop production responds negatively to male, but not female, migration. The authors argue that this result could be related to the fact that males (in contrast to females) are more likely to be employed in production and wage labor activities prior to migration and that the availability of substitutes for their labor in production activities is limited. Also, the positive impact of remittances on the demand for leisure may be significant enough to decrease production. The positive production effects that are observed only for female migration may be because females participate less than males in production activities prior to migrating or else work only in a subset of activities, such as the cultivation of maize and beans. Thus, the positive remittance and insurance effects of female migration counterbalance the smaller negative effects of lost labor.

With respect to household expenditure patterns, this chapter finds that households with female migrants spend significantly less on education than otherwise similar households without female migrants. These findings may result from female migrants in low-skilled service jobs abroad sending home a signal that there are low returns from schooling in international migration work (see chapter 6 for a discussion of labor market performance abroad of educated female migrants from Mexico). Alternatively, it is possible that females who have migrated lose the ability to monitor their household's schooling investments (as discussed in chapter 5). These findings indicate that the sex of the migrant might have an impact on expenditure patterns in remittance-receiving households in the country of origin.

The subsequent chapter (chapter 5) on impacts of migration and remittances focuses on Ghana. This chapter, by Guzmán, Morrison, and Sjöblom, marries the literature on remittances with the literature on intra-household bargaining by exploring two questions: first, whether or not the sex of the household head affects household budget allocations of remittance-receiving households and, second, whether or not the sex of the remitter has any impact on household expenditure allocations in these households. The chapter draws on data from the nationally representative 1998/99 Ghana Living Standards Survey and uses the adjusted Working-Leser curve and the fractional logit model to estimate the effects.

With respect to the first research question, the results indicate that, after controlling for total income, international remittances have a significant impact on the budget allocations for food, consumer and durable goods, housing, health, and other goods in female-headed households, while there is no such impact on expenditure patterns in male-headed households. Internal remittances from within Ghana have a positive effect on expenditure shares on health and education in female-headed households, but again there is no impact on expenditure shares in male-headed households. Comparing female-headed households receiving international and internal remittances reveals interesting differences: female-headed households receiving internal remittances spend a larger percentage of their budget on education and health, and female-headed households receiving international remittances spend a lower share of their budget on food and a greater share on consumer and durable goods, housing, health, and other goods. Hence, there is heterogeneity in expenditure patterns between female- and male-headed households, but there is also heterogeneity among female-headed households receiving remittances. The authors conclude that only the expenditure pattern for female-headed households receiving internal remittances corresponds to the traditional view of women's specific spending patterns, as described in the literature on intra-household bargaining.

In response to the second research question, the authors find that households receiving remittances from females have a different expenditure pattern than those that receive remittances from males, after controlling for the remitter's ability to monitor how the remittance-receiving household allocates its resources. Households with female remitters allocate a larger expenditure share to health and other goods, but a lower share to food. This chapter indicates that households receiving remittances from the wife allocate much less of their budget to education than households that receive remittances from the husband. Two reasons possibly explain this result. First, men tend to spend less money on education than women, so households where the wife is absent are likely to spend less on education. Second, when the wife leaves the household, it is plausible to assume that children leave with her or that she leaves when the children are beyond school age, therefore resulting in a smaller share of education in total expenditures of the household left behind. Overall, the chapter highlights that changes in the composition of households associated with migration are likely to affect the relative influence of female and male household members, which in turn may influence expenditure patterns.

Labor Market Insertion of Women Migrants

Chapter 6, by Özden and Neagu, explores the labor market participation and performance of female migrants in the United States, using census data from 1990 and 2000. They use two measures of performance: wage income and average educational requirement in the occupation in which the migrant is employed. The latter measures whether the migrant is in a higher- or lower-skilled profession relative to her education level, especially compared to migrants from other countries with similar educational backgrounds. This is the first time that this type of measure has been used in an analysis of the labor market performance of women migrants, and it constitutes an important contribution of this chapter.

Overall, the authors find that there is significant variation in labor market participation and performance of female migrants according to their country of origin and their level of education. In fact, regardless of country of origin, the most important determinants of labor force participation are education level (+), years in the United States (+), number of children in the household (−), and marital status (single women and women married to American men are the most likely to work). Controlling for these and other personal characteristics, the authors conclude that labor market participation is lower among female migrants from South Asia (India, Pakistan, and Bangladesh) and the Middle East and North Africa, while it is higher among migrants from Europe, Sub-Saharan Africa, the Caribbean, and East Asia.

Wage levels are higher for migrants from Europe, followed by East and South Asia and Africa; female migrants from Latin America have the lowest wages. After controlling for probability of employment, the most important determinants of wage rates and placement levels are education and years in the United States. In terms of placement in higher-skilled jobs, European migrants and migrants from English-speaking developing countries (such as India, Pakistan, South Africa, and Ghana) perform the best. Latin American and Eastern European migrants are placed in the lower-skilled job categories for identical education levels. The traditional measure of success in the labor market—namely, wage level—provides cross-regional results that are consistent with those of the innovative measure of placement used in this analysis.

Looking Ahead: Future Directions for Research and Policy

The final chapter, by Morrison and Schiff, discusses some of the most important findings of this research volume, relates them to policy, and highlights some of the burning research and policy issues in the field of gender and international migration. The chapter is structured around five issues: the determinants of women's migration, the economic impacts of female migration, the non-economic impacts of female migration, and issues related to temporary and circular migration (including Mode IV). The final section addresses some methodological issues.

The chapter discusses the relationships among gender inequality, women's empowerment, and migration, how wages in sending countries are affected by female migration, and other issues related to the economic impacts of this phenomenon. It also highlights various understudied aspects of migration, such as the impact of migration on family cohesion and children's welfare as well as the trafficking of women.

In addition, the chapter examines temporary migration and concludes that source countries would benefit from it. Host countries would benefit as well, but some of the temporary migrants might overstay illegally. We argue that the temporary movement of service providers under Mode IV-type trade in services is a superior solution to temporary migration because it would minimize the overstaying problem. The chapter provides reasons why the provision of services that use female labor intensively (for example, nurses, nannies, and maids) may be superior to the provision of male-dominated services in a Mode IV-type agreement. Additional policy suggestions are made that should improve the chances of reaching an agreement on Mode IV-type trade in services at the bilateral, regional, or multilateral levels.

In terms of methodological issues, the chapter notes that these models of the determinants of migration can be improved by incorporating joint decision making, given that decisions on the migration of wives and husbands are not independent of one another. This would enable models to capture a number of interrelated factors, including the decision to migrate, the migrant's characteristics, such as gender (and others), the migrant's location and sector of employment, and the sequencing of migration (if any).

Endnotes

1. A billion is 1,000 million.
2. The migration flows within the FSU often represent country-border movements that occurred on the breakup of the Soviet Union and not necessarily the relocation of households across country borders.
3. For definitions of regions, see United Nations (2006).
4. As the author recognizes, data constraints limit the confidence that can be placed in this conclusion. First, sex-disaggregated data on migrant flows simply do not exist for many important destination countries such as France and Russia, and Guzmán's final sample of countries covers less than half of the world's total migrant population. Second, there are inconsistencies in data coverage even among those countries for which data are available. For instance, the data from some countries include illegal migrants, while the data from other countries do not.

References

Bhargava, Alok, and Frédéric Docquier. 2006. Panel Data on Migration of Physicians. Available online at http://www.econ.worldbank.org/programs/migration.

Docquier, Frédéric, and Abdeslam Marfouk. 2006. "International Migration by Education Attainment, 1990–2000." In *International Migration, Remittances, and the Brain Drain*, ed. Çağlar Özden and Maurice Schiff, 151–99. New York: Palgrave Macmillan.

Docquier, Frédéric, Lindsay B. Lowell, and Abdeslam Marfouk, "A Gendered Assessment of the Brain Drain." 2007. Preliminary draft. World Bank, Washington, DC.

Dumont, Jean-Christophe, John P. Martin, and Gilles Spielvogel. 2007. "Women on the Move: The Neglected Gender Dimension of the Brain Drain." Institute for the Study of Labor (IZA), Germany.

Guzmán, Juan Carlos. 2006. "Trends in International Migration: Is There a Feminization of Migration Flows?" Unpublished mss. World Bank, Gender and Development Group, Washington, DC.

Özden, Çağlar, and Maurice Schiff, eds. 2006. *International Migration, Remittances, and the Brain Drain*. New York: Palgrave Macmillan.

———, eds. 2007. *International Migration, Economic Development, and Policy*. New York: Palgrave Macmillan.

Parsons, Christopher, Ronald Skeldon, Terrie L. Walmsley, and L. Alan Winters. 2007. "Quantifying International Migration: A Database of Bilateral Migrant Stocks." In *International Migration, Economic Development, and Policy*, ed. Çağlar Özden and Maurice Schiff, 17–58. New York: Palgrave Macmillan.

United Nations. 2006. "Trends in Total Migrant Stock: The 2005 Revision. CD-ROM Documentation." POP/DB/MIG/Rev.2005/Doc. New York: United Nations.

2

GENDER IN ECONOMIC RESEARCH ON INTERNATIONAL MIGRATION AND ITS IMPACTS: A CRITICAL REVIEW

Lisa Pfeiffer, Susan Richter,
Peri Fletcher, and J. Edward Taylor

The determinants and impacts of international migration have been the subject of a prolific and growing literature in economics and the other social sciences. More than 190 million people live outside their country of birth. Since the 1960s, the number of females who have participated in international migration has been nearly as great as the number of males, and today the share of females in the world's international migrant population is close to half.

Sociologists and anthropologists have long recognized the important role of women in migration (for example, see Fernández-Kelly 1983; Pessar 1986, 1988). Through the 1980s and 1990s, migration research, mostly qualitative, explored the gendered characteristics of immigrants, the impact of women's migration on their household and community of origin, and the cultural factors affecting women's migration decisions (for example, see Mahler and Pessar 2003; Goldring 2003; Hondagneu-Sotelo 1994; Mills 1997; Gamburd 2000). From sociology and

This chapter benefited enormously from comments by three referees, by members of the Gender and Development Unit of the World Bank, and by participants at the Gender and International Migration Workshop, held on December 16, 2005, at the World Bank.

anthropology came both an increasing attention to the larger issues of gender and a critique of the perceived male bias in quantitative research (Boyd and Grieco 2003). Feminist research in particular challenged both the notion of decisions being made by a male head of household and the assumption that households act in a unified manner. It conceives of households as sites of struggle, in which men and women often pursue different goals and strategies (Gabaccia et al. 2006).

Despite what some researchers have called the feminization of international migration (Gabaccia et al. 2006), economists have been slow to incorporate gender into their migration research in a substantive way. When gender enters into economic migration models, it is rarely the focus, but rather, a simple control variable—what Boyd and Grieco (2003) call an "add women, mix, and stir" approach. This stands in contrast to other social science research that makes women's experience of migration a center of inquiry. This is illustrated by the recent publication of a special issue of the *International Migration Review* on gender and migration, the product of a Social Science Research Council initiative (Gabaccia et al. 2006).[1] Yet, economists are conspicuously absent from the issue's table of contents.

Gender Patterns in International Migration

Even the most highly aggregated data suggest that the patterns of international migration vary between men and women. For example, the 2000 U.S. decennial census uncovered more male than female immigrants from El Salvador, but more female than male immigrants from the Dominican Republic.[2] Migration from India to the United States is dominated by males, while immigration from China and the Republic of Korea to the United States is dominated by females.

Differences in gender ratios between temporary and permanent migrants are similarly intriguing. The 2002 Canadian census found about twice as many foreign-born female as male permanent residents. The female-to-male ratio is smaller for Canadian immigrants from the United States and Central and South America than for other regions, but females still predominate. In contrast, temporary migrant entries from the top sending countries in 2002, including China, France, Germany, India, Mexico, and the United States, were dominated by males.[3] On a more microscale, data from the 2003 Mexico National Rural Household Survey show that most villages in Mexico send more males than females to the United States, but some send more females.[4]

What can explain these differences in migratory patterns between men and women? There are many potential hypotheses. Gender segmentation of the immigrant labor market in receiving countries undoubtedly influences the gender composition of immigration flows. For example, the U.S. economy draws large numbers of low-wage laborers from Mexico to work in male-dominated agricultural and service jobs, including construction, gardening, and janitorial work. Asian cities attract large numbers of nurses and domestic-service workers from the Philippines. Immigration laws also can affect the gender mix. The gender composition of permanent and temporary immigrant visas reflects historical and current policies, which may affect women differently than men. Some policies promote family reunification, some aim to fill low-paying jobs that cannot be filled by domestic workers, and others attract high-skilled workers in competitive fields in which one gender may dominate. Immigration laws can induce temporary or permanent migration, individual or family movement, and legal or illegal border crossings, all of which may have different implications for men than for women.

The level of economic development in destination countries also seems to matter. Females tend to claim a larger proportion of total immigrants in developed than in developing countries, possibly because of a tendency for immigration laws to evolve toward a greater emphasis on family reunification as incomes rise or because developed countries offer women access to a wide variety of educational and employment opportunities, autonomy, and independence not found at home. Nevertheless, developing countries are attracting an increasing number of female immigrants as dependents of migrant workers or to fill positions in female-dominated professions, including nursing and teaching (Zlotnik 2003).

Models of international migration that disregard gender have a difficult time explaining these migration patterns. In any international migration model, considerations of gender are likely to become increasingly critical as the female share of international migration rises. The gender composition of world migration reflects a complex interaction among social, political, and economic conditions, migration histories, labor demands in destination countries, and household and community dynamics. As Kanaiaupuni (2000) states, "Migration is a profoundly gendered process, and the conventional explanations of men's migration in many cases do not apply to women." Theoretical models and empirical findings focusing on male migration do not adequately describe migration by females, and studies that do not distinguish between males and females may yield findings that are biased for both genders. Furthermore, research that does not consider structural differences between the genders may yield unreliable policy prescriptions.

Objectives of This Review

Economic research grounded in recent advances in theory and quantitative methods is needed to complement the existing discussion of gender and migration. In this spirit, this chapter offers a critical review of the treatment of gender in economic models of international migration and discusses priorities for "gendering" international migration research. It is organized into five sections. The first sketches out a simple conceptual framework as a starting point for thinking about gender's role in shaping international migration and its impacts. The second offers a critique of the treatment of gender in economics research focusing on individuals. The third discusses gender in household migration models. "Joint" models describe migration by entire households; women typically are viewed as tied movers. "Split" models describe migration by some, but not all, household members and are a staple of research inspired by the so-called "new economics of labor migration" (NELM, now more than two decades old). The fourth is dedicated to the role of international migration networks, the study of which has entailed an increasing focus on gender in recent years. We conclude in a final section by suggesting some priorities for incorporating gender into future economic research on international migration.

Our objective in this review is neither to propose a comprehensive modeling framework nor to provide a complete catalog of theoretical and empirical studies of international migration in the social sciences. Rather, it is to represent the current state of social science thinking about the role of gender in international migration, with a particular focus on economics. To this end, we have chosen studies that we believe represent the major theoretical and empirical approaches that have been used to incorporate gender into international migration research. While the focus of this review is on international migration, research on internal migration is occasionally cited to illustrate key theoretical and empirical points.

"We Go to Get Ahead": A Conceptual Framework for Thinking about Gender and Migration

The existing social science literature on international migration lacks a single coherent theoretical framework. Massey et al. (2005), conclude,

> At present, there is no single theory . . . by social scientists to account for the emergence and perpetuation of international migration throughout the world, only a fragmented set of theories that have developed largely in isolation from one another, sometimes but not always segmented by disciplinary boundaries.

This state of international migration research persists. Moreover, relatively little work on international migration explicitly addresses gender issues.

Most researchers would agree that, in the majority of cases, people migrate internationally in an effort "to get ahead" (Malkin 2004), to provide a better life for themselves, their children, or their family members left at home. Migration decision makers—be they individuals, households, or some complex combination of the two—presumably use all of the information that is available to them to perform what an economist might call "a cost-benefit analysis" of international migration. The information at their disposal may be limited, and they may face severe constraints on their migration (and other) choices, but if the benefits of participating in international migration exceed the costs (however these benefits and costs may be defined and subject to information and other constraints), an economic model would predict that international migration will result. Models of migration determinants attempt to describe the ways in which international migration selects on characteristics of individuals and the households and larger social units (for example, communities or nations) in which they live prior to migrating. Economic models generally emphasize monetary costs and benefits, including wages, the probability of employment, opportunity costs, and transportation costs, along with risks. These are undoubtedly important. However, other considerations also may affect the benefits and costs of international migration, particularly if one defines those benefits and costs more broadly. The legal viability of migration, the social impacts of loss of contact with friends and family, and cultural norms may significantly increase or decrease the benefits and costs, while limiting the viability of international migration as an option for some individuals and households.

A cost-benefit analysis is at the heart of any migration decision model, either explicitly or implicitly. Migration can be conceived as an outcome of individual or household decisions—or both. It can encompass a wide variety of benefits, costs, and risks, including ones that are not traditionally thought of as being "economic," and it can be shaped by individual, household, or community characteristics, some of which can be observed and others not.

Despite the increasing sophistication and diversity of economic models of migration, human capital theory continues to be a foundation of how economists envision and model the migration cost-benefit analysis. In its most basic form, this theory posits that individuals' productivity depends on their education, work experience, and other human capital variables. If wages reflect individuals' productivity, then they, too, depend on these variables. A prolific literature on labor markets and discrimination, motivated by Becker (1971), finds differences in the economic returns to human capital between men and women. A prolific literature on migration grounded in Sjaastad's (1962) human capital model finds differences in the returns to human capital between migrant-sending and -receiving areas.

A gendered human capital model of international migration would posit that the differences in the returns to human capital across borders are not the same for women and for men (see chapter 3). This could help to explain why women migrate more to some places than to others and why they leave some places more than others.

In the most general migration models, the benefits and costs of international migration depend on both individual and household characteristics, regardless of whether the migration decision maker is an individual, a household, or both. Particular variables may "explain" migration because of their influence on a wide variety of benefits, costs, and risks that shape migration decisions. Such variables include, but are not limited to, the human capital of migrants and other household members.

The opportunity cost of migration may be a wage or an expected wage at the origin in an individual migration model, or it may represent the value produced by the individual in household production activities in a household model. Other variables potentially affecting migration costs include immigration laws, risk aversion, the loss of family contact, and the rupture of societal norms.

The migration benefits might be a wage or expected wage abroad in a wage-driven model or be remittances in a household model. The benefits include outcomes of international migration besides income, including those that are not traditionally emphasized by economic studies, such as increased autonomy and independence, the formation of a migration network, or greater opportunities for future generations. The benefits of migration may be influenced by characteristics of other households in the migrant-sending or -receiving area (for example, see Stark and Taylor 1991), and there may be external costs and benefits as well (Taylor and Adelman 1996).

The key argument of this review is that any or all of these costs and benefits are likely to be gender specific. A model that pools men and women can be justified only if the parameters reflecting how explanatory variables affect migration do not vary by gender. However, few studies test for pooling or even control for gender, besides including a gender dummy among their explanatory variables. That is, with the exception of the intercept, all model parameters usually are assumed to be the same for men and for women.

Figure 2.1 illustrates the models and interactions that are the focus of the rest of this review. The models include individual, wage- and employment-driven models of migration and household models, both joint and split. Human capital theory and the consideration of networks have influenced theoretical and especially empirical research in all of these models, as illustrated by the arrows in the figure. Models of individual migration decisions have influenced household models by emphasizing the heterogeneity of characteristics among family members. The new economics of labor migration theory (Stark 1991) has primarily influenced primarily split household migration models. Finally, models of the local economywide impacts of migration "nest" many different kinds of households in

Figure 2.1. Illustration of Migration Models and Their Interactions

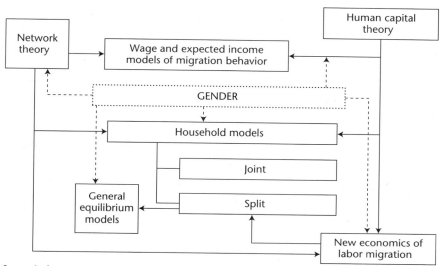

Source: Authors.

migrant-sending areas, including split (but logically not joint) migration house-holds. Gender potentially influences all aspects of migration and its impacts, as illustrated by the broken lines in the figure. Reviews of economic models of migration and its impacts are available elsewhere (for example, see Massey et al. 2005; Taylor and Martin 2001). This review is unique in exploring the role of gender in all of these models.

The (Mis)treatment of Gender in Economic Models of International Migration Focusing on Individuals

The key prediction of most individual migration models is that the people who migrate are the ones for whom the difference in discounted future earnings (or expected earnings) streams between destination and origin is greatest (given migration costs) or for whom migration costs are lowest (given earnings differentials; Sjaastad 1962). This implication leads to several testable hypotheses that economists have not thoroughly examined through a gendered lens, even though researchers in other social sciences have hypothesized that wages, migration costs, and the returns to education, the key elements of these models, are almost certainly different for men than for women.

Hypothesis One: Individuals' Human Capital Drives Migration

Individuals' potential earnings at home and abroad clearly shape the benefits from migrating. According to human capital theory, wages are a function of productivity, which in turn depends on human capital variables including education and work experience.[5] The little applied migration research that has focused on gender produces evidence that human capital variables influence migration differently for the two sexes. The economic rewards from schooling in destination and sending areas may be different for men and women if labor markets at destinations and origins are segmented by gender or if other factors create gender disparities in the returns to human capital. If this is the case, then one would expect migration to select differently on men's than on women's schooling.[6]

Elnajjar (1993), in his analysis of international migration from the Gaza Strip, finds that migrants have significantly higher levels of education than nonmigrants and that those with higher education levels are more likely to be employed. However, he also finds that women and men have different likelihoods of employment in the sending community and that female and male migration seems not to respond to unemployment and education in the same way. Kanaiaupuni (2000) finds that international migration from Mexico selects positively on education for females; for males it does the opposite. High unemployment rates in the country of origin increase men's propensity to migrate but have no effect on migration by women. This empirical finding is supported by qualitative studies that describe how women with higher education feel constrained by social norms and a lack of employment opportunities in their origin country and how crossing a border provides new employment as well as social opportunities (Hondagneu-Sotelo 1994). Thus empirical studies focusing on wages or expected incomes, which fail to explain most of the variation in migration among individuals (Massey et al. 2005), may do a poorer job of explaining female than male migration. Separate modeling approaches allowing for variables that differentially affect the benefits and costs of migration for the sexes may be needed.

The role of home-country characteristics, such as investment in female education, can affect productivity and thus the propensity to migrate. Borjas (1987) estimates the impact of home-country characteristics on the observed wages of foreign-born wives in the United States, arguing that differences in the economic performance of immigrants with the same measured skills may be the result of selectivity in unobserved characteristics. Thus the "quality" of immigrants, in terms of their ability to succeed in the United States, depends on which foreigners have an incentive to emigrate. Cobb-Clark (1993) empirically applies Borjas's work by using country characteristics to control for these unobservable individual characteristics. She finds that greater income inequality, returns to education, and GDP in the country of origin are all positively related to the wages of female immigrants in the United States. Moreover, women who immigrate as family members earn significantly higher wages than those who immigrate as individuals. These findings point to the importance of linking female immigrants' labor market performance not only to their own characteristics at the time of immigration but also to other variables that influence the decision of whether or not to migrate, including origin-country characteristics.

All of these studies indicate that an individual's human capital is an important variable shaping migration decisions. However, the economic literature has only begun to consider how human capital variables might differentially affect international migration by males and females.

Hypothesis Two: The Young Are More Mobile Than the Old

In an expected-income model, individuals migrate if the sum of their expected income gains from migrating (appropriately discounted) is positive. This implies that, other things being equal, the young are more mobile than the old and an increase in the cost of migrating, holding wages constant, decreases migration more for older than for younger individuals.

There has been limited research on the topic of age and international migration by the two sexes, but some suggestive findings are available. Kanaiaupuni (2000) finds that rural Mexican men are more likely to migrate than women except after the age of 50. This finding is consistent with the argument that women often migrate to reunite with family members or to join their husband abroad once their children are older.

Gender differences in the effect of age on international migration could be an important topic for future research, particularly if the motivations for migration by females are distinct or are contingent on past migration by males. For instance, if family reunification is an important motive for female but not for male migration, one could observe migration by women being delayed or the apparently paradoxical outcome of female migration being associated with a negative expected income differential.

Hypothesis Three: High Costs and Risks Discourage Migration

A third hypothesis of the human capital model is that migration between locales is negatively related to migration costs and risks. While distance is the most logical correlate of migration costs, migration networks have been shown to decrease these costs. If individuals have contact with migrants who can help them to cross a border, provide information to arrive safely, and help with locating a job, the costs of migration can fall dramatically. The literature on migration networks is vast and has important implications for migration by men and women; thus we dedicate a separate section to it.

Other variables could explain migration costs and opportunity costs, particularly when these are defined more broadly. For example, individuals who are married and have children will have higher costs of family migration and perhaps an incentive to split the family between locales (for example, the male migrates, while the female remains at home). These variables have been included in models of migration and immigrant employment, a step toward developing more gendered models of human capital migration. Kanaiaupuni (2000) finds that civil status and number of children of the migrant affect international migration propensities differently for males and for females. Also Kossoudji and Ranney (1984), in their evaluation of wage rates among Mexican immigrants, find that differences are not explained by education or work experience, but instead by civil status and number of children. Maxwell (1988) finds that employment differences among men and women vary according to civil status. Cackley (1993) looks at wage differentials by sex and their impacts on migration within Brazil and finds that single women respond to positive wage differentials between the sending and receiving communities, but married women do not. These studies indicate that women and men may evaluate the costs and benefits of migration differently; correct delineation by gender is essential to estimate international migration propensities.

Hypothesis Four: The Probability of Employment Affects International Migration

The probability of employment is central to most economic models of migration: Even if wage rates are relatively high at a prospective migrant destination, a low probability of employment reduces the expected income differential. Contacts with migrant networks can increase migrants' probability of employment. Immigration laws also can be a critical component in a person's migration decision. For example, if a migrant can earn the same wage, with the same employment probability, in two different countries, but immigration laws are more lenient in one country than in the other, the expected income differential will be higher in the country with the more lenient laws. Immigration laws may discriminate by gender—for example, if a country has a perceived shortage of nurses, a profession that is often intense in female labor, (or the political will to rely on a foreign source for nurses), it may provide work visas for nurses, but not for other (for example, agricultural) workers. Such a policy clearly would affect the gender composition of immigration if labor markets tend to be gender segregated.

One example of an immigration law that changed the propensity for international migration and had a gender bias is the Bracero program. Male workers from rural Mexico were recruited under this program to alleviate U.S. labor shortages created by World War II. From 1942 to 1964, more than 4.5 million Mexican *braceros* worked temporarily in U.S. agriculture (Donato and Patterson 2004; Durand, Massey, and Parrado 1999). Not only did the Bracero program increase the flow of male Mexican migrants into the United States, it also established migration networks that altered the benefits, risks, and costs of migration for many years to come, including for females.

The demand for and supply of migrant labor by gender may be affected by migrant labor recruitment strategies as well as by the economic activities in which male and female migrants concentrate. Tyner (1996) finds that migrant labor recruiters in the Philippines match men and women with specific kinds of jobs abroad. Men typically are employed in professional jobs, while women work in domestic services or in the health profession. The probability of obtaining a job as a lawyer is lower for Philippine female than for male migrants, while the probability of obtaining a nursing job is higher for female than for male migrants. King and Zontini (2000) find that a rise in female immigration to Southern Europe can be explained predominately by an increase in jobs in the service and informal sectors.

In 1986 the U.S. Congress passed the Immigration Reform and Control Act (IRCA), which had three main components aimed at curtailing and controlling immigration (Cerrutti and Massey 2004). The first was to legalize migrants who had worked in the country continuously and in an unauthorized status since 1982. Legalization of migrants decreased circular migration and stimulated new migration for family reunification. Cornelius (1990) argues that female immigration was positively affected by the IRCA, as wives and children in Mexico crossed the border to reunite with husbands and fathers in the United States. One study estimates that 300,000 persons per year migrated illegally for family reunification, while another finds that a family member legalized by the IRCA increased the probability of illegal entry by a factor of seven (Durand, Massey, and Parrado 1999). Researchers are only beginning to explore the ways in which females may respond differently than males to migration policy shocks.

Hypothesis Five: Migration Equalizes Wages over Space

Human capital theory implies that migration will narrow wage differentials for specific types of workers between sending and receiving areas over time by reallocating workers from low- to high-wage labor markets (driving wages up in the former and down in the latter; for example, see Rosenzweig 1988). If female and male workers are not perfect substitutes at the origin and destination, migration will tend to equalize female and male wages separately across space, but not necessarily between the genders.[7] An increase in demand for female labor at the destination would induce more female migration, which in turn would raise female wages at the origin until a new equilibrium in the female labor market is achieved. The same would hold for males. However, one could imagine a scenario in which wage differentials between men and women at the origin might decrease as males migrate. Other things being equal, higher substitutability between male and female labor at the destination would promote wage equity at the origin, and vice versa. To our knowledge no empirical studies have tested this gender-specific wage equalization hypothesis.

Obstacles to Incorporating Gender into Wage- and Employment-Driven Models

In a gendered neoclassical model of international migration, gender-specific wage differentials between origin and destination countries would be the primary drivers of migration by both sexes. If migration costs are significant, as is usually the case for international migration, a wedge between source- and destination-area wages will reflect those costs. If migration costs differ between men and women, so will equilibrium wages. Furthermore, the probability of employment at the origin and destination may be a function of gender. Incorporating gender into wage and expected-income models of international migration thus is critical, but researchers face obstacles in doing so.

Three problems hamper researchers' efforts to conduct empirical studies of migration and its impacts using individual-based-wage and expected-wage models.

First, wages and employment often simply are not observed. Data on wages are available only for those individuals who are in the wage labor force, and many people—particularly women—do not earn wages prior to migrating. The fact that wages are not observed if individuals choose not to work for a wage creates a potential endogenous selection problem that may require bringing household variables into the analysis. For example, an individual from a household with large assets (for example, landholdings) is likely to be more productive on the farm and thus to have a high reservation wage and low ex ante likelihood of working for a wage. As a result, it will take an unusually high wage to draw this individual into the wage labor force.

Second, in many migrant-sending areas, economic activities are carried out by households that employ and supply little wage labor. Women may be employed entirely in unpaid family work prior to migrating. This makes the women's wages unobservable and their departure a cost to the household. If women are employed in the production of household nontradables—that is, Becker's (1965) "Z-goods," such as raising children and cooking—one does not have access to market prices to help to determine the opportunity costs of migrating. This is an important drawback, inasmuch as the "reproduction" sector appears to be economically important. Estimates of the value of reproduction activities (cooking and cleaning; home repair; home-produced furniture and clothes; care of children, the sick, and the elderly; and personal, social, and community support services) in the least-developed countries have ranged as high as 26 percent of conventional GDP (for example, see Fontana and Wood 2000). Implicit wages for these individuals must be estimated in a household context.

Third, imperfect labor and capital markets affect the opportunity cost of migrating. Labor markets at the origin often are imperfect (for example, the household cannot hire a perfect substitute for the family members who migrate or demand or supply the amount of labor it desires). In this case, the wages that are observed at the origin may not accurately represent the opportunity cost of migration for the household or the sending economy.[8] The substitution between male and female labor in household activities is critical in determining the costs and benefits of migration by individual family members. If males and females are engaged in different activities in the source economy, then the opportunity costs of migration almost certainly will depend on gender. For example, if women are employed largely in unpaid household work while men work the fields, it is possible that women's migration will not reduce crop production, but that men's migration will. However, if the "missing" females pull male labor out of the fields and into activities traditionally dominated by women, then female migration could reduce crop production via a labor substitution effect. Conversely, migration by males could pull females into the fields.

Still another limitation of wage-based models is that some economic benefits from migration are associated with *other people's* earnings. Some studies suggest that an increase in income resulting from a "better marriage" creates an economic pull for women to migrate. Thadani and Todaro (1984) revise the Todaro (1969) model to include the benefits of a "better marriage" as a reason for a female to migrate. In their model female migration is a function of the expected wage gap, a "mobility marriage" differential, and a "customary marriage" differential. The "mobility marriage" differential is a single female migrant's probability of achieving a certain income through marriage to a male at the destination, while the "customary marriage" differential is the probability that a single female migrant can find *any* husband at the destination. Behrman and Wolfe (1984) empirically test this model for internal migration in Nicaragua. They find that women moving from rural to urban areas generally do so for employment reasons. Nevertheless, the probability of finding a spouse motivates a significant amount of migration. Findley and Diallo (1993) use this model to study the movement of women in Mali. They find that women respond to source-region economic and social variables and not just to the probability of marriage to a rich husband.[9]

In short, while researchers frequently encounter difficulties estimating the expected income gains from migration, these difficulties tend to be magnified when the migrant is a woman. When individuals engage in household production or reproduction activities prior to migration or migrants share their earnings with the household after migration, there is a need to model migration decisions within the context of households. Increasingly, the consensus among social science researchers is that it is unlikely that individuals make migration decisions independently from the household of which they are members (for example, see Aguilera and Massey 2003; Curran and Rivero-Fuentes 2003; Munshi 2003). This observation implies moving beyond classical, neoclassical, and "neo-neoclassical" expected-income models focusing on individuals.

Beyond Individuals: Gender and Household Migration Models

Economic studies of migration that take into account the role of the household generally take two forms: split migration and joint migration. Split migration refers to migration by one or more household members, but not entire household units. Joint migration is migration by the entire household unit (the bane of panel surveys). The differences between split migration and joint migration sometimes are subtle and often are not clearly spelled out in the literature. The main distinction is that, in the case of split migration, the household unit does not change location, whereas in the case of joint migration, the household's location changes, either all at once or via sequential moves in which other household members follow the initial migrant.

Joint Household Models of Migration

Joint migration models might conveniently be viewed as an extension of the individual expected-income model, as in Mincer (1978). In a household context, household members maximize their net family gain, G_f, instead of their individual gains, G_i. The net gain for the household from migration is defined as $G_f = R_f - C_f$, where R_f is the sum of the revenues and C_f is the sum of the costs of migration across family members. Costs and revenues can assume all of the forms mentioned in the previous section. If there are only two household members with expected gains from migration equal to G_1 and G_2, respectively, then the overall gain for the household is $G_f = G_1 + G_2$. The individual decision to migrate will not conflict with the overall family decision to migrate if G_1 and G_2 are of the same sign. If individual gains are not of the same sign, one individual will be tied to the other (Mincer 1978).

A tied mover is one whose individual gain from migration is negative when the overall family gain from migration is positive. In contrast, a tied stayer is one whose individual gain from not migrating is negative when the overall family gain from not migrating is positive. When the externality imposed on the tied individual is not internalized by the household and exceeds the gain from marriage, the marriage will dissolve. Family migration is less likely than individual migration (Compton and Pollack 2004; Mincer 1978), given this formalization.[10]

Few studies have analyzed the role of joint migration in international migration or in developing countries. Smith and Thomas (1998) analyze the migration moves of wives and husbands in Malaysia. They find that joint moves constitute less than two-thirds of all migration moves and that a wife's characteristics matter little in determining postmarriage moves. Solo moves, or split migration, are distinctively different for men and women. Solo moves by women are made for familial reasons, such as relocating to be with other family members for the birth of a first child. Men make solo moves to generate income. In a separate study of Malaysian migration patterns, Chattopadhyay (1998) finds that joint migration negatively affects women's economic achievements and favors men's.

The majority of economic studies of joint migration moves have found that migration has a negative impact on a married woman's labor force participation, employment, weeks worked, hours worked, income, and attitudes toward work, but the assumption that women are tied movers is problematic. One study assumes that all women are tied movers and uses that assumption as a basis for dropping all female migrants from the analysis (Aguilera and Massey 2003). Cerrutti and Massey (2001) assume that women are tied movers if they migrate after other family members. Cooke (2003) uses a data set that matches incomes of husbands and wives over two time periods and then documents whether or not they migrate during this time. This approach hinges on the ability to observe wages for the same individual at both the origin and the destination. Cooke finds that a positive effect of migration on income results from an increase in the husband's, not the wife's, income. The effect of women's income is not statistically different from zero. All of these studies are hampered by obstacles that include unobservable wages, economic activities performed at the household level, and imperfect labor markets.

Mincer (1978) defines tied movers as individuals who do not enjoy an individual gain from migration when the overall family gain is positive. Previous joint migration studies did not measure whether individual gains from migration are positive or negative. This may not be a major problem when modeling migration if the husband's gain from migration always exceeds the wife's loss (in absolute value). However, it is likely to create serious problems when modeling female migration if the rest of the household is not taken into account. Husbands may move first, in order to set up a house, find a stable job, save money, or establish other connections that will aid the arrival of the rest of the family. Meanwhile, females may stay behind, even if their expected net income gain from migration is positive. One can also imagine a scenario in which female migrants gain from moves in which they follow their husband, but these women are excluded from migration studies on the assumption that they are tied movers. Males may migrate to supplement a family's income on the assumption that the move is temporary, but over time they may decide to settle at the destination, thereby delaying an eventual move by the female. The potential biases when estimating female migration are manifold.

The joint migration model does not consider possible frictions between household members over migration decisions. Each individual is assumed to have the same amount of bargaining power (Cooke 2003). Most split household migration models share this limitation; however, the limitation seems less glaring in a split than in a joint model in which the entire household moves, even when the gains from migration may be negative for one or more household members.[11]

Few researchers have collected data on joint migration, due to considerations of cost and feasibility. When a household migrates, it is costly for a survey team to search for it in the destination country. When surveys are conducted at the destination, reliable data on income and wealth prior to migration are difficult to gather. The majority of the international migration literature focuses on split migration decisions, for which data collection is easier, with the justification that households rarely move all at once to another country. Still, the joint migration literature suggests some promising avenues for future research. It highlights the complexity of potential benefits and costs of international migration within households, and it offers an explanation for why some individuals (particularly women) move even when migration does not maximize their (individual) expected incomes.

Gender in "Split" Household Models of International Migration

In split household models, individual household members may migrate and the household's demographic composition thus may change, but the household survives as an economic and social unit in the migrant-sending area. The new economics of labor migration (Stark 1991) integrates the study of migration into a theoretical framework in which migration may be undertaken by individuals as members of larger social units, usually households, and both determinants and impacts of migration are analyzed in the context of households or communities. NELM models expand the list of objectives underlying migration decisions beyond the goal of maximizing income or expected income. Households are assumed to allocate their members' time to work and nonwork activities at home and abroad so as to maximize household welfare, which can take various forms. Primary interest usually is placed on the nature of the household objective function and on the market context within which migration decisions take place. These, in turn, determine the nature of the opportunity costs and benefits of migration by a given household member.

The simplest household modeling framework that can be used to study international migration is that of a unitary household that maximizes its utility obtained from the consumption of goods, subject to a time and cash income constraint. The household's time allocated to leisure, migration, and local work cannot exceed its total endowment of time. The household's cash outlay on tradables cannot exceed its cash income. Cash income may include the sum of wages of household members who participate in a labor market; household profits from producing goods for which there are markets (that is, tradables); migrant remittances; and other income, including nonearned income and nonremittance transfers. If a perfect labor market exists, then labor is a tradable and is valued at the market wage. The time of an individual who migrates is valued not at the local wage but at the destination wage if the individual is considered to be part of the household after migrating. Implicitly, migration raises the value of an individual's time above the local wage; otherwise the individual would not migrate.

Assuming that all prices are determined in markets and all goods and labor are tradable, household utility maximization in this model implies income maximization. This, in turn, implies that each household member's time will be allocated to the labor market (local or migrant) in which his or her contribution to household income will be greatest.

In practice, identifying the benefits, costs, and even the decision maker can be challenging; this has been a source of disagreement in the social sciences literature. The NELM perspective does not posit a specific form for any one of these. As mentioned, its main contribution is to view migration decisions and impacts within the context of larger social units. It is up to the researcher to specify what these social units, the decision maker, and the costs and benefits of international migration might be, as well as the role that gender plays in each of these.

The most well-known migration-development interactions in the NELM framework revolve around market failures in migrant-sending areas. For example, Stark (1978) argues that migrants, through remittances or the promise of remittances in the event of adverse shocks, provide households with capital and insurance that may facilitate the transition from familial to commercial production. This argument implies that households lack access to capital and income insurance to begin with—that is, capital and insurance markets are missing or incomplete. When households in migrant-sending areas also face imperfect labor markets, this has important implications for the conceptualization of the opportunity costs of migration.

From a household perspective, the opportunity costs of migration can take on three different forms, depending on an individual's involvement with the labor market and the household's involvement in markets for the commodities that it produces. They are as follows:

1. The market wage, for household members who are actively engaged in wage labor
2. The market value of the marginal product of labor in household production, for those who are not actively engaged in the labor market but dedicate their work time primarily to household production activities—for example, cultivation of staples for sale in markets or for home consumption; determining this market value, of course, assumes the existence of markets for the goods produced
3. The shadow value of labor in reproduction activities, including subsistence production when high transaction costs isolate households from markets, as in de Janvry, Fafchamps, and Sadoulet (1991)[12]

The NELM perspective is particularly germane to the study of gender and migration because of the household context in which women's activities often are carried out and the frequency with which wages for females are not observed prior to migration. In addition, productivity in different activities, and thus the opportunity costs of migration, may differ between the genders.

There is a growing realization in the microdevelopment economics literature that gender is a critical source of intra-household heterogeneity that can shape resource allocations (for example, see Udry 1996; Schultz 1990). Alternative household modeling approaches have heretofore unexplored implications for understanding the effects of gender on the determinants and impacts of migration, including models with risk (David 1974; Taylor 1986; Rosenzweig and Stark 1989; Stark and Katz 1986; Levhari and Stark 1982), collective models of household behavior (Bourguignon and Chiappori 1992), Nash-bargained models (McElroy and Horney 1981), and models to test for Pareto optimality of intra-household resource allocations (Udry 1996).

In a Nash-bargained rural household containing migrants, household utility might be represented by the product of net utility gains deriving from household membership for female and male migrants and other household members. Migrants' utility as nonmembers of the household—that is, the utility they would enjoy by severing their ties with the household—represents the threat point in this game. Threat points, preferences, and control over household resources are likely to differ between men and women, and migration may influence these in important ways. The more insecure that migrants perceive their future prospects to be outside the household, ceteris paribus, the smaller this threat point will be, the less likely migrants will sever their ties with the household, and the more income migrants will remit. While a model of pure altruism would predict a negative association between migrant earnings and rural-household wealth, a game-theoretic model might predict just the opposite. Chen (2006) and de Laat (2005) consider how asymmetric information may induce opportunistic behavior by the members of the household who do not migrate; consideration of this information failure increases the costs of migration for the potential migrant. Intra-household economic research may hold promise for bringing gender into theoretical models of the pattern and impacts of international migration, offering an avenue to model potentially competing interests of migrants and other household members and responding to criticisms of unitary household models.

Migration and Remittance Determinants in Split Household Models

Split household models have a potentially rich set of implications for predicting international migration and remittance behavior by men and women. For example, asset-rich households, in which the productivity of family members' labor at home is high, other things being equal, are likely to have a lower probability of sending members with similar human capital abroad than asset-poor households. Findings by Donato (1993) and Cerrutti and Massey (2001) support this prediction; they find that land, home, and business ownership decrease the probability of migration by women. On the one hand, if households participate in migration to overcome risk and liquidity constraints on production, then migration will be lower for wealthy households, which have access to liquidity, are less risk averse, and may enjoy other forms of income insurance. On the other hand, if migration itself is costly and risky, poor households may not be able to afford the costs or be willing to bear the risks of sending migrants abroad. Cerrutti and Massey (2001) also find that homeownership increases the probability of migration for males. It may be that opportunity costs constrain women's decisions, while actual costs constrain men's.

Individual human capital characteristics undoubtedly affect migration propensities, and it is important to include these in any household model. It is reasonable to expect that many characteristics will affect migration differently for men than for women. For example, Kanaiaupuni (2000) finds that women are more likely to migrate internationally if they are single or no longer married and that international migration selects positively on schooling for females but not for males.

Remittances, in addition to potentially being influenced by household wealth, may reflect migrants' insurance role. If migrants are insurance substitutes, one would expect remittances to respond positively to adverse income shocks in sending areas. If households get disutility from being relatively deprived within the reference group, then greater income inequality in the sending area might stimulate migration as well as influence remittances.

Taylor's (1987) empirical analysis of Mexico-to-U.S. migration finds that both expected remittances and nonmigration contributions of cash income are significantly lower for females than for males. Low nonmigration contributions for women are almost certainly due, in part, to women's participation in nonpecuniary (such as household production) activities. Lower remittances by women may be due either to lower earnings at the destination or less willingness to share these earnings with the household of origin. The analysis does not test for differences in the effects of human capital and other variables on migration by gender; however, migration determinants and net returns could be estimated separately for males and females.

In one of the most influential efforts to test the NELM risk hypothesis, Lucas and Stark (1985) find evidence that sons remit more to households with large herds, consistent with a strategy to maintain favor in inheritance. They also find evidence that remittances provide income insurance to migrant-sending households; in a drought year, remittances are higher to households with assets most sensitive to drought. Hoddinott (1994) also finds that sons' remittances are positively related to their parent's inheritable assets. However, neither study tests for differences in remittances by male and female migrants, and both use data on internal, not international, migrants.

De la Brière et al. (2002) find that the determinants of remittances to the rural Dominican Republic vary with the migrant's gender and destination. They reject the null hypothesis that the effects of gender can be captured by simply including a dummy variable in the remittance equation; interactions of gender with other hypothesized determinants of remittances are jointly significant. This suggests that there are structural differences in the remittance behavior of men and women. Other things being equal, female migrants in the United States send home significantly more remittances than male migrants. Moreover, remittances from female but not male migrants respond positively to the number of lost working days by parents. The authors conclude that female migrants, particularly those located in the United States, perform an insurance function for their households of origin, while male migrants only fulfill this insurance function when they are the sole migrant in the family. It appears that men remit more to invest, while women do so to insure their family and assist siblings. A limitation of this study is that it does not estimate separate remittance functions for males and females and for internal and international migrants or test for three-way interactions among gender, destination, and other explanatory variables in the pooled migrant sample.

Outside economics, studies by Ribas (2000) and Semyonov and Gorodzeisky (2005) find that Philippine male migrants abroad are more likely to remit than females, while a study in Cuba found that a higher percentage of female than male migrants remitting (Blue 2004). However, Ramírez, Domínguez, and Morais (2005) advise caution when interpreting this result because labor exporting tends to be highly gender segregated.[13]

Gender and the Economic Impacts of International Migration in Sending Areas

NELM models lead to a richer set of potential impacts of international migration on sending areas as well. The effects of international migration on sending areas are not very interesting in models in which individuals are studied in isolation from households. There are no direct benefits from international migration to the sending area in a model that lacks a rationale for the migrant to continue her involvement in the sending economy via remittances or other means. In a classical model, the opportunity cost of international migration to the sending area is assumed to be zero (Lewis 1954). In a neoclassical model, it is equal to the marginal value product of the migrant's labor; when individuals migrate, the sending-area labor supply shifts inward, wages increase slightly, but employment and output fall.

There have been a few attempts to test the prediction of the NELM that migration and remittances influence production in migrant-sending households. Lucas (1987); Rozelle, Taylor, and de Brauw (1999); Taylor (1992); and Taylor, Rozelle, and de Brauw (2003) find evidence of negative lost-labor and positive remittance effects on production. These models treat household labor as homogeneous, without regard to gender, and model the allocation of this labor to migration and nonmigration activities. The assumption frequently made in household economy models that family labor is fungible is questionable if the activity spheres of female and male time are different.

Some economic research has addressed gender differences in productivity and activity participation in rural households. In a study of labor allocation in Mexico, Amuedo-Dorantes and Pozo (2006) find no significant effect of remittances on monthly hours worked by males in rural or urban areas. Instead, their study indicates that males choose to increase monthly work hours in the informal sector and decrease participation in both self-employment and the formal sector. Females, in contrast, show an overall decrease in their monthly hours worked in rural areas, specifically in the informal sector and in unpaid work. Jacoby (1988) finds a gendered division of labor in household production in the Peruvian sierra, with females specializing in livestock production. Adult male labor is found to contribute more than female labor to farm output at the margin; the use of animal traction and land affects the marginal productivity of male and female labor differently. Udry (1996) rejects Pareto optimality in the allocation of resources across plots controlled by males and females in Burkina Faso.

Anthropological and sociological studies have a long history of examining gender roles in production (for example, Wolf 1992). From these fields comes evidence that women's participation in agriculture in some countries has been increasing, due at least in part to migration by males in search of wage work and women's lower opportunity costs of working on the farm (Deere and León 1982; Crummet 1987; Pou et al. 1987; Lago 1987). A reallocation of family labor between household and production activities when individuals migrate is consistent with the predictions of agricultural household models, particularly where labor markets are imperfect.

A critical question, addressed in chapter 4, is whether output changes in response to migration and whether the output effect depends on the gender of the migrants. We are not aware of other gender-specific tests of migration impacts on agricultural production in migrant-sending households.

There is some economic evidence that migration and remittance effects on schooling expenditures may be influenced by gender. The "brain drain" is an increasingly important topic in international migration research, because international migration often selects positively on education (for example, see Özden and Schiff 2005). Nevertheless, migration and remittances also may influence the incentives to invest in schooling. If the economic returns to schooling are higher in migrant labor markets than at the origin, then a strictly positive probability of migration may stimulate investments in human capital formation (Stark and Wang 2002). In addition, remittances may provide sending households with liquidity to invest in education.

Hanson and Woodruff (forthcoming) find that migration to the United States is associated with more years of completed education for 13- to 15-year-old girls, but only for those whose mothers have three years or fewer of education. They cite a positive effect of migration on liquidity and thus on households' ability to invest in schooling. Research by Edwards and Ureta (2003) supports these findings. They conclude that parents' schooling is the main determinant of school attendance, but remittances have a positive and significant effect on the probability that children stay in school. Receiving at least the median amount of remittances reduces the hazard of leaving school by 14 percent in rural households. In urban households, it reduces the hazard by 54 percent for children in grades 1–6 and 27 percent in grades 7–12.

Remittances may provide liquidity to invest in education, but the incentive to migrate and the presence of migrant networks may have the opposite effect. McKenzie and Rapoport (2006) find evidence of a significant negative effect of migration on schooling attendance and attainment for 12- to 18-year-old boys and 16- to 18-year-old girls. They cite a negative incentive effect of migration on schooling. Kandel and Massey (2002) interviewed both males and females at various levels of education to ascertain their aspirations of migrating to the United States and how these aspirations affected schooling investments. They found that individuals were motivated to migrate by cultural expectations about life-course trajectories. Many young men were expected to migrate as part of their experience, while women were not. However, family migration networks increased women's propensity to migrate. For both males and females, advancement in schooling became less important as the aspiration to migrate abroad increased, echoing the finding by Mora and Taylor (2005) and others that international migration does not select positively on schooling in some settings.

When migration and remittances enable households to overcome liquidity and risk constraints, they may influence income indirectly, in various ways. Income insurance and liquidity offered by migrants may stimulate productive investments, creating an income multiplier within the sending household similar to that created by public transfers (for example, see Sadoulet, de Janvry, and Davis 2001).[14] Household expenditures stimulated by migration also may generate local demand for goods and services, creating income and investment multipliers outside the household.

General Equilibrium Considerations

An important implication of split migration is that part of the household remains behind, and it can transmit the impacts of migration to others in the migrant-sending area. General equilibrium effects of migration and remittances on rural economies have been estimated using economywide modeling techniques. A few studies have used economywide modeling techniques to examine the impacts of international migration and remittances on national (Taylor et al. 1996) and rural (Taylor and Adelman 1996; Taylor 1996; Adelman, Taylor, and Vogel 1988) economies. They find evidence that migrant remittances have a multiplier effect on migrant-sending economies. For example, Adelman, Taylor, and Vogel (1988) estimate a village "remittance multiplier" from international migration equal to

1.78; that is, $1 of international migrant remittances generates $1.78 in additional village income, or $0.78 worth of second-round effects. The additional income is created by expenditures from remittance-receiving households, which generate demand for locally produced goods and services, bolstering the income of other households in the village. There is also evidence that migration competes with local production for scarce family resources, raising rural incomes but in some cases producing, in the short run, a "Dutch disease" effect on migrant-sending economies. In the long run, however, remittance-induced investments appear to create positive effects of migration on the income of communities (Taylor and Adelman 1996) and whole rural sectors; for example, see Taylor and Yúnez-Naude's (2005) study of short- and long-run impacts of international migration on the rural economies of El Salvador, Guatemala, Honduras, and Nicaragua. The economywide effects of migration depend critically on how migrants and remittances are distributed across households, on households' access to markets, on expenditure patterns in both migrant and nonmigrant households, and on production constraints. All of these may be influenced by the gender composition of nonmigrant as well as migrant households. No economywide studies of the impacts of international migration on sending areas incorporate gender in their analysis.

Via these diverse pathways, access to migration opportunities by some households may influence a variety of variables of interest in complex ways, including poverty, inequality, health, education, productivity, and choice of activity. The influences of migration thus may be found in households with migrants as well as in those with which migrant households interact in sending economies. All of these influences may be shaped by the gender of the migrants, the remittance recipients, the other members of the migrant-sending household, or the members of other households in migrant-sending areas.

Gender and Migration Networks

Migrant networks convey information and provide assistance to prospective migrants, and these reduce the costs and risks while increasing the benefits of future migration. Network ties can decrease migration costs by providing would-be migrants with critical information about border crossings and employment. Past migrants also may assist in financing the costs of future migrants and provide job market information and contacts. As a result, they can positively influence the probability of migration and also the economic returns from migration (Winters, de Janvry, and Sadoulet 1999). Networks are thus a form of capital that, together with human and physical capital, creates disparities in the costs and benefits of migration across households and individuals.

Networks are central to most models of international migration behavior. In the social sciences, international migration is widely recognized as a network-driven process (for example, see Massey et al. 1987). There are compelling reasons to expect that the effects of networks are gender specific. If networks' value stems from their provision of job information, and if males and females are concentrated in different sectors of the destination economy, then networks with male migrants may have little effect on female migration, and vice versa. The gender composition of networks can affect not only international migration incentives but also settlement patterns (Curran and Saguy 2001; Hondagneu-Sotelo 1994; Lindstrom 1997; Pedraza 1991; Pessar 1999).

The gender composition of networks has empirically been shown to be an important variable shaping international migration. Davis and Winters (2001) find that male and female networks are significant in explaining migration by both genders, but female's location decisions are influenced more heavily by female networks. Curran and Rivero-Fuentes (2003), using cross-sectional data from the Mexican Migration Project, find that male migrant networks are more important determinants of international migration for men than for women. Controlling for other variables, the estimated probability of migration is 2.5 times higher for young adult men with male migrant networks than for those without; however, the presence of male migrants abroad does not affect women's migration. In contrast, female networks increase the odds of female migration 3.8 times. Female networks diminish the probability of men's migration 30 percent compared to men without female networks. Richter and Taylor (chapter 3 in this volume), using retrospective panel data, find that female networks significantly affect the odds of migration by both genders.

When motivations for international migration differ between men and women, women may seek out information and assistance only from female migrants (Davis and Winters 2001). Kandel and Massey (2002) conclude that a "rite of passage" factor influences international migration by young males, while kinship ties exert more influence on the migration of young women. The information conferred by each type of network affects the costs and benefits of international migration differently by gender. For instance, in his work on migration in rural Thailand, de Jong (2000) finds that low income, landlessness, and crop loss are important determinants of migration by men, while expectations, gender roles, networks, and norms are more important for women.

Hondagneu-Sotelo (1994) argues that women must rely on "women's networks" composed of female family members and friends because social norms prevent women from migrating independently or with males, unless they are spouses. Social norms may place constraints on female migration, while increasing the value of migration networks for women relative to men. For instance, it may not be culturally permissible for women to live outside of the familial unit or to cross the border without relatives' assistance.

Both the quality and type of information provided by female and male networks may differ. Menjivar (2000) finds that Central American female migrants are more likely to have extensive social networks than their male counterparts. This finding is supported by Curran and Rivero-Fuentes (2003), who find that female migrant networks within Mexico are more useful to both men and women than are male migrant networks. Male and female migrant networks offer different resources and information crucial for the success of migration by each gender. Despite the finding by some studies that females provide a more extensive support system, Hagan (1998) and Livingston (2006) show that, over time, men have more employment opportunities than women because of their network ties.

Other studies also find that female migration networks are more comprehensive (Curran et al. 2003), and this may reflect findings by Grassmuck and Pessar (1991) and Pedraza (1991) that women migrants are more likely to settle permanently. Women's networks reach outside immigrant enclaves and take advantage of social services required to make ends meet. One reason for this may be that females tend to have divergent interests and plans regarding settlement in the United States, with men more interested in returning to Mexico (Grassmuck and Pessar 1991; Massey and Espinosa 1997; Goldring 1996; Hondagneu-Sotelo 1994; Malkin 1998). Hondagneu-Sotelo (1994) points out that Mexican immigrant men usually find themselves in a subordinate position in the United States compared to their situation in Mexico, in terms of social status or patriarchal privilege, despite possible improvements in their standard of living. In contrast, women are more likely to experience either a relative gain in status in the United States or not as great a loss of status. Working outside the home for wages can improve women's ability to negotiate "patriarchal bargains" (Hondagneu-Sotelo and Messner 1994; Kandiyoti 1988). For women, going back to Mexico might involve the reassertion of stronger patriarchal authority and a return to the premigration gender division of labor in a setting where household work is taxing and implies a loss of the autonomy that female migrants gain working abroad. The permanent settlement motivation for migration could explain why some studies find that females benefit more from mature migrant networks. Curran et al. (2003), in their study of internal migration from rural Thailand, find that female migrant social capital has a greater impact when it is mature—that is, when it is composed of females who have lived at the destination for a long period. This is not the case for male migrant social capital. If members of the female migration network return often to the home village, the effect of the network on female migration is diminished. The importance of the maturity of migration networks is also highlighted by Kanaiaupuni (2000).

Comprehensive female migrant networks may be self-perpetuating if female migrants decide not to return to their origin location. Ellis, Conway, and Bailey (1996) find the migration has the potential to "modify gender relations and alter future migration decision making as women gain experience in the labor market and exposure to new social and cultural environments." Curran and Saguy (2001) expand on Portes and Sensenbrenner's (1993) hypothesis that migration networks transmit not only information but also culture and values. Curran and Saguy define two functions of networks for females: obligation and relative deprivation. Family members remaining at the origin can use networks to find their family members who have migrated and enforce village norms of remitting. This is the obligation function. If women's networks are stronger than those of men, remittances from female migrants should be larger. The authors hypothesize that the relative deprivation effects of networks are stronger for females than for males, because women have few possibilities for upward mobility within the village. The knowledge that female friends have newfound freedoms at the destination may spur women to migrate.

Some researchers have hypothesized that networks modify gender relations as well as future migration decisions. Ellis, Conway, and Bailey (1996) hypothesize that migration may modify gender relations as "women gain experience in the labor market and exposure to new social and cultural environments." From a household perspective, networks may be endogenous; households may strategically invest in establishing networks that influence their future economic returns from migration. Gender considerations may influence household investments in network formation, because female networks may generate different economic returns than male networks. If the information and assistance value of family networks is gender specific, then a family's optimal choice is to invest in the gender network that maximizes future net benefits—for example, keeping the only son at home to work on the farm, while sending abroad the oldest daughter, who can constitute a network to facilitate migration by her younger female siblings in the future. The role of gender in endogenous network formation has not been a subject of quantitative research to our knowledge. Most research takes networks as predetermined and, with few exceptions, ignores the endogeneity of network formation.

Conclusions

Economists and other social scientists have begun to address some pieces of the puzzle of how gender shapes international migration and its impacts. These include gender differences in remittance behavior, in the effects of human capital and household variables on migration probabilities, in family migration networks, in the impacts of policy shocks on international migration by males and females, and in labor market outcomes at destinations. When gender is introduced into empirical models, it generally is found to be an important variable shaping migration and its outcomes.

The Need for a Coherent Framework

Nevertheless, the existing research on gender in international migration lacks any kind of coherent theoretical framework, and the empirical record is thin and often difficult to interpret. Rarely has gender made an appearance in theoretical models of international migration in economics. As a result, when gender is included in empirical models, it is usually relegated to being a control variable rather than a focus of hypothesis tests. Empirical studies focusing on differences in international migration determinants, remittances, and impacts between the sexes are few, and often they lack grounding in economic theory or the use of appropriate instruments to enable one to reliably identify gender effects. Critical pieces of the gender-and-international-migration puzzle largely have been ignored. These include differences between males and females with regard to the opportunity costs of migration; the influences of migration and remittances on household investments, production and technology choices, and expenditures; and the linkages that transmit migration influences through migrant-sending economies. Some of the most thorny migration research challenges are magnified when gender is brought into the analysis. For example, women often are not observed in the workforce prior to migration, and many benefits produced by women in households have unobserved "shadow values" instead of market prices. Development economics research using nonseparable household models have made some inroads into understanding economic behavior when markets are not available. These approaches need to be brought more squarely into international migration research, particularly if one wishes to understand differences in the opportunity costs of international migration between men and women.

Nearly all researchers agree that networks are a key variable influencing international migration, and there is now some empirical evidence that the effects of networks are gender specific. There is a need to provide these empirical studies with a mooring in network and information theory, with an emphasis on gender. With only a few exceptions, researchers take networks as predetermined and exogenous; little if any attention is given to how networks are formed, how the endogeneity of networks might bias empirical findings, or what methods might be used to avoid such bias and better identify relationships of interest. Do households take gender into account when establishing migration networks abroad? Once established, how does the gender composition of a household's network influence the future gender composition of migration? Do international migrant networks outside the household influence male and female migration similarly, or does the gender composition of these networks shape the future gender composition of migration in ways that might explain differences across origins and destinations? Where formal recruitment plays a role in international labor migration, how do recruitment networks select on gender, why, and what are the implications for origins, destinations, and the migrants themselves?

A similar problem of empirical analysis getting ahead of theory is evident in research on remittance behavior by men and women. There is some evidence that women remit different amounts than men, and some variables appear to affect remittances by the two genders differently. However, here, as in the case of remittance behavior in general, theory has lagged. To carry out gendered research on remittance behavior, data are needed on both wages and remittances by migrants as well as on sending-household characteristics that influence these remittances. The high cost of "tracer surveys" of migrants is an obvious impediment to such research.

The impacts of international migration and remittances on migrant-sending households have been a focus of so-called new economics of labor migration research over the past two decades. Theoretical and empirical models of migration's impacts need to incorporate gender to address critical questions, including the following: Do remittances by men affect production and household expenditures differently than remittances by women? If so, why? Does the gender of remittance recipients matter? The gender composition of the sending household? Women's access to microcredit? There is a pressing need to recast international migration-and-development research in a gender framework. This requires a gendered household modeling approach, tests of the effects of the gender of remitters and receivers on household expenditures, and most likely a departure from unitary household models.

The impacts of international migration do not end in the households that send migrants and receive remittances. Expenditure linkages transmit impacts to other households in the migrant-sending economy. Economywide impacts of migration and remittances have been addressed using microsurvey data and both aggregate and disaggregated general equilibrium modeling techniques. A gender focus needs to be brought into this research as well, in order to understand ways in which gender may shape the transmission of impacts through sending economies. The economywide effects of international migration are likely to be different when one gender migrates and remits while the other stays at home.

The starting point for bringing gender into economic research on international migration is to design theoretical models that highlight gender and provide a foundation for rigorous empirical analysis. At a minimum, a "gender subscript" should be attached to every key variable in international migration models. Beyond this, new directions need to be explored. Grounding the analysis of how gender shapes migration and its impacts on the household (and possibly larger social units) is critical. Over the past two decades, economic research on migration has directed its attention outside the household, to consider market imperfections under which separability breaks down and the set of potential impacts of migration proliferates. Gender has been absent, for the most part, from this interesting literature. Future research also needs to turn its attention inside the household, to understand the ways in which gender may affect migration decisions and impacts, particularly when benefits and costs of international migration are gender specific. This review has discussed some implications of gender in joint and split household models of international migration, but little is known about the gender dynamics underlying international migration decisions. Recent advances in intra-household economic research, including some that have a gender focus, may be a useful starting point for doing this.

Data and Survey Design

Theory guides data collection, and a key implication of this review is that "gendering" economic research on international migration also means bringing a gender focus into surveys supporting this research. This includes obtaining a gender breakdown of information on migration, remittances, and other variables that may influence the opportunity costs, returns, and impacts of international migration for prospective migrant-sending households. At present, few data sets offer anywhere near the detail required to do this type of analysis. There are many tradeoffs inherent in designing household surveys, and any additional question that is added to a survey instrument comes at a high cost. However, the cost of ignoring gender is likely to be higher.

It is particularly costly to add questions to a national population census, given the large number of households being surveyed. Fortunately, most population censuses already provide information on gender and birthplace of household members. This, together with the ability to generalize to whole country populations, makes census data useful for some kinds of international migration research that have been discussed in this review.

The greatest opportunity to acquire better data for gender and international migration research is through modifications in national income and expenditure surveys and new surveys designed specifically to generate data on migration, in both sending and receiving countries. In many cases, simply adding a question or two to an existing survey can create valuable data to support gender and international migration research at a relatively low cost. Any survey whose main motives include creating data for research on migration, at a minimum, should collect all migration, migrant network, and remittance information by gender.[15]

Some existing income and expenditure surveys, including some living standards measurement surveys, ask respondents how many family members were living abroad in the year prior to the survey. This question should be asked separately for men and women, in order to obtain measures of the household's international migration network by gender. Information on new migration (occurring during the year covered by the survey) also should be gathered by gender. This would make it possible to model new migration by men and women as a function of gender-specific migration networks. To explore interactions between migration and marriage, information on the sequencing of these two variables is essential. Obtaining international migration by gender, in our view, is the top priority for modifying existing surveys to support gender and international migration research.

Increasingly, remittances are included in large-scale surveys, because often they are an important component of total income in the least-developed countries. When this is done, rarely is there sufficient information from the survey to treat remittances as anything other than an exogenous income transfer. There is now considerable evidence that remittances are endogenous. Obtaining gender-specific information on international migration as well as on international migrant remittances may allow one to take the first step toward properly treating remittances as endogenous income transfers. As we have seen, there is reason to believe that the gender of the migrant who sends remittances matters, not only to the amount of remittances that are sent but also for the potential impacts of the remittances on the receiving household. A breakdown of international migrant remittances by the gender of the sender would facilitate the integration of gender into the analysis of remittances. If one has a gender breakdown of international migration but not remittances, it might still be possible to study gender differences in remittances using regression methods; however, much information will be lost.

We have also seen that gender may influence the impacts of migration and remittances within migrant-sending households. All good household surveys collect information on the gender of nonmigrating household members. Few record the gender of the survey respondent. This is important to test for a gender bias in survey response. Almost no surveys ask the gender of the household members who receive the remittances. This may be critical for understanding the ways in which remittances may influence household expenditures on consumption, production activities, and investments. Linking individuals with the production and other income activities in which they participate is indispensable if there is to be any hope of identifying opportunity costs of international migration for men and women. Information on wages and days in wage work should be gathered for each household member; there is likely to be a close affinity between wages and opportunity costs of migration if local labor markets function reasonably well.

If a survey is sufficiently detailed to quantify family labor inputs in household production activities, as in agricultural household models, this should be done for each household member rather than in the aggregate. Not only might this enable researchers to include gender-specific family labor in household production functions; it also is likely to produce a more reliable estimate of total family labor in these activities.

In destination surveys of immigrant households, researchers should do their best to obtain disaggregated information on remittances abroad by individual household members. This, together with socioeconomic and income data by household member, would greatly facilitate research on some aspects of remittance behavior by men and women living outside their country of origin. Ideally, one would want to include in such surveys questions about individuals' household of origin. This could facilitate analyses of the ways in which (origin) household characteristics influence motivations to remit by migrants abroad, as a complement to those currently being conducted with data from sending-area surveys.

Final Thoughts

In short, for research as well as the design of gender-focused development policies, empirical analysis needs to be grounded in a coherent "gendered" theory of international migration that can serve as a guide for new data collection, estimation, and interpretation of empirical results. To date, the lack of a structured and coherent gender focus has compromised our understanding of how even basic characteristics, such as human capital, affect international migration decisions and impacts for men and women. What little we do know makes it clear that gender cannot be ignored or represented simply as a dummy variable in economic studies of international migration and its impacts.

Endnotes

1. The study was carried out by the Gender and Migration Working Group of the Social Science Research Council's International Migration Program.

2. Information on the 2000 census is available at http://www.census.gov/main/www/cen2000.html.

3. Citizenship and Immigration Canada (2002).

4. See the Encuesta Nacional a Hogares Rurales de México (ENHRUM) area at http://precesam.colmex.mx.

5. However, studies of discrimination in labor markets find that the effects of these variables on wages often are not the same, depending on an individual's ethnicity, gender, or even looks (for

evidence on the latter, see Hamermesh and Biddle 1994; chapter 6 of this volume, by Özden and Neagu).

6. Human capital theory posits that individuals with more human capital, other things being equal, locate themselves in the labor market in which the economic returns to this human capital are highest. This may imply that relatively educated individuals have a higher propensity to migrate abroad than do less educated individuals. However, the reverse may be true if the returns to human capital are higher at home (Mora and Taylor 2006; Boucher, Stark, and Taylor 2005). Thus the finding of a negative association between education and international migration may be perfectly consistent with human capital theory.

7. Males and females need to be perfect substitutes at only one locale in order to obtain an equalization of wages between the genders at both locales.

8. The opportunity cost of migration for the sending economy is equal to the marginal value product of the migrant's labor. This can be assumed to be the same as the wage only when a perfect labor market exists.

9. Another study, by Liang and Chen (2004), does not support the marriage mobility hypothesis. It separately analyzes the employment opportunities and professions of male and female migrants in China and finds that women primarily migrate from rural to urban areas for employment reasons; rarely are they motivated by marriage prospects. The study also concludes that the majority of the difference between male and female migrant wages can be attributed to the fact that female migrants, in general, have lower levels of education than male migrants.

10. Mincer (1978) finds that married persons are less likely to move than are singles, and the mobility of separated and divorced partners is higher than that of married partners. There is evidence that migration rates are lower for families with working wives. Distance is found to be a deterrent to migration. Women are more likely than men to be tied movers, while husbands are more likely to be tied stayers than tied movers (Compton and Pollack 2004). Women are generally disadvantaged by moves (Smith and Thomas 1998). Compton and Pollack (2004) find that couples tend to locate in large metropolitan areas because of the husband's and not the wife's education.

11. There may be dynamic considerations that are overlooked by joint migration models as well. Women may choose career paths that are easy to move, such as nursing or primary education, and gender roles may encourage the betterment of the husband's, at the expense of the wife's, career. Compton and Pollack (2004) find that women chose occupations that are more transferable; thus only the male's education or income matters in determining relocation decisions. This could conceal tied-mover effects, making women's moves appear to be less tied than they really are. If this is the case, then the effects of family migration on women may be more negative than studies indicate.

12. The shadow wage is the shadow value on the individual's time constraint divided by the marginal utility of income; see Skoufias (1994); Jacoby (1988); Benjamin (1992).

13. There may be differences in savings as well as remittances between male and female migrants. Grassmuck and Pessar (1991) find that men view migration as a temporary move from the Dominican Republic and begin to save money for return and for remittances. But women, hoping to avoid returning, spend their income abroad and fail to remit. Pedraza (1991) finds that male migrants save money, while women attempt to deplete funds to foreclose the option of returning to the home country and relinquishing newfound freedoms enjoyed abroad. These studies contradict some of the findings of remittance studies; that is, that women have a higher propensity to remit than men.

14. Migration also may disrupt household labor allocation and social norms, with implications for children's health. Kanaiaupuni and Donato (1999) find that in the short run migration increases infant mortality, but in the long run mortality risks decrease as the village as a whole experiences an increase in economic resources from migration. Donato, Kanaiaupuni, and Stainback (2001) find that increases in income have a positive effect on boys' health relative to girls', but in migrant households the gap between boys' and girls' health narrows.

15. Even when the data are not intended for migration research, it is rare that economic behavior by households can be modeled reliably without taking into account the portfolio of activities, including migration, in which families may participate.

References

Adelman, Irma, J. Edward Taylor, and Stephen Vogel. 1988. "Life in a Mexican Village: A SAM Perspective." *Journal of Development Studies* 25 (5): 5–24.

Aguilera, Michael, and Douglas S. Massey. 2003. "Social Capital and the Wages of Mexican Migrants: New Hypotheses and Tests." *Social Forces* 82 (2): 671–701.

Amuedo-Dorantes, Catalina, and Susan Pozo. 2006. "Migration, Remittances, and Male and Female Employment Patterns." *American Economic Review* 96 (2): 222–26.

Becker, Gary. 1965. "A Theory of the Allocation of Time." *Economic Journal* 75 (299): 493–576.

———. 1971. *The Economics of Discrimination.* Chicago: University of Chicago Press.

Behrman, Jere R., and Barbara Wolfe. 1984. "Micro Determinants of Female Migration in a Developing Country: Labor Market, Demographic Marriage Market, and Economic Marriage Market Incentives." In *Research in Population Economics,* Vol. 5, ed. T. Paul Schultz and Ken Wolpin, 137–66. Greenwich, CT: JAI Press.

Benjamin, Dwayne. 1992. "Household Composition, Labor Markets, and Labor Demand: Testing for Separation on Agricultural Household Models." *Econometrica* 60 (2): 287–322.

Blue, Sarah A. 2004. "State Policy, Economic Crisis, Gender, and Family Ties: Determinants of Family Remittances to Cuba." *Economic Geography* 80 (1): 63–82.

Borjas, George. 1987. "Self-Selection and the Earnings of Migrants." *American Economic Review* 77 (4): 531–53.

Boucher, Stephen, Oded Stark, and J. Edward Taylor. 2005. "A Gain with a Drain? Evidence from Rural Mexico on the New Economics of the Brain Drain." Paper prepared for the 14th World Congress of the International Economic Association, Marrakech, Morocco, August 29–September 2.

Bourguignon, François, and Pierre-Andre Chiappori. 1992. "Collective Models of Household Behavior: An Introduction." *European Economic Review* 36 (2–3): 355–64.

Boyd, Monica, and Elizabeth Grieco. 2003. "Women and Migration: Incorporating Gender into International Migration Theory." Migration Policy Institute, *Migration Information Source,* March. (www.migrationinformation.org/Feature/print.cfm?ID=106.)

Cackley, Alicia Puente. 1993. "The Role of Wage Differentials in Determining Migration Selectivity by Sex: The Case of Brazil." In *Internal Migration of Women in Developing Countries.* New York: United Nations, Department for Economic and Social Information and Policy Analysis.

Cerrutti, Marcela, and Douglas S. Massey. 2001. "On the Auspices of Female Migration from Mexico to the United States." *Demography* 38 (2): 187–200.

———. 2004. "Trends in Mexican Migration to the United States, 1965–1995." In *Crossing the Border: Research from the Mexican Migration Project,* ed. Jorge Durand and Douglas S. Massey. New York: Russell Sage Foundation.

Chattopadhyay, Arpita. 1998. "Gender, Migration, and Career Trajectories in Malaysia." *Demography* 35 (3): 335–44.

Chen, Joyce. 2006. "Non-Cooperative Behavior among Spouses: Child Outcomes in Migrant-Sending Households." Unpublished mss. Harvard University, Department of Economics. (http://www.agecon.ucdavis.edu/uploads/seminars/chen_paper.pdf.)

Citizenship and Immigration Canada. 2002. *Facts and Figures 2002: Immigration Overview; Permanent and Temporary Residents.* Department of Citizenship and Immigration Canada.

Cobb-Clark, Deborah. 1993. "Immigrant Selectivity and Wages: The Evidence for Women." *American Economic Review* 83 (4): 986–93.

Compton, Janice, and Robert Pollack. 2004. "Why Are Power Couples Increasingly Located in Large Cities?" NBER Working Paper 10918. National Bureau of Economic Research, Cambridge, Mass., November.

Cooke, Thomas J. 2003. "Family Migration and the Relative Earnings of Husbands and Wives." *Annals of the Association of American Geography* 93 (2): 338–49.

Cornelius, Wayne. 1990. "Mexican Immigrants in California Today." Keynote presentation to the conference "California Immigrants in a World Perspective," Immigration Research Program, University of California, Los Angeles, April 26–27.

Crummet, María de los Angeles. 1987. "Rural Women and Migration in Latin America." In *Rural Women and State Policy: Feminist Perspectives on Latin American Agricultural Development*, ed. Carmen Deere and Magdalena León de Leal. Boulder, CO: Westview Press.

Curran, Sara R., Filiz Garip, Chang Chung, and Kanchana Tangchonlatip. 2003. "Migration, Cumulative Causation, and Gender: Evidence from Thailand." Paper prepared for the conference "African Migration in Comparative Perspective," Johannesburg, South Africa, June 4–7.

Curran, Sara R., and Estela Rivero-Fuentes. 2003. "Engendering Migrant Networks: The Case of Mexican Migration." *Demography* 40 (2): 289–307.

Curran, Sara R., and Abigail C. Saguy. 2001. "Migration and Cultural Change: A Role for Gender and Social Networks." *Journal of International Women's Studies* 2 (3): 54–77.

David, Paul A. 1974. "Fortune, Risk, and the Microeconomics of Migration." In *Nations and Households in Economic Growth*, ed. Paul A. David and Melvin W. Reder. New York: Academic Press.

Davis, Benjamin, and Paul Winters. 2001. "Gender, Networks, and Mexico-U.S. Migration." *Journal of Development Studies* 38 (2): 1–26.

Deere, Carmen D., and Magdalena León de Leal, eds. 1982. *Rural Women and State Policy: Feminist Perspectives on Agricultural Development in Latin America.* Boulder, CO: Westview Press.

De Janvry, Alain, Marcel Fafchamps, and Elisabeth Sadoulet. 1991. "Peasant Household Behavior with Missing Markets: Some Paradoxes Explained." *Economic Journal* 101 (409): 1400–17.

de Jong, Gordon. 2000. "Expectations, Gender, and Norms in Migration Decision Making." *Population Studies* 54 (November): 307–19.

de Laat, Joost. 2005. "Moral Hazard and Costly Monitoring: The Case of Split Migrants in Kenya." Brown University, November.

de la Brière, Bénédicte, Alain de Janvry, Elisabeth Sadoulet, and Sylvie Lambert. 2002. "The Roles of Destination, Gender, and Household Composition in Explaining Remittances: An Analysis for the Dominican Sierra." *Journal of Development Economics* 68 (2): 309–28.

Donato, Katharine M. 1993. "Current Trends and Patterns of Female Migration: Evidence from Mexico." *International Migration Review* 27 (4): 748–71.

Donato, Katharine M., Shawn M. Kanaiaupuni, and Melissa Stainback. 2001. "The Effects of Migration, Household Income, and Gender on Mexican Child Health." Working Paper 2001-10. University of Wisconsin, Madison, Center for Demography and Ecology.

Donato, Katharine M., and Evelyn Patterson. 2004. "Women and Men on the Move: Undocumented Border Crossing." In *Crossing the Border: Research from the Mexican Migration Project*, ed. Jorge Durand and Douglas Massey. New York: Russell Sage Foundation.

Durand, Jorge, Douglas S. Massey, and Emilio Parrado. 1999. "The New Era of Mexican Migration to the United States." *Journal of American History* 86 (2): 518–36.

Edwards, Alejandra Cox, and Manuelita Ureta. 2003. "International Migration, Remittances, and Schooling: Evidence from El Salvador." *Journal of Development Economics* 72 (2): 429–61.

Ellis, Mark, Dennis Conway, and Adrian J. Bailey. 1996. "The Circular Migration of Puerto Rican Women: Towards a Gendered Explanation." *International Migration* 34 (1): 31–64.

Elnajjar, Hassan. 1993. "Planned Emigration: The Palestinian Case." *International Migration Review* 27 (1): 34–50.

Fernández-Kelly, María Patricia. 1983. *For We Are Sold, I and My People: Women and Industry in Mexico's Frontier.* Albany: State University of New York Press.

Findley, Sally, and Assitan Diallo. 1993. "Social Appearances and Economic Realities of Female Migration in Rural Mali." In *Internal Migration of Women in Developing Countries.* New York: United Nations, Department for Economic and Social Information and Policy Analysis.

Fontana, Marzia, and Adrian Wood. 2000. "Modeling the Effects of Trade on Women, at Work and at Home." *World Development* 28 (7): 1173–90.

Gabaccia, Donna, Katharine M. Donato, Jennifer Holdaway, Martin Monalansan IV, and Patricia R. Pessar, eds. 2006. *International Migration Review [special issue on Gender and Migration Revisited]* 40 (Spring).

Gamburd, Michele R. 2000. *The Kitchen Spoon's Handle: Transnationalism and Sri Lanka's Migrant Housemaids.* Ithaca: Cornell University Press.

Goldring, Luin. 1996. "Blurring Borders: Constructing Transnational Community in the Process of Mexico-U.S. Migration." *Research in Community Sociology* 6: 69–104.

———. 2003. "Gender, Status, and the State in Transnational Spaces: The Gendering of Political Participation and Mexican Hometown Associations." In *Gender and U.S. Immigration: Contemporary Trends,* ed. Pierrette Hondagneu-Sotelo, 341–58. Los Angeles: University of California Press.

Grassmuck, Sherri, and Patricia R. Pessar. 1991. *Between Two Islands: Dominican International Migration.* Los Angeles: University of California Press.

Hagan, Jaqueline Maria. 1998. "Social Networks, Gender, and Immigration Incorporation: Resources and Constraints." *American Sociological Review* 63 (1): 55–67.

Hamermesh, Daniel S., and Jeff E. Biddle. 1994. "Beauty and the Labor Market." *American Economic Review* 84 (5): 1174–94.

Hanson, Gordon H., and Christopher Woodruff. Forthcoming. "Emigration and Educational Attainment in Mexico." *Journal of Development Economics.*

Hoddinott, John. 1994. "A Model of Migration and Remittances Applied to Western Kenya." *Oxford Economic Papers* 46 (3): 459–76.

Hondagneu-Sotelo, Pierrette. 1994. *Gendered Transitions: Mexican Experiences of Immigration.* Berkeley: University of California Press.

Hondagneu-Sotelo, Pierrette, and Michael A. Messner. 1994. "Gender Displays and Men's Power: The 'New Man' and the Mexican Immigrant Man." In *Theorizing Masculinities,* ed. Harry Bord and Michael Kaufman, 200–18. London: Sage.

Jacoby, Hanan. 1988. "Productivity of Men and Women and the Sexual Division of Labor in Peasant Agriculture of the Peruvian Sierra." *Journal of Development Economics* 37 (1–2): 265–87.

Kanaiaupuni, Shawn M. 2000. "Reframing the Migration Question: An Analysis of Men, Women, and Gender in Mexico." *Social Forces* 78 (4): 1311–47.

Kanaiaupuni, Shawn, and Katharine Donato. 1999. "Migradollars and Mortality: The Effects of Migration on Child and Infant Survival." *Demography* 36 (4): 332–53.

Kandel, William, and Douglas S. Massey. 2002. "The Culture of Mexican Migration: A Theoretical and Empirical Analysis." *Social Forces* 80 (3): 981–1004.

Kandiyoti, Deniz. 1988. "Bargaining with Patriarchy." *Gender and Society* 2 (3): 274–490.

King, Russell, and Elizabeth Zontini. 2000. "The Role of Gender in the South European Immigration Model." *Revista de Sociologia* [Universitat Autònoma de Barcelona] 60 (1): 35–52.

Kossoudji, Sherrie A., and Susan I. Ranney. 1984. "The Labor Market Experience of Female Migrants: The Case of Temporary Mexican Migration to the U.S." *International Migration Review* 18 (4): 1120–43.

Lago, María Soledad. 1987. "Rural Women and the Neo-Liberal Model in Chile." In *Rural Women and State Policy: Feminist Perspectives on Agricultural Development in Latin America,* ed. Carmen D. Deere and Magdalena León de Leal. Boulder, CO: Westview Press.

Levhari, David, and Oded Stark. 1982. "On Migration and Risk." *Economic Development and Cultural Change* 31 (1): 191–98.

Lewis, W. Arthur. 1954. "Economic Development with Unlimited Supplies of Labor." *Manchester School* 22 (May): 139–91.

Liang, Zai, and Yiu Por Chen. 2004. "Migration and Gender in China: An Origin-Destination Linked Approach." *Economic Development and Cultural Change* 52 (4): 423–44.

Lindstrom, David P. 1997. "The Impact of Temporary U.S. Migration on Fertility of Female Migrants: The Case of Temporary Migration in a Rural Mexican Township." Working Paper Series. Population Studies and Training Center, Brown University, Providence, RI.

Livingston, Gretchen M. 2006. "Gender, Job Searching, and Employment Outcomes among Mexican Immigrants." *Population Research and Policy Review* 25 (1): 43–66.

Lucas, Robert E. B. 1987. "Emigration to South Africa's Mines." *American Economic Review* 77 (3): 313–30.

Lucas, Robert E. B., and Oded Stark. 1985. "Motivations to Remit: Evidence from Botswana." *Journal of Political Economy* 93 (5): 901–18.

Mahler, Patricia, and Sarah Pessar. 2003. "Transnational Migration: Bringing Gender in." *International Migration Review* 37 (3): 812–46.

Malkin, Victoria. 1998. "Migration, Modernity, and Respect." In *The Family and Gender in Transmigrant Circuits: A Case Study of Migration between Western Mexico and New Rochelle, New York.* Ph.D. diss., University College of London, Department of Social Anthropology, December.

———. 2004. "We Go to Get Ahead: Gender and Status in Two Mexican Migrant Communities." *Latin American Perspectives* 31 (5): 75–99.

Massey, Douglas, Rafael Alarcón, Jorge Durand, and Humberto González. 1987. *Return to Aztlán: The Social Process of International Migration from Western Mexico.* Los Angeles: University of California Press.

Massey, Douglas, Joaquin Arango, Graeme Hugo, Ali Kouaouci, Adela Pellegrino, and J. Edward Taylor. 2005. *Worlds in Motion: Understanding International Migration at the End of the Millennium.* Oxford: Oxford University Press.

Massey, Douglas, and Kristin Espinosa. 1997. "What's Driving Mexico-U.S. Migration? A Theoretical, Empirical, and Policy Analysis." *American Journal of Sociology* 102 (4): 939–99.

Maxwell, Nan L. 1988. "Economic Returns to Migration: Marital Status and Gender Differences." *Social Science Quarterly* 68 (1): 108–21.

McElroy, Marjorie B., and Mary Jean Horney. 1981. "Nash Bargained Household Decisions." *International Economic Review* 22 (2): 333–50.

McKenzie, David, and Hillel Rapoport. 2006. "Can Migration Reduce Educational Attainment? Evidence from Mexico." Policy Research Working Paper 3952. World Bank, Washington, DC.

Menjivar, Cecilia. 2000. "The Intersection of Work and Gender: Central American Immigrant Women and Employment in California." *American Behavioral Scientist* 42 (4): 601–27.

Mills, Mary Beth. 1997. "Contesting the Margins of Modernity: Women, Migration, and Consumption in Thailand." *American Ethnologist* 24 (1): 37–61.

Mincer, Jacob. 1978. "Family Migration Decisions." *Journal of Political Economy* 86 (5): 749–73.

Mora, Jorge, and J. Edward Taylor. 2006. "Determinants of Migration, Destination, and Sector Choice: Disentangling Individual, Household, and Community Effects." In *International Migration, Remittances, and the Brain Drain,* ed. Çağlar Özden and Maurice Schiff. New York: Palgrave Macmillan.

Munshi, Kaivan. 2003. "Networks in the Modern Economy: Mexican Migrants in the U.S. Labor Market." *Quarterly Journal of Economics* 118 (2): 549–99.

Özden, Çağlar, and Maurice Schiff, eds. 2005. *International Migration, Remittances, and the Brain Drain.* New York: Palgrave Macmillan.

Pedraza, Silvia. 1991. "Women and Migration: The Social Consequences of Gender." *Annual Review of Sociology* 17: 303–25.

Pessar, Patricia R. 1986. "The Role of Gender in Dominican Settlement in the United States." In *Women and Change in Latin America,* ed. June Nash and Helen Safa, 273–94. South Hadley, MA: Bergin and Garvey.

———. 1988. "The Constraints on and Release of Female Labor Power: Dominican Migration to the United States." In *A Home Divided: Women and Income in the Third World,* ed. Daisy Dwyer and Judith Bruce, 195–215. Palo Alto: Stanford University Press.

———. 1999. "Engendering Migration Studies: The Case of New Immigrants in the United States." *American Behavioral Scientist* 42 (4): 577–600.

Portes, Alejandro, and Julia Sensenbrenner. 1993. "Embeddedness and Immigration: Notes on the Social Determinants of Economic Action." *American Journal of Sociology* 98 (6): 1320–50.

Pou, F., B. Mones, P. Hernández, L. Grant, M. Dottin, A. Arango, B. Fernández, and T. Rosado. 1987. *La mujer rural dominicana.* Santo Domingo: Centro de Investigación para la acción femenina.

Ramírez, Carlota, Mar G. Domínguez, and Julia Morais. 2005. "Crossing Borders: Remittances, Gender, and Development." Working Paper. United Nations, International Research and Training Institute for the Advancement of Women, Washington, DC.

Ribas, Natalia. 2000. "Presentación del monográfico inmigración femenina en el Sur de Europa." *Papers* 60: 13–34.

Rosenzweig, Mark R. 1988. "Labor Markets in Low-Income Countries." In *Handbook of Development Economics*, Vol. 1, ed. Hollis Chenery and T. N. Srinivasan, 714–63. New York: Elsevier Science Publishers.

Rosenzweig, Mark R., and Oded Stark. 1989. "Consumption Smoothing, Migration, and Marriage: Evidence from Rural India." *Journal of Political Economy* 97 (4): 905–26.

Rozelle, Scott, J. Edward Taylor, and Alan de Brauw. 1999. "Migration, Remittances, and Productivity in China." *American Economic Review* 89 (2): 287–91.

Sadoulet, Elisabeth, Alain de Janvry, and Benjamin Davis. 2001. "Cash Transfer Programs with Income Multipliers: PROCAMPO in Mexico." *World Development* 29 (6): 1043–56.

Schultz, T. Paul. 1990. "Testing the Neoclassical Model of Family Labor Supply and Fertility." *Journal of Human Resources* 25 (4): 599–634.

Semyonov, Moshe, and Anastasia Gorodzeisky. 2005. "Labor, Migration, Remittances, and Household Income: A Comparison between Filipino and Filipina Overseas Workers." *International Migration Review* 39 (1): 45–68.

Sjaastad, Larry A. 1962. "The Costs and Returns of Human Migration." *Journal of Political Economy* 70 (5): 80–93.

Skoufias, Emmanuel. 1994. "Using Shadow Wages to Estimate Labor Supply of Agricultural Households." *American Journal of Agricultural Economics* 76 (2): 215–27.

Smith, James P., and Duncan Thomas. 1998. "On the Road: Marriage and Mobility in Malaysia." *Journal of Human Resources* 33 (4): 805–32.

Stark, Oded. 1978. *Economic-Demographic Interactions in Agricultural Development: The Case of Rural-to-Urban Migration.* Rome: United Nations Food and Agricultural Organization.

———. 1991. *The Migration of Labor.* Cambridge, U.K.: Basil Blackwell.

Stark, Oded, and Eliakim Katz. 1986. "Labor Migration and Risk Aversion in Less Developed Countries." *Journal of Labor Economics* 4 (1): 134–49.

Stark, Oded, and J. Edward Taylor. 1991. "Migration Incentives, Migration Types: The Role of Relative Deprivation." *Economic Journal* 101 (408): 1163–78.

Stark, Oded, and Yong Wang. 2002. "Inducing Human Capital Formation: Migration as a Substitute for Subsidies." *Journal of Public Economics* 86 (1): 29–46.

Taylor, J. Edward. 1986. "Differential Migration, Networks, Information, and Risk." In *Migration Theory, Human Capital, and Development*, ed. Oded Stark, 147–71. Greenwich, CT: JAI Press.

———. 1987. "Undocumented Mexico-U.S. Migration and the Returns to Households in Rural Mexico." *American Journal of Agricultural Economics* 69 (3): 626–38.

———. 1992. "Remittances and Inequality Reconsidered: Direct, Indirect, and Intertemporal Effects." *Journal of Policy Modeling* 14 (2): 187–208.

———. 1996. "International Migration and Economic Development: A Micro Economy-Wide Analysis." In *Development Strategy, Employment, and Migration: Insights from Models*, ed. J. Edward Taylor. Paris: Organisation for Economic Co-operation and Development.

Taylor, J. Edward, and Irma Adelman. 1996. *Village Economies: The Design, Estimation, and Use of Villagewide Economic Models.* Cambridge, U.K.: Cambridge University Press.

Taylor, J. Edward, and Philip L. Martin. 2001. "Human Capital: Migration and Rural Population Change." In *Handbook of Agricultural Economics*, vol. 1, ed. Bruce Gardener and Gordon Rausser, 457–511. Amsterdam: Elsevier.

Taylor, J. Edward, Douglas S. Massey, Joaquin Arango, Graeme Hugo, Ali Kouaouci, and Adela Pellegrino. 1996. "International Migration and National Development." *Population Index* 62 (2): 181–212.

Taylor, J. Edward, Scott Rozelle, and Alan de Brauw. 2003. "Migration and Incomes in Source Communities: A New Economics of Migration Perspective from China." *Economic Development and Cultural Change* 52 (1): 75–101.

Taylor, J. Edward, and Antonio Yúnez-Naude. 2005. "Análisis de los impactos en los mercados y en los factores de producción en el ámbito rural del Tratado de Libre Comercio entre América Central y los Estados Unidos de América (CAFTA): Efectos en la migración laboral." Unpublished mss. Inter-American Development Bank, Washington, DC.

Thadani, Veena, and Michael P. Todaro. 1984. "Female Migration: A Conceptual Framework." In *Women in the Cities of Asia: Migration and Urban Adaptation,* ed. James T. Fawcett, Siew-Ean Khoo, and Peter C. Smith. Boulder, CO: Westview.

Todaro, Michael P. 1969. "A Model of Labor Migration and Urban Unemployment in Less Developed Countries." *American Economic Review* 59 (1): 138–48.

Tyner, James A. 1996. "The Gendering of Philippine International Labor Migration." *Professional Geographer* 48 (4): 405–16.

Udry, Christopher. 1996. "Gender, Agricultural Production, and the Theory of the Household." *Journal of Political Economy* 104 (5): 1010–46.

Winters, Paul, Alain de Janvry, and Elisabeth Sadoulet. 1999. "Family and Community Networks in Mexico-U.S. Migration." ARE Working Paper 99-12. University of New England, Graduate School of Agricultural and Resource Economics.

Wolf, Diane. 1992. *Factory Daughters: Gender, Household Dynamics, and Rural Industrialization in Java.* Berkeley: University of California Press.

Zlotnik, Hania. 2003. "The Global Dimensions of Female Migration." *Migration Information Source.* (http://www.migrationinformation.org/Feature/display.cfm?ID=109.)

3

GENDER AND THE DETERMINANTS OF INTERNATIONAL MIGRATION FROM RURAL MEXICO OVER TIME

Susan Richter and J. Edward Taylor

There is a growing awareness in social science research that the consideration of gender is critical when studying the motivations, outcomes, and barriers to international migration (see chapter 2). Nevertheless, there has been little effort to model explicitly the differences between men and women with respect to the determinants of international migration and their changes over time. This oversight is a serious shortcoming. Theoretical models and empirical findings focusing on male migration may not adequately describe migration by females, and studies that do not distinguish between males and females may misstate the effect of independent variables on migration for both genders. The lack of a structured and coherent gender focus has compromised our understanding of how even basic characteristics, including human capital, affect international migration by men and women. What little we do know makes it clear that gender cannot be ignored or represented simply as a dummy variable in econometric models.

A lack of panel data has further impeded research on international migration by gender, because such data permit researchers to investigate how trends in migration have changed and differed by gender over time. Panel data also make it possible to explore the ways in which immigration policies, economic shocks, and other key variables may affect female and male migration, perhaps in different ways.

This chapter presents the findings of an empirical study of gender and the determinants of migration from rural Mexico, using unique data from the Mexico National Rural Household Survey. This survey collected 20-year migration histories on all household members as well as on children living outside the household at the time of the survey. The migration histories make it possible to construct a retrospective panel data set to which discrete-choice econometric methods can be applied.

This chapter addresses three questions. First, what are the determinants of international migration from rural Mexico, and how have they changed over time? Second, have male and female propensities to migrate changed over time, and what are the gender differences in international migration trends? Third, how do international migration determinants and the impacts of policy and macroeconomic shocks on international migration differ between men and women?

In the first section we present a brief review of the treatment of gender in models of migration determinants, highlighting the need for gender-focused micro-econometric studies of migration dynamics. A framework to estimate the gender dynamics of international migration is proposed in the second section. The third section describes how migration histories were collected and used to construct the panel. The fourth section reports our econometric findings, and a final section presents our conclusions.

Gender in Econometric Models of Migration Determinants

Human capital models posit that variables increasing the expected earnings difference between migrant destination and origin raise the probability of migration. More recent models, in the tradition of the new economics of labor migration (NELM), expand the list of variables affecting migration beyond earnings to include other considerations, including income risk and liquidity constraints on production in the migrant's household of origin.

Gender, Human Capital, and Migration

Human capital models have focused on four categories of variables that capture an individual's expected earnings difference between migrating and staying at home: (1) earnings potential, (2) age, (3) costs of migration, and (4) probability of employment. These four categories are central to understanding the probability of migration and have guided data collection and econometric analysis. However, existing econometric studies, based primarily on cross-sectional data analysis, often have produced conflicting findings with respect to these four types of migration determinants for men and women.[1]

The first category of migration determinants relates to individuals' productivity and thus potential earnings. Economists have used total years of schooling or work experience as proxies for productivity. Experience is a key determinant of earnings in human capital models, with or without migration (Sjaastad 1962; Mincer 1974). In practice, one usually cannot distinguish the effect of experience from age in modeling earnings or migration determinants, because the first is generally a linear transformation of the second.[2]

Total years of schooling are a key variable of interest in human capital studies of migration. Most studies of migration determinants find that educational levels of migrants are higher than those of nonmigrants and that increases in schooling stimulate migration. As we discussed in chapter 2, a few empirical studies investigate the relationship between migration and education. In the Mexican context, Kanaiaupuni 2000 finds that international migration selects positively on female education. Mora and Taylor (2006), using cross-sectional data from rural Mexico, confirm this result for female and male internal migrants but find that international migration, primarily to low-skilled agricultural and service jobs, does not select positively on schooling.

As discussed in more detail in chapter 2, there are various explanations for these findings related to the economic returns to education for different individuals and in different sectors of the economy. An alternative explanation, presented by Hondagneu-Sotelo (1994), is that women with higher education feel constrained by social norms and a lack of employment opportunities in their origin country, and migration provides new opportunities for these women.

Most studies posit that, other things being equal, the young are more mobile than the old, and an increase in the cost of migrating, when wages are held constant, decreases migration more for older than for younger individuals. This is because older people have a shorter future time horizon over which to spread fixed migration costs. In chapter 2, we presented an overview of the limited empirical research available on this topic.

Regarding the cost of migration, it is typically proxied by distance to the border or the destination, on the assumption that distance is linearly related to costs. As we discussed in the previous chapter, migration costs could also be influenced by civil status, need to care for children, and migration networks. Several studies have found that single women are more likely to migrate than are married ones (Kossoudji and Ranney 1984; Cackley 1993; Kanaiaupuni 2000) and that the probability of men's migration increases with the number of children in the household, while this relationship is not observed for female migrants (Kanaiaupuni 2000).

Migration costs are also a function of an individual's migration networks, as these convey information and provide assistance to prospective migrants. In chapter 2, we discussed the reasons to expect that the effects of networks are gender specific, as well as some of the empirical evidence in this area. In terms of Mexico-specific studies, Curran and Rivero-Fuentes (2003), using cross-sectional data from the Mexican Migration Project, find that male migrant networks are more important determinants of international migration for men than for women. Richter et al. (2005) find similar results in their analysis of longitudinal data from the 2003 Mexico National Rural Household Survey. None of these studies uses individual-level panel data, however. Furthermore, there has been minimal theoretical work that investigates the benefits of networks according to gender.

Finally, the probability of employment can be affected by policy variables. Because male and female immigrants tend to be concentrated in specific sectors of the economy, immigration policies that are easier to enforce in some sectors than in others may affect migration differently for the two sexes. For example, the U.S. Immigration Reform and Control Act of 1986 made it illegal for employers to knowingly hire unauthorized immigrants. Enforcement of this act is likely to be easier and more complete in relatively formal jobs than, for example, in informal domestic service jobs in which female immigrants concentrate. Testing for the impacts of policy changes on international migration is complicated by the fact that panel data spanning the period before and after the policy shock are required. Because of the lack of detailed panel data, researchers are only beginning to explore ways in which females may respond differently than males to policy reforms.

Household Variables

While the human capital model of migration has provided researchers with intuition on the fundamental determinants of individual migration, most social science researchers agree that migration decisions take place within the context of households (for example, see Aguilera and Massey 2003; Curran and Rivero-Fuentes 2003; Munshi 2003). Ethnographic studies, including those critical of the unitary household assumption common to economic studies (Wolf 1992), highlight the importance of the household as a social unit influencing behavior. Thus household as well as individual variables influence migration probabilities.

Most household models of migration involve "split" household migration, in which individual household members may migrate and the household's demographic composition thus may change, but the household survives as an economic and social unit in the migrant-sending area.[3] In theory, any household variable affecting the opportunity cost of migrating, migrant earnings, and remittance behavior, as well as the indirect effects of migration and remittances on household incomes via their influence on liquidity and risk should be included in a model of migration determinants. In practice, the household variables that are included in migration models, with few exceptions, include physical and human capital assets, proxies for risk aversion and access to credit, and stochastic variables like weather shocks, in addition to family networks. Family migration networks are a form of capital, which, together with human and physical capital, creates disparities in the costs and benefits of migration across households and individuals.

There has been little effort to test for differences in household-level variables on international migration by men and women, but there is reason to think that gender matters. The influences of many household variables on international migration by either gender are ambiguous a priori. For example, if access to land increases potential income contributions at home by males but not by females, one would expect land to have a negative effect on migration by men but not by women. Household wealth, as a (negative) proxy for risk aversion or a (positive) proxy for access to insurance, might be expected to increase the probability of international migration, if migration is perceived to be a relatively risky activity, or the reverse, if perceived to be less risky. The effects of household wealth on male and female migration will depend on the perceived risk of migration for each gender. As a proxy for access to liquidity to finance production activities at home, wealth might be expected to decrease the probability of migration. Donato (1993) and Cerrutti and Massey (2001) suggest that land, home, and business ownership decreases the probability of migration by women. Cerrutti and Massey (2001) also find that homeownership, an indicator of wealth, increases the probability of migration for males. Kanaiaupuni (2000) supports the finding that agricultural land decreases the probability of migration for females, but she finds that it increases the propensity of migration for males. She also finds that business ownership decreases the probability of migration for both males and females.

The remittance behavior of the migrant influences the probability of migration. If male migrants remit to finance investments at home, while females remit mostly to support their household of origin at times of adverse shocks, as suggested by de la Brière et al. (2002), then household wealth might decrease the probability of migration by both genders.

Other household variables that may be included in empirical models of migration are household size, household education, and number of children. One might expect the presence of adults who can fill in for the migrant's labor on the farm to reduce the opportunity cost of migration. The education of other household members may affect the productivity of the migrant's labor at home and thus the opportunity cost of migrating. Taylor (1987) finds no significant effect of land holdings or family size on international migration from rural Mexico. Mora and Taylor (2006) find significant negative effects of land and household education, positive effects of wealth, and no effect of family size. Kanaiaupuni (2000) finds no effect of the number of children on the migration propensity of females.

Econometric Model

A human capital model compares the costs and benefits of migration with what individuals would earn if they did not migrate. A household model expands the notion of opportunity costs to include the market or imputed value of lost productivity due to the loss of the migrant's labor, and benefits may include remittances as well as other, indirect effects of migration on household welfare, including income risk.

Suppose that the opportunity cost of migration by person i of gender g at time t, w_{0igt}, is a function of a vector of observable variables denoted x_{0igt}, while the benefits of international migration by the same individual, w_{1igt}, are a function of variables x_{1igt}, such that

$$w_{0igt} = f_{0g}(x_{0igt}; \beta_{0g}) + \eta_{0ig} + \varepsilon_{0igt}$$
$$w_{1igt} = f_{1g}(x_{1igt}; \beta_{1g}) + \eta_{1ig} + \varepsilon_{1igt}$$
(3.1)

The vectors β_{0g} and β_{1g} contain parameters representing the effects of the observed explanatory variables x_{0igt} and x_{1igt} on w_{0igt} and w_{1igt}, respectively; η_{0ig} and η_{1ig} are unobserved individual characteristics, and ε_{0igt} and ε_{1igt} are error terms. The opportunity cost of migration, w_{0igt}, may be a wage or an expected wage at the origin or the value produced by the individual in household production activities. Thus it is influenced by both individual human capital characteristics and household assets that influence productivity. Migration benefits, w_{1ig}, include remittances, which depend both on earnings abroad and on the migrant's willingness to share these earnings with the household. They, too, are influenced by the migrant's human capital, household variables that influence success at the destination (for example, family migration networks), and motivations to remit (inheritable assets, altruism) as well as by unobserved variables.

Let

$$c_{igt} = c_g(x_{cigt}; \gamma_g) + \eta_{cig} + \varepsilon_{cigt}$$
(3.2)

denote migration costs, which are a function of x_{cigt}, a vector of observed individual and household characteristics, whose effect on migration costs is given by the parameters γ_g; let η_{cig} be unobserved characteristics that influence migration costs; and let ε_{cigt} denote the error term in this migration cost equation. Migration costs include travel, border crossing, and financial support until the migrant finds productive employment at the destination. Costs are affected by individual characteristics as well as household migration networks.

Migration costs and benefits are affected by unobserved individual and household variables. For example, individuals' unobserved ability affects their productivity and earnings at home and thus the opportunity costs of migrating. It also affects economic success at the destination, motivations to remit, and even the likelihood of a successful border crossing. Unobserved household characteristics, including the ability of the household head and other members, their willingness to take risks, and their access to information, certainly influence both the economic as well as the noneconomic costs of and returns to international migration by individual household members. Societal norms and attitudes may have different effects on migration by women than by men. To the extent that these norms and attitudes vary from household to household and individual to individual, they represent unobserved variables in a model of migration determinants. If correlated with other variables in the model, failure to account for these unobservables may result in biased econometric estimates of the effects of included variables on migration probabilities.

Migration decision makers, be they individuals or households, presumably make use of all of the information that is available to them to perform "a cost-benefit analysis" of international migration. That is, migration is observed if

$$w_{1igt} > w_{0igt} + c_{igt}.\qquad(3.3)$$

Equation 3.3 states that the benefit of migration is greater than the cost of migrating. Substituting from 3.1 and 3.2, and assuming that the benefit and cost functions are linear in their parameters,

$$\varepsilon^*_{igt} < \eta^*_{ig} + x'_{igt}\beta_g,\qquad(3.4)$$

where

$$\begin{aligned}
x_{igt} &= [x_{1igt}, x_{0igt}, x_{cigt}] \\
\beta_g &= [\beta_{1g}, \beta_{0g}, \gamma_g] \\
\eta^*_{ig} &= \eta_{1ig} - \eta_{0ig} - \eta_{cig} \\
\varepsilon^*_{igt} &= \varepsilon_{0igt} + \varepsilon_{cigt} - \varepsilon_{1igt}
\end{aligned}\qquad(3.5)$$

We can define a dichotomous migration variable, M_{igt}, which takes on the value of 1 if person i of gender g is observed as a migrant at time t and 0 otherwise. The probability of migration, then, is

$$\Pr[M_{igt} = 1 | x'_{igt}, \beta_g, \eta^*_{ig}] = \Lambda(\eta^*_{ig} + x'_{igt}\beta_g),\qquad(3.6)$$

where $\Lambda(\cdot)$ is the logistic cdf, $\Lambda(z) = e^z/(1 + e^z)$. Other distributions may be assumed. In cross-sectional analyses, it is common to assume a standard normal cdf, which yields a probit instead of a logit.

A model that pools men and women can be justified only if the parameters β_g do not vary by gender. Few microeconomic studies of migration determinants test for pooling or even control for gender, besides including a gender dummy in the list of explanatory variables. Therefore, in most studies all elements of β_g are assumed to be the same for men and women. Furthermore, unobserved characteristics of individuals, households, and communities affect the observed outcomes of migration. Few migration studies control for unobserved characteristics of individuals and households. Cross-sectional studies must assume that η_{ig}^* is the same for all individuals i (or, if a gender dummy is included, for all individuals of the same gender).

Unobserved variables are a concern unless (a) they do not explain migration behavior and (b) they are not correlated with other explanatory variables that do explain migration. It is generally unwise to make these assumptions. For example, unobserved ability is likely to be correlated with both schooling and migration behavior, and aversion to labor market participation by women is likely to affect current and past migration (and thus the existence of female migration networks), education, and other variables. Household variables in the vector x_{igt} may not be truly exogenous even if they are predetermined. For example, household wealth, education, and so forth, together with current migration, may be correlated with past migration decisions, and all may be correlated with unobserved variables.

The main econometric concern surrounding endogeneity is that the inclusion of "contaminated" explanatory variables may bias findings with respect to both these and other explanatory variables in the model. For example, if past migrants provided remittances that enabled households to accumulate wealth, then it is not clear whether it is past migration or wealth that "explains" current migration. More disconcerting is the possibility that unobserved variables may be correlated with both migration and observed household variables, confounding the interpretation of econometric estimates.

It is important to control for unobservables, η_{ig}^*, as much as possible when estimating models of migration determinants. Controlling for unobservables implies carefully selecting explanatory variables (the vector x_{igt}) and controlling for fixed effects when possible. Fixed-effects methods can control for unobservables that are time invariant.

The panel structure of the data used in this study permits the estimation of both random-effects (RE) and fixed-effects (FE) migration models. FE estimation is possible for the panel logit, but not for the probit. A drawback to fixed-effects versus random-effects estimation is that, in the former, one cannot estimate the effect of time-invariant explanatory variables on migration behavior. We use FE estimation to test for differences in migration determinants between males and females and to provide a check on the robustness of estimated parameters with respect to unobserved variables. For example, if migration persistence or policy effects change when one switches from a RE to a FE model, there is reason to be concerned about the influence of unobserved variables.

Data and Descriptive Statistics

The data used in this chapter were generated through a nationwide rural household survey—the Mexico National Rural Household Survey (Encuesta Nacional a Hogares Rurales de México, or ENHRUM)—carried out jointly by the University of California, Davis, and El Colegio de México, Mexico City. The ENHRUM survey provides retrospective data on migration by individuals from a nationally representative sample of rural households. The survey, which was carried out in January and February of 2003, reports on a sample of 22 households in 80 villages. INEGI (Instituto Nacional de Estadística, Geografía e Información), Mexico's National Census Office, designed the sampling frame to provide a statistically reliable characterization of Mexico's population living in rural areas, defined by the Mexican government as communities with fewer than 2,500 inhabitants. For reasons of cost and tractability, individuals in hamlets or dispersed populations of fewer than 500 inhabitants were not included in the survey. The resulting sample is representative of more than 80 percent of the population that the Mexican National Census Office considers to be rural.

The ENHRUM survey assembled complete labor migration histories from 1980 through 2002 for (a) the household head, (b) the spouse of the household head, (c) all the individuals who lived in the household for three months or more in 2002, and (d) a random sample of sons and daughters of either the head or his or her spouse who lived outside the household for longer than three months in 2002. The latter includes individuals who migrated but did not return to the village as well as temporary migrants. For each of these individuals, the survey asked whether the individual had worked as an internal or international migrant and, if so, in which of the 23 years, whether the work was for a wage or self-employment, and whether it was agricultural or nonagricultural. This information makes it possible to reconstruct detailed migration work histories for each individual from 1980 through 2002. The data set is unbalanced by nature because not every individual in the sample was alive in 1980.

The ENHRUM survey provides the most reliable and representative historical data available on domestic and international migration from rural Mexico. The most widely used data for analyzing Mexico-to-U.S. migration are from the Mexican Migration Project (MMP). The MMP, like the ENHRUM, collected retrospective migration data. However, the ENHRUM has several advantages over the MMP. First, the ENHRUM has a random sampling design that is nationally representative, while the MMP communities are disproportionately in high-migration areas. Second, the MMP community surveys span more than two decades, with two to five communities surveyed each year. Because of these factors, it is generally not appropriate to pool data from all of the communities in the MMP sample. Given that migration is increasing over time, differences in migration between MMP communities may simply reflect the years in which the communities were surveyed. The ENHRUM was carried out at the same time in all 80 villages; thus it can be used to analyze the determinants of migration and the effects of policy variables for the entire sample. Finally, historical information on migration in the MMP is limited to the number of trips and years of first and last migration. The ENHRUM collected its retrospective information for each year from 1980 through 2002; thus it permits analysis of circular migration and the probability of migration each year.

The major limitation of the ENHRUM, shared by the MMP, stems from joint migration (chapter 2)—that is, when all members of a household migrated prior to the survey. When this happens, no migration histories can be elicited, resulting in an underestimation of migration and migration trends over time.[4] The extent of this problem will not be known for certain until after the second round of ENHRUM is carried out in 2008. What is known is that children are significantly more likely to migrate than are household heads (for example, see Mora and Taylor 2006), and as long as at least one parent remains in the village, the survey is able to collect migration histories on all of the children. In a panel survey of two villages in a high-migration zone of West-Central Mexico, Taylor and Adelman 1996: ch. 4) find an average household attrition rate due to migration of 10 percent over a 10-year period. The relevant question for our purposes is whether the loss of whole households in the past biases the estimated effects of individual, household, and policy variables on migration presented here. If there are such biases, they generally cannot be signed a priori. However, an underestimation of migration at the end of the period, especially of female migrants, may make it more difficult to identify positive effects of policy shocks on migration.

The survey asked household members to recall employment and labor migration histories for each family member who was not present at the time of the survey. Individuals may be unable to remember their (or their migrant sons' and daughters') employment history for 23 years. However, when employment is coupled with a life event such as international migration, there is a smaller likelihood that data will be misreported. A study by Smith and Thomas (2003) shows that when respondents are asked to recall information linked to salient events, such as marriage or birth of a child, misreporting is insignificant. Moreover, individuals asked to recall labor or migration histories also report more accurately moves that involved either a long distance or an extended stay.

Only those 15 years or older were included in the analysis at any point in time. Thus 23 years of observed migration are available for individuals who were 38 years or older at the time of the survey, but only 20 years are available for an individual who was 35 at the time of the survey. There are 6,456 individuals in the sample in 2002, but 2,746 in 1980. In total, the sample contains 102,026 person-year observations on migration.

Information on education (years of completed schooling and number of repeated years) was collected for all family members. Age is included as both a demographic variable and a proxy for work experience (the Mincer experience variable).

The retrospective migration data make it possible to include in the model not only human capital variables but also previous migration work experience and family migration networks, which change over time. International migration work experience at time t is measured as the number of years prior to t that an individual worked at some time as an international migrant since 1980, the beginning of the survey time period; likewise for internal migration work experience. Following Mincer, we also include work experience squared, inasmuch as there may be decreasing returns to work experience.

The family migration network variable for person i at time t is calculated as the number of family members besides person i who were migrants at time $t - 1$ (this precludes an individual from being his or her own network). While the focus of this chapter is on international migration, family migration networks are calculated for both national and international migration. Having a family network to an internal migrant destination at time $t - 1$ has an ambiguous effect on international migration at time t. It may increase the propensity to migrate internationally, for example, if internal migrants provide individuals with general information about migration. However, it may decrease the likelihood of international migration by providing access to migrant work opportunities at internal destinations. Separate network variables are also constructed for men and women, in order to test for own- and cross-gender network effects. For example, for a given individual at time t, the female internal network variable is the sum of female family members who were internal migrants at $t - 1$.

The ENHRUM provides detailed data on household assets and other variables for 2002. However, asset histories for 1980–2002 are not available. Fixed effects can control for time-invariant unobservables at both the individual and household levels. Only higher-level fixed effects (village dummies) can be included in the RE versions of the migration models; however, a time trend is used to control for time-varying unobservables affecting all individuals and households similarly (for example, changing attitudes toward Mexican immigrants in the United States or general amenability to migration in rural Mexico over time). The time trend cannot be included in the FE model, because the differencing used to solve this model would convert it into a constant. There is no way, here or in any other migration model that we know of, to control for time-varying unobservables at either the individual or household level.

Descriptive Statistics

Tables 3.1–3.3 present descriptive statistics by person-year for the variables used in the analysis. Table 3.1 compares migrants and nonmigrants. Table 3.2 provides summary statistics by gender and migrant status. Over the entire 23-year period

Table 3.1. Descriptive Statistics, by Person-Year for Full Sample and Migrants versus Nonmigrants

Variable	Full sample	Migrant	Nonmigrant
Number of observations	102,026	5,240	96,786
Percent of total	100.0	5.1	95
Dependent variables (percent)			
International migrant	5.1	n.a.	n.a.
Agricultural sector	1.3	26	n.a.
Nonagricultural sector	3.8	76	n.a.
Individual variables			
Gender (percent female)	51	15	52
Age	35	30.7	35.24**
Years of schooling	5.08	6.3	5.01**
Family international migration networks (percent)			
Member	13.4	42.0	12.0**
Female	4.8	11.0	4.5**
Male	12.0	35.8	10.7**
Family international migration networks (number)			
Member	0.149	0.401	0.099**
Female	0.023	0.099	0.044**
Male	0.125	0.347	0.088**
Family internal migration networks (percent)			
Member	17	13.2	17.4**
Female	8.4	7.2	8.5**
Male	13.2	8.7	13.5**
Family internal migration networks (number)			
Member	0.199	0.120	0.156**
Female	0.072	0.071	0.087
Male	0.127	0.074	0.112**

Source: 2003 ENHRUM data.

** Difference in means between migrants and nonmigrants are statistically significant at 5 percent.

n.a. Not applicable.

Table 3.2. Descriptive Statistics for Person-Year, by Gender and Migrant Status

Variable	Males Full sample	Nonmigrant	Migrant	Females Full sample	Nonmigrant	Migrant
Number of observations	50,476	46,023	4,453	51,550	50,763	787
Percent of total	49.5	91.2	8.8	50.53	98.5	1.5
Dependent variables (percent)						
International migrant	8.8	n.a.	n.a.	1.5	n.a.	n.a.
Agriculture	2.5	n.a.	28	0.2	n.a.	10
Nonagriculture	6.5	n.a.	73	1.4	n.a.	89.5
Individual variables						
Age	35.2	35.6	30.9**	35	34.87	29.82**
Years of schooling	5.2	5.14	6.08**	4.9	4.89	7.63**
Family international migration networks (percent)						
Member	12.4	9.9	40.1**	14.4	13.8	54.5**
Female	4.9	4.4	9.9**	4.7	4.5	16.2**
Male	10.9	8.8	34.7**	12.9	12.5	41.8**
Family international migration networks (number)						
Member	0.140	0.096	0.611**	0.157	0.149	0.684**
Female	0.024	0.018	0.087**	0.023	0.021	0.173**
Male	0.117	0.079	0.524**	0.134	0.128	0.510**
Family internal migration networks (percent)						
Member	15.3	15.6	12.5**	19.2	19.4	21.2**
Female	8.6	8.7	7.1**	8.2	8.25	7.7
Male	10.9	11.2	7.4**	15.6	15.6	15.9
Family internal migration networks (number)						
Member	0.175	0.178	0.136**	0.223	0.223	0.231
Female	0.073	0.073	0.071	0.070	0.070	0.064
Male	0.102	0.105	0.065**	0.153	0.153	0.167

Source: 2003 ENHRUM data.

** Difference in means between migrants and nonmigrants are statistically significant at 5 percent.

n.a. Not applicable.

Table 3.3. Descriptive Statistics for Policy Variables

Variable	Mean
Trend	14
Lagged U.S. GDP (billion, 2000 US$)	7,543.4
Lagged Mexican GDP (billion, 1990 pesos)	799.7
Percent change in border control expenditures	0.15
Percent change in exchange rate	0.01
NAFTA (dummy = 1 in 1994)	0.49
IRCA (dummy = 1 in 1986)	0.82

Source: 2003 ENHRUM.

covered by our data, an average of 5.1 percent of the individual-year observations (over the age of 15) were international migrants; 1.3 percent worked in the agricultural sector and 3.8 percent worked in the nonagricultural sector. Of the individual-year observations 51 percent are females, but only 1.5 percent of these females are international migrants. The majority of international migrants are males; an average of 8.8 percent of the individual-year observations for males involves international migration. The low percentage of female migrants could indicate a pattern of permanent migration in which the male household head migrates first, followed eventually by the wife accompanied by the remaining family members. If female migration is more likely to be associated with joint migration, there could be a systematic undercounting of female migrants in surveys carried out in migrant-sending localities. It will not be possible to address this question until after the second round of the ENHRUM survey is conducted in 2008. An alternative explanation is that female migrants are less likely to work than male migrants. If this is the case, then the ENHRUM count of labor migration underestimates total migration more for females than for males. Analysis of 2002 total versus labor migration data indicates that this may be the case. In 2002, the only year in which we have information on both residence and work in the United States, 16 percent of labor migrants but 26 percent of all migrants were females. This finding suggests that there is, indeed, a difference in work propensity between male and female migrants.[5]

Figure 3.1 illustrates gross trends in the shares of males and females from rural Mexico who are observed as international labor migrants over time. Figure 3.1 reveals that the share of female migrants is less than that of males in every year of the series. The trend for female migration, although increasing, does not exhibit the same upturn observed for male migration in the mid-1990s. These trends do not control for other variables that may differentially affect migration by gender over time.

Figure 3.1. International Migration, by Gender, 1980–2002

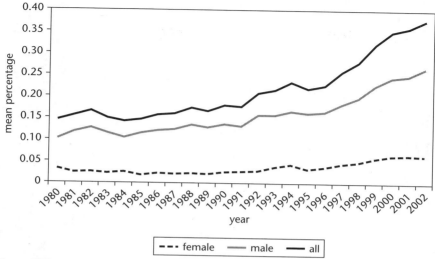

Source: 2003 ENHRUM data.

When the migration data are disaggregated by sector of employment (figure 3.2), it becomes clear that nonagricultural work absorbs an increasing share of international migrants from rural Mexico over time. Migration into nonagricultural jobs is larger than agricultural migration in all time periods, but it exhibits a much steeper climb in the 1990s. There is a slight increase in agricultural employment in 1996.

Female migrants are overwhelmingly employed in the nonagricultural sector (figure 3.3). The trend in female migration to nonagricultural jobs changes over the time period, with drops in 1980, 1984, and 1994. However, in 1996 it begins to increase at a steady rate. Male migrants are also employed primarily in nonagricultural jobs, but a higher share of males than females are in agricultural jobs (figure 3.4). There is a consistent upward trend in the graph, but once again in 1997 it increases sharply.

The average individual in the sample was 35 years of age and had 5.08 years of completed schooling. Schooling levels were slightly higher for males than for females (5.2 versus 4.9 years of completed schooling, respectively) and higher for international migrants than for nonmigrants (6.3 and 5.01, respectively; see tables 3.1 and 3.2). The difference between schooling of migrants and non-migrants was larger for females than for males. Female migrants averaged

Figure 3.2. International Migration, by Sector of Employment, 1980–2002

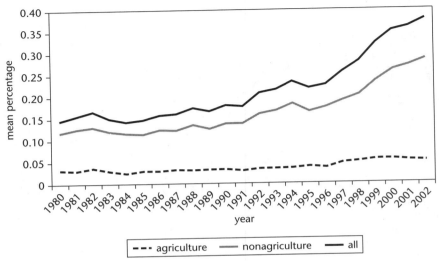

Source: 2003 ENHRUM data.

Figure 3.3. Female International Migration, by Sector of Employment, 1980–2002

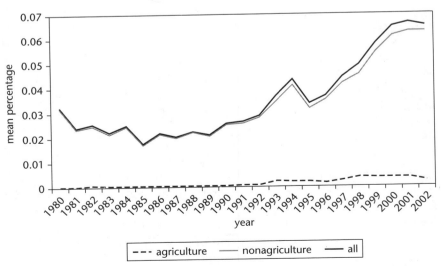

Source: 2003 ENHRUM data.

Figure 3.4. Male International Migration, by Sector of Employment, 1980–2002

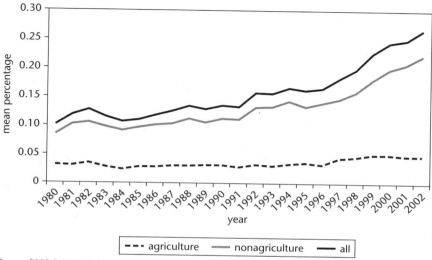

Source: 2003 ENHRUM data.

7.63 years of schooling, compared with only 4.89 years for female nonmigrants. Male migrants had 6.08 years of schooling, while male nonmigrants had 5.14. Internal migrants had a higher level of schooling than international migrants in the case of males (6.4 years), but not females (not shown in table).

Household migration networks can be defined by the location of the migrants, international or internal, as well as the migrants' gender. Of all individuals in the sample, 13.4 percent had at least one family member in the United States in the previous year; that is, they had access to a migrant network. The composition of the network was predominantly male: 12.0 percent of all individuals had access to a male migrant network and 4.8 percent to a female network. Slightly more females than males had family members who were international migrants in the previous year, 14.4 percent compared with 12.4 percent. Of male international migrants 40.1 percent had an international family migration network, compared with only 9.9 percent of male nonmigrants. Of female migrants, 54.5 percent had access to an international family network, compared with 13.8 percent of females who did not migrate abroad.[6]

There are also differences between international migrants and nonmigrants with respect to access to internal migration networks. A larger share of male non-migrants than international migrants had access to family internal migration networks. However, for females it is the reverse: more female international migrants than nonmigrants had family members at internal migrant destinations. Table 3.3 summarizes the policy variables that are used in the analysis, including U.S. and Mexican gross domestic product (GDP), exchange rates, and dummy variables indicating the periods following North American Free Trade Agreement (NAFTA, 1994) and the Immigration Reform and Control Act (IRCA, 1986).

Econometric Findings

In our econometric models of international migration, as in equation 3.6, the dependent variable takes M_{igt} on the value of 1 if person i of gender g is observed as an international migrant at time t and 0 otherwise. For each gender, the model is estimated using the XTLOGIT procedure in Stata 9 with both fixed and random effects. The advantage of the fixed-effects model is that it is able to control for (time-invariant) unobservables when estimating the effect of time-varying variables on migration propensities. Examples of time-varying variables include migration experience and networks and policy variables. There are two disadvantages to using a conditional logistic regression like XTLOGIT. First, the effects of observed variables that do not vary over time cannot be considered. This includes important variables like schooling, which changes very little for individuals over 15 years of age. It also includes the time trend and individual's age, which vary over time but by a constant amount. The second disadvantage is that the model is identified by changes in migration status; individuals whose migration status does not change over the 23-year time period covered by our data are discarded from the sample. This omission can lead to the loss of many observations. Random-effects models do not have these disadvantages; however, they do not permit one to control for unobservables.

The XTLOGIT has other advantages. It predicts the log odds of migrating while taking into account several properties of the data that otherwise could produce inconsistent and inefficient estimates. First, the sample is unbalanced; we do not have an observation for each individual in each year. XTLOGIT produces robust parameter estimates for an unbalanced panel. Second, XTLOGIT corrects the standard errors of the estimates to take into account repeated observations across time for given individuals (Maume 2004). Therefore, it allows us to obtain coefficient estimates that are consistent and efficient, while exploiting the dynamics implicit in the panel data. In light of the advantages and disadvantages of the two methods, estimation results using both are presented in the three sets of tables that follow for female and male international migration (tables 3.4–3.6), migration to U.S. farm jobs (tables 3.7–3.9), and migration to U.S. nonfarm jobs (tables 3.10–3.12). In each of these tables, columns 1 and 2 present the estimated coefficients for the fixed effects model with and without macroeconomic and policy variables, while columns 3 and 5 present the estimated coefficients for the random-effects model. The marginal effects of explanatory variables on the migration probability are presented in columns 4 and 6 of each table. Marginal effects are not available for the fixed-effects model inasmuch as the individual effects, which are needed to calculate the marginal effect, are not consistently estimated (Corts and Singh 2002; Wooldridge 2002). However, we can compare odds ratios between the two models. Odds ratios for select variables are presented in tables 3.6 (international migration), 3.9 (international agricultural migration), and 3.12 (international migration to nonfarm jobs).[7] The Hausman specification test is also presented for each model that is estimated with both fixed and random effects. In the majority of cases we reject the null hypothesis that the random-effects model produces consistent and efficient coefficient estimates.

In all models we control for previous migration experience by including on the right-hand side the sum of the individual's total years of experience in international and national migration from 1980 up until year t as well as the square of each of these variables. Not surprising, the own-effect (for example, of international migration experience at time $t - 1$ on the probability of being observed as an international migrant at time t) is always positive and highly significant. Reminiscent of Mincer's experience variable, the quadratic own-effects generally are negative. Cross-effects (for example, of internal migration experience on international migration probabilities) are negative in some cases (suggesting competition between destinations) and positive in others (consistent with stepwise migration or a general migration experience effect).

Gender and International Migration

Both male and female international migration exhibits the quadratic experience effect described above: experience as a migrant abroad increases migration probabilities, but at a decreasing rate in both the fixed- and random-effects models (see tables 3.4 and 3.5). The marginal effect of international migration experience is larger for males than for females in the random-effects model (1.07 versus 0.12, column 4, tables 3.4 and 3.5). The cross-destination effect is negative for males (that is, internal migration experience decreases the international migration probability). In contrast, for females it is insignificant.

Family migration networks are differentiated by destination, international or internal, as well as by gender. For females, having female family members who were international migrants at time $t - 1$ increases the probability of being observed as an international migrant at time t. The own-gender effect of internal networks is not significant for females or males.

Table 3.4. Logit Results for Female International Migration

| Variable | Fixed-effects (FE) model | | | Random-effects (RE) model | | | |
	Estimated coefficients (1)	Estimated coefficients (2)	Estimated coefficients (3)	Marginal effect[a] (4)	Estimated coefficients (5)	Marginal effect[a] (6)
Time-invariant variables						
Constant	n.a.	n.a.	−4.912	n.a.	−3.683	n.a.
			(11.60)***		(−1.71)	
Trend	n.a.	n.a.	−0.023	−0.001	0.117	0.005
			(1.51)		(−0.88)	
Age	n.a.	n.a.	−0.087	−0.004	−0.088	−0.004
			(7.39)***		(7.39)***	
Years of schooling	n.a.	n.a.	0.05	0.002	0.051	0.002
			(−1.58)		(−1.63)	
Work experience						
International	2.131	2.298	2.61	0.12	2.615	0.11
	(14.74)***	(12.72)***	(26.63)***		(26.64)***	
International squared	−0.141	−0.149	−0.114	−0.005	−0.115	−0.005
	(13.88)***	(12.96)***	(23.61)***		(23.59)***	
National	−0.66	−0.591	−0.073	−0.003	−0.071	−0.003
	(−1.62)	(−1.4)	(−0.56)		(−0.54)	
National squared	0.049	0.046	0.001	<0.001	0.001	< 0.001
	(−1.27)	(−1.16)	(−0.07)		(−0.05)	

Migration networks

Family members who were international migrants in t−1						
Number of females	1.714 (2.19)**	1.74 (2.32)**	1.386 (4.33)***	0.06	1.369 (4.28)***	0.058
Number of males	0.992 (3.75)***	1.02 (3.88)***	0.82 (6.00)***	0.04	0.82 (5.99)***	0.035
Family members who were internal migrants in t−1						
Number of females	0.274 (−0.53)	0.358 (0.69)	−0.043 (−0.13)	−0.002	−0.059 (−0.18)	−0.003
Number of males	0.969 (2.12)**	0.943 (2.06)*	0.28 (−1.31)	0.01	0.274 (−1.28)	0.012
Macroeconomic and policy variables						
Percent change in exchange rates	n.a.	1.191 (−1.53)	n.a.	n.a.	0.695 (−1.17)	0.03
Lagged Mexican GDP	n.a.	−0.004 (−0.7)	n.a.	n.a.	0 (0)	<0.001
Lagged U.S. GDP	n.a.	0 (−0.44)	n.a.	n.a.	0 (−0.48)	<0.001
Percent change in border control	n.a.	−2.715 (2.41)**	n.a.	n.a.	−2.453 (2.68)***	−0.11

(Table continues on the following page)

Table 3.4. Logit Results for Female International Migration (Continued)

| Variable | Fixed-effects (FE) model | | | | Random-effects (RE) model | | | |
	Estimated coefficients (1)	Estimated coefficients (2)	Estimated coefficients (3)	Marginal effect[a] (4)	Estimated coefficients (5)	Marginal effect[a] (6)
NAFTA	n.a.	−0.204	n.a.	n.a.	−0.462	−0.002
		(0.51)			(−1.18)	
IRCA	n.a.	0.074	n.a.	n.a.	−0.798	−0.05
		(−0.12)			(−1.5)	
Joint test of policy variables −χ^2	n.a.	9.08	n.a.	n.a.	11.78*	n.a.
Overall goodness of fit −χ^2	824.57***	833.87***	888.06	n.a.	888.23	n.a.
Hausman −χ^2	1,450.67***	201.31***	n.a.	n.a.	n.a.	n.a.
Number of observations	1,734	1,734	49,828	n.a.	49,828	n.a.
Number of id	112	112	3,249	n.a.	3,249	n.a.

Source: 2003 ENHRUM.

Note: Absolute value of *z* statistics is in parentheses. The number of id refers to the number of individuals.

*** Significant at 1 percent.

** Significant at 5 percent.

* Significant at 10 percent.

n.a. Not applicable.

a. Marginal effects presented as percentage points.

Table 3.5. Logit Results for Male International Migration

Variable	Fixed-effects (FE) model		Random-effects (RE) model			
	Estimated coefficients (1)	Estimated coefficients (2)	Estimated coefficients (3)	Marginal effect[a] (4)	Estimated coefficients (5)	Marginal effect[a] (6)
Time-invariant variables						
Constant	n.a.	n.a.	n.a.	n.a.	n.a.	n.a.
Trend	n.a.	n.a.	−0.037 (5.23)***	−0.022	−0.177 (3.36)***	−0.11
Age	n.a.	n.a.	−0.094 (17.18)***	−0.056	−0.094 (17.21)***	−0.056
Years of schooling	n.a.	n.a.	−0.007 (−0.41)	−0.004	−0.006 (−0.37)	−0.004
Work experience						
International	1.284 (31.88)***	1.48 (28.20)***	1.789 (48.42)***	1.07	1.787 (48.42)***	1.06
International squared	−0.073 (27.64)***	−0.08 (26.93)***	−0.07 (41.54)***	−0.042	−0.07 (41.53)***	−0.042
National	−0.181 (2.62)***	−0.105 (−1.47)	−0.17 (4.07)***	−0.101	−0.166 (3.99)***	−0.098
National squared	0.008 (2.18)**	0.007 (−1.87)	0.011 (4.25)***	0.0063	0.01 (4.15)***	6.00E-03

(Table continues on the following page)

Table 3.5. Logit Results for Male International Migration (Continued)

Variable	Fixed-effects (FE) model			Random-effects (RE) model		
	Estimated coefficients (1)	Estimated coefficients (2)	Estimated coefficients (3)	Marginal effect[a] (4)	Estimated coefficients (5)	Marginal effect[a] (6)
Migration networks						
Family members who were international migrants in $t-1$						
Number of females	1.11 (4.68)***	1.175 (4.94)***	1.143 (6.09)***	0.68	1.113 (5.92)***	0.66
Number of males	0.403 (3.20)***	0.531 (4.07)***	1.1 (12.69)***	0.65	1.079 (12.44)***	0.64
Family members who were internal migrants in $t-1$						
Number of females	0.135 (−0.67)	0.197 (−0.98)	0.187 (−1.29)	0.11	0.185 (−1.28)	0.11
Number of males	−0.219 (−0.97)	−0.129 (−0.56)	−0.148 (−0.94)	−0.088	−0.149 (−0.95)	−0.088
Macroeconomic and policy variables						
Percent change in exchange rates	n.a.	0.189 (−0.71)	n.a.	n.a.	−0.174 (−0.75)	−0.103
Lagged Mexican GDP	n.a.	0 (−0.06)	n.a.	n.a.	0.002 (−1.2)	1.30E-03
Lagged U.S. GDP	n.a.	0 (−0.67)	n.a.	n.a.	0 (−1.71)	<0.001

Percent change in border control	n.a.	0.508	n.a.	0.521	0.309
		(−1.6)		(−1.8)	
NAFTA	n.a.	−0.559	n.a.	−0.151	−0.089
		(3.83)**		(−0.9)	
IRCA	n.a.	0.075	n.a.	0.258	0.14
		(−0.37)		(−1.19)	
Joint test of policy variables ($-\chi^2$)	n.a.	55.42***	n.a.	17.49***	n.a.
Overall goodness of fit ($-\chi^2$)	2,368.6***	2,425***	2,852.66***	2,882.75***	n.a.
Hausman $-\chi^2$	0	1,064.4***	n.a.	n.a.	n.a.
Number of observations	8,978	8,978	48,535	48,535	n.a.
Number of id	565	565	3,153	3,153	n.a.

Source: 2003 ENHRUM.

Note: Absolute value of z statistics in parentheses.

*** Significant at 1 percent.

** Significant at 5 percent.

* Significant at 10 percent.

n.a. Not applicable.

a. Marginal effects presented as percentage points.

For females as well as for males, cross-gender network effects differ from own-gender effects. For females, the own-gender effect is larger than the cross-gender effect and the marginal effect is larger as well (columns 4 and 6, table 3.4). Not so for males in the FE model (table 3.5). Cross-gender internal migration network effects are insignificant for males (table 3.5); however, past internal migration by males is associated positively with international migration by females.

A look at the migration odds ratios (table 3.6) confirms that, for both genders, having access to international migration networks of either gender significantly increases the odds of international migration. It has been suggested elsewhere that males provide information and other kinds of support for safe passage across the border and that cultural norms discourage women from traveling abroad unaccompanied by males. However, some studies conclude that females create more extensive migration networks than males. Our finding that the cross-gender network effect is larger for male than for female migration (3.24 versus 1.70) lends cautionary support to the finding suggested by other studies that female migration networks are more influential than male migration networks.[8]

Table 3.6. Odds Ratio for Select Variables for International Migration, by Gender

Variable	Fixed effects		Random effects	
	Female (1)	Male (2)	Female (3)	Male (4)
Previous work experience				
International	9.95	4.39	13.67	5.86
International squared	0.86	0.92	0.89	0.93
National	0.55	0.90	0.93	0.85
National squared	1.05	1.01	1.00	1.01
Family members who were international migrants in t − 1				
Female	5.7	3.24	3.93	2.92
Male	2.77	1.70	2.27	2.89
Family members who were internal migrants in t − 1				
Female	1.43	1.22	0.94	1.2
Male	2.57	0.88	1.31	0.87
Macroeconomic and policy variables				
Percent change in border control	0.07	1.66	0.09	1.68

Source: 2003 ENHRUM.

Macroeconomic and policy variables are included in the models summarized in columns 2, 4, and 5 of tables 3.4 and 3.5. In the fixed-effects models for both males and females (column 2), we can reject the null hypothesis that the coefficients on these variables are jointly zero. The border control expenditure variable is significant for females in both the fixed- and random-effects models (column 2 and 4 in tables 3.4 and 3.5).[9] For males, the NAFTA dummy variable is negative and significant in the FE model.

The sign of the estimated effect of border control expenditures is different between genders. Other things being equal, an increase in border expenditures decreases the likelihood of female migration to the United States. The sign on border control expenditures in the male model is positive; however, it is not statistically significant. A 1 percentage point increase in border control expenditures decreases female migration by 0.11 percent (column 6, tables 3.4 and 3.5). The odds ratio changes associated with a 1 percent increase in border control expenditures are presented in table 3.6. In the fixed- (random-) effects model, a 1 percentage point increase in border expenditures decreases the odds of female migration by 93 percent (91 percent). These findings lend support to studies suggesting that women are more risk averse than men with respect to crossing borders illegally and without documents (Donato and Patterson 2004). Legal documents are generally not available to new migrants from rural Mexico, and smugglers charge high fees for providing their clients with "documented" entry (that is, entry through U.S. immigration checkpoints with falsified documents). Although an increase in border enforcement increases the costs of unauthorized entry for new migrants, it may also discourage migrants from returning to Mexico (and having to repeat the border entry) once they are in the United States. It appears that, overall, border controls are more of a deterrent to female than to male migrants.

NAFTA's potential effects on Mexico-to-U.S. migration are complex. Trade reforms were expected to offer alternatives to emigration by stimulating export production in Mexico. However, NAFTA also was expected to trigger a contraction in the production of importables for which protections were phased out. Studies by Levy and van Wijnbergen (1994) and by Robinson et al. (1993), using computable general equilibrium models, predicted that employment created by increasing production of exportables would be insufficient to absorb workers displaced from the importables sector, leading to a rise in rural out-migration. The major catalyst for migration in these models is an anticipated decrease in maize production, which did not materialize (Taylor et al. 2005). Agricultural exports from Mexico to the United States increased sharply after 1994, when Mexico joined NAFTA, but worker productivity in Mexican agriculture also increased, depressing the demand for farm labor. The findings reported in table 3.4 suggest that, on balance, migration pressures for rural Mexican males but not females decreased with Mexico's entry into NAFTA in 1994.

Unlike the FE model, the RE model (columns 3–6 in tables 3.4 and 3.5) permits inclusion of a time trend and individual characteristics, including human capital variables, which do not change significantly over time.[10] Controlling for other variables, including migration experience and networks, the time trend effect is negative for both males and females, but it is insignificant for females (column 3, tables 3.4 and 3.5). The effect of age is negative for both males and females, consistent with the prediction of human capital theory that younger people are more mobile than older people. The RE model yields different results with regard to the effect of education on migration by females and males. Other things being equal, an increase in years of completed schooling increases the likelihood of international migration for women, but not for men.

Gender and Choice of Foreign Employment Sector

Human capital and networks not only influence whether or not an individual will migrate but also the migrant's sector of employment. Most migrants know the sector in which they are likely to be employed before they migrate, based on their education, access to networks, and policies affecting job placement. To test for differences between men and women with regard to the determinants of sector of U.S. employment, we reestimated both the RE and FE models for international migration to agricultural and nonagricultural jobs. In these models, the migration variable M_{sigt} takes on the value of 1 if person i of gender g is observed as an international migrant in sector s (agricultural or nonagricultural) at time t, and 0 otherwise.

International Agricultural Labor Migration

The results of the RE and FE estimation of the agricultural migration model are presented in tables 3.7 and 3.8, with the odds ratios of select variables presented in table 3.9. The number of observations for females in international agricultural migration is low, and there are insufficient cases of women migrating internally to include female internal migration networks in the model.[11] For female participation in international agricultural migration, there are insufficient observations to run the FE model. Thus table 3.7 only presents results from the RE model.

For females, international migration experience increases the probability of working in a U.S. farm job, regardless of which sector the experience is in. However, the cross-sector effect is slightly smaller than the own-sector effect. This contrasts with the results for male agricultural migration, presented in table 3.8. For males, past international migration experience working in farm jobs significantly

Table 3.7. Logit Results for Female International Migration to Agricultural Jobs

Variable	Random-effects (RE) model			
	Estimated coefficients (3)	Marginal effect[a] (4)	Estimated coefficients (5)	Marginal effect[a] (6)
Time-invariant variables				
Constant	−7.138 (5.06)***	n.a.	0.945 (−0.1)	n.a.
Trend	−0.043 (−0.85)	<0.001	0.382 (−0.68)	<0.001
Age	−0.063 (1.88)*	<0.001	−0.065 (1.93)*	<0.001
Years of schooling	−0.048 (−0.43)	<0.001	−0.057 (−0.5)	<0.001
Work experience				
International agriculture	6.658 (9.56)***	<0.001	6.959 (9.25)***	<0.001
International agriculture squared	−0.355 (9.38)***	<0.001	−0.374 (8.95)***	<0.001
International nonagriculture	4.812 (3.29)***	<0.001	4.901 (3.44)***	<0.001
International nonagriculture squared	−1.378 (2.24)**	<0.001	−1.362 (2.38)**	<0.001
National agriculture	−26.801 (0)	<0.001	−17.872 (0)	<0.001
National agriculture squared	1.262 (0)	<0.001	0.788 (0)	<0.001
National nonagriculture	−30.938 (0)	<0.001	−20.794 (0)	<0.001
National nonagriculture squared	1.28 (0)	<0.001	0.86 (0)	<0.001
Migration networks				
Family members who were international migrants in $t-1$				
Number of females agriculture	−24.361 (0)	<0.001	−14.318 (0)	<0.001
Number of females nonagriculture	1.634 (2.27)**	<0.001	1.828 (2.50)**	<0.001
Number of males agriculture	−1.589 (2.31)**	<0.001	−1.55 (2.18)**	<0.001
Number of males nonagriculture	−18.232 (6.66)***	<0.001	−18.869 (6.67)***	<0.001

(*Table continues on the following page*)

Table 3.7. Logit Results for Female International Migration to Agricultural Jobs (Continued)

| Variable | Random-effects (RE) model | | | |
	Estimated coefficients (3)	Marginal effect[a] (4)	Estimated coefficients (5)	Marginal effect[a] (6)
Family members who were internal migrants in $t - 1$				
Number of females agriculture	−29.101 (0)	<0.001	−18.572 (0)	<0.001
Number of females nonagriculture	−28.163 (0)	<0.001	−19.299 (0)	<0.001
Number of males agriculture	1.646 (−1.63)	<0.001	1.46 (−1.32)	<0.001
Number of males nonagriculture	−28.069 (0)	<0.001	−18.082 (0)	<0.001
Macroeconomic and policy variables				
Percent change in exchange rates	n.a.	n.a.	4.151 (−1.82)	<0.001
Lagged Mexican GDP	n.a.	n.a.	0.016 (−0.94)	<0.001
Lagged U.S. GDP	n.a.	n.a.	0.00 (−0.03)	<0.001
Percent change in border control	n.a.	n.a.	5.754 (−1.30)	<0.001
NAFTA	n.a.	n.a.	0.444 (−0.29)	<0.001
IRCA	n.a.	n.a.	0.663 (−0.32)	<0.001
Joint test of policy variables (χ^2)	n.a.	n.a.	4.37	n.a.
Overall goodness of fit (χ^2)	139.53***	n.a.	132.34***	n.a.
Number of observations	49,828	n.a.	49,828	n.a.
Number of id	3,249	n.a.	3,249	n.a.

Source: 2003 ENHRUM.

Note: Absolute value of z statistics in parentheses. There are insufficient observations to run the FE model, but the numbering of the columns is retained to remain consistent with other tables.

*** Significant at 1 percent.

** Significant at 5 percent.

* Significant at 10 percent.

n.a. Not applicable.

a. Marginal effects presented as percentage points.

Table 3.8. Logit Results for Male International Migration to Agricultural Jobs

Variable	Fixed-effects (FE) model		Random-effects (RE) model			
	Estimated coefficients (1)	Estimated coefficients (2)	Estimated coefficients (3)	Marginal effect[a] (4)	Estimated coefficients (5)	Marginal effect[a] (6)
Time-invariant variables						
Constant	n.a.	n.a.	−3.124 (9.04)***	n.a.	−4.827 (3.18)***	n.a.
Trend	n.a.	n.a.	−0.078 (6.30)***	−0.003	−0.198 (2.28)**	−0.008
Age	n.a.	n.a.	−0.096 (9.95)***	−0.004	−0.096 (9.98)***	−0.004
Years of schooling	n.a.	n.a.	−0.042 (−1.45)	−0.002	−0.042 (−1.44)	−0.002
Work experience						
International agriculture	1.007 (16.92)***	1.275 (16.52)***	1.821 (28.64)***	0.074	1.824 (28.59)***	0.007
International agriculture squared	−0.057 (14.38)***	−0.066 (14.96)***	−0.073	−0.003	−0.073 (23.29)***	−0.003
International nonagriculture	−0.859 (5.36)***	−0.812 (4.64)***	−1.074 (7.81)***	−0.044	−1.074 (7.81)***	−0.043
International nonagriculture squared	0.023 (−1.27)	0.022 (−1.06)	0.049 (7.28)***	0.002	0.049 (7.29)***	0.002
National agriculture	−1.072 (4.11)***	−1.071 (3.77)***	−0.185 (−1.43)	−0.003	−0.181 (−1.39)	−0.003

(Table continues on the following page)

Table 3.8. Logit Results for Male International Migration to Agricultural Jobs (Continued)

Variable	Fixed-effects (FE) model		Estimated coefficients (3)	Random-effects (RE) model		
	Estimated coefficients (1)	Estimated coefficients (2)		Marginal effect[a] (4)	Estimated coefficients (5)	Marginal effect[a] (6)
National agriculture squared	0.04 (3.26)***	0.044 (3.25)***	0.011 (−1.45)	<0.001	0.011 (−1.43)	<0.001
National nonagriculture	0.144 (−0.77)	0.298 (−1.53)	−0.07 (−0.84)	−0.008	−0.068 (−0.82)	−0.007
National nonagriculture squared	−0.002 (−0.23)	−0.006 (−0.5)	0.007 (−1.18)	<0.001	0.007 (−1.16)	<0.001
Migration networks						
Family members who were international migrants in $t-1$						
Number of females nonagriculture	0.673 (−1.23)	1.101 (−1.93)	0.89 (1.98)**	0.036	0.883 (−1.95)	0.035
Number of males agriculture	0.781 (2.99)***	0.877 (3.23)***	1.759 (8.89)***	0.072	1.76 (8.86)***	0.07
Number of males nonagriculture	−0.227 (−0.86)	0.039 (−0.14)	−0.139 (−0.57)	−0.006	−0.152 (−0.62)	−0.006
Family members who were internal migrants in $t-1$						
Number of females agriculture	−0.493 (−0.42)	−0.285 (−0.24)	−0.54 (−0.51)	−0.022	−0.637 (−0.59)	−0.025
Number of females nonagriculture	0.921 (2.03)**	0.921 (2.10)**	0.561 (2.31)**	0.023	0.562 (2.31)**	0.022
Number of males agriculture	−1.155 (−1.23)	−1.144 (−1.16)	−0.79 (−0.96)	−0.032	−0.83 (−1.00)	−0.033
Number of males nonagriculture	0.944 (−1.41)	0.847 (−1.26)	−0.288 (−0.86)	−0.012	−0.295 (−0.88)	0.001

Macroeconomic and policy variables					
Percent change in exchange rates	n.a.	0.659	n.a.	0.22	0.009
		(−1.67)		(−0.63)	
Lagged Mexican GDP	n.a.	−0.006	n.a.	−0.003	< 0.001
		(−1.92)		(−1.13)	
Lagged U.S. GDP	n.a.	0	n.a.	0.001	< 0.001
		(−0.81)		(2.03)**	
Percent change in border control	n.a.	0.697	n.a.	0.723	0.029
		(−1.38)		(−1.58)	
NAFTA	n.a.	−0.443	n.a.	0.102	0.004
		(−1.88)		(−0.36)	
IRCA	n.a.	−0.585	n.a.	−0.057	−0.002
		(−1.86)		(−0.17)	
Joint test of policy variables (X^2)	n.a.	45.32***	n.a.	8.39	
Overall goodness of fit (X^2)	584.6***	631.70***	998.01***	997.76***	n.a.
Hausman X^2	922.4***	9,521.25**	n.a.	n.a.	n.a.
Number of observations	3,037	48,535	48,535	48,535	48,535
Number of id	187	3,153	3,153	3,153	3,153

Source: 2003 ENHRUM.

Note: Absolute value of z statistics in parentheses.

*** Significant at 1 percent.

** Significant at 5 percent.

* Significant at 10 percent.

n.a. Not applicable.

a. Marginal effects presented as percentage points.

Table 3.9. Odds Ratio for Select Variables for International Agricultural Migration, by Gender

Variable	Fixed effects Male (1)	Random effects Female (2)	Random effects Male (3)
Work experience			
International agriculture	3.58	1,052.61	6.19
International agriculture squared	0.94	0.69	0.93
International nonagriculture	0.44	134.43	0.34
International nonagriculture squared	1.02	0.26	1.05
National agriculture	1.35	0.00	0.93
National agriculture squared	0.99	2.20	1.01
National nonagriculture	0.34	0.00	0.83
National nonagriculture squared	1.04	2.36	1.01
Family members who were international migrants in t − 1			
Female agriculture	2.18	0.00	4.36
Female nonagriculture	3.01	6.22	2.42
Male agriculture	2.4	0.21	5.81
Male nonagriculture	1.04	0.00	0.86
Family members who were internal migrants in t − 1			
Female agriculture	0.75	0.00	0.53
Female nonagriculture	2.51	0.00	1.75
Male agriculture	0.32	4.31	0.44
Male nonagriculture	2.33	0.00	0.74
Macroeconomic and policy variables			
Percent change in border control	2.01	0.00	2.06

Source: 2003 ENHRUM.

increases the likelihood of agricultural labor migration, but past experience in nonfarm jobs does the opposite. That is, there is evidence of competing U.S. sector effects for men, but not for women. The effects of internal migration networks on U.S. agricultural labor migration also differ between men and women. They are insignificant for women, but for men there is evidence of competition between Mexican and U.S. farm jobs.

Network effects on agricultural labor migration, like the effects of experience, differ between sectors as well as between genders. Female networks to agricultural jobs do not have a significant effect on female agricultural labor migration. (This finding most likely is due to the paucity of such networks in the ENHRUM data: few females migrate to U.S. farm jobs, and thus few females have access to female agricultural migration networks.) However, female networks associated with nonagricultural jobs increase the likelihood of female migration to agricultural jobs (as well as to nonagricultural jobs, suggesting a general migration network effect for females). Female agricultural networks significantly increase the probability of male migration to farm jobs in the RE but not the FE model (table 3.8). Networks of male migrants in U.S. agricultural jobs significantly increase the probability of male migration to these jobs in all models (table 3.8). However, if the male family member is a nonagricultural migrant, there is no significant effect on male agricultural migration. Male networks decrease the likelihood of female migration to farm jobs (but not to nonfarm jobs).

Internal agricultural networks do not significantly affect male agricultural migration to the United States in any model. However, female internal migration networks to nonfarm jobs have a significant negative effect on male migration to U.S. farm jobs in both models.

In short, the effects of migration networks to international farm jobs are both sector and gender specific.

The effects of policy and macroeconomic variables on international agricultural migration are presented in columns 5 and 6 in table 3.7 and columns 2, 5, and 6 in table 3.8. Although the coefficients are not statistically significant, the estimates suggest that NAFTA and IRCA decreased the likelihood of female and male international migration to farm jobs.

The effects of human capital variables in the RE model have the predicted signs, but the only significant variable is age in the international farm labor migration equation for males. Education does not significantly explain international farm labor migration for either gender. For males, the effect of schooling is negative, but not quite significant at the 90 percent level.

International Nonagricultural Migration

The results of both the RE and FE estimation of the nonagricultural international migration model are presented in tables 3.10 and 3.11. Odds ratios for select variables are presented in table 3.12. As before, the results from the FE model are presented in columns 1 and 2, while the RE results are presented in columns 3 through 4.

Inasmuch as most international migration from rural Mexico goes to nonfarm jobs in the United States, the results of this regression are similar in many ways to those of the total international migration model. In the FE version of the model, nonagricultural international migration experience increases the probability that a woman will be observed as a nonagricultural international labor migrant at time t (although at a decreasing rate). However, having experience as an agricultural migrant negatively affects the probability of nonagricultural labor migration for

Table 3.10. Logit Results for Female International Migration to Nonagricultural Jobs

Variable	Fixed-effects (FE) model			Random-effects (RE) model		
	Estimated coefficients (1)	Estimated coefficients (2)	Estimated coefficients (3)	Marginal effect[a] (4)	Marginal coefficients (5)	Marginal effect[a] (6)
Time-invariant variables						
Constant	n.a.	n.a.	n.a.	n.a.	n.a.	n.a.
Trend	n.a.	n.a.	−0.01 (−0.62)	<0.001	0.077 (−0.54)	0.0023
Age	n.a.	n.a.	−0.095 (7.31)***	−0.003	−0.096 (7.32)***	−0.0028
Years of schooling	n.a.	n.a.	0.061 (1.79)*	0.002	0.063 (1.84)*	0.0019
Work experience						
International agriculture	−2.791 (−1.54)	−2.918 (1.65)*	−0.765 (−1.22)	−0.024	−0.843 (−1.37)	−0.025
International agriculture squared	0.566 (−1.26)	0.603 (−1.38)	0.043 (−0.63)	0.0014	0.048 (−0.76)	0.0014
International nonagriculture	2.241 (13.1)***	2.344 (11.08)***	2.759 (25.38)***	0.087	2.763 (25.34)***	0.082
International nonagriculture squared	−0.148 (11.98)***	−0.153 (11.06)***	−0.116 (22.44)***	−0.0037	−0.116 (22.34)***	−0.0034
National agriculture	−13.831 (−0.01)	−14.261 (0.01)	0.159 (−0.29)	0.005	0.169 (−0.3)	0.005
National agriculture squared	1.763 (−0.01)	1.819 (−0.01)	−0.016 (−0.24)	<0.001	−0.016 (−0.25)	<0.001

National nonagriculture	−0.711 (1.65)*	−0.661 (−1.5)	−0.112 (−0.77)	−0.0035	−0.109 (−0.74)	−0.003
National nonagriculture squared	0.042 (−1.06)	0.038 40(−0.96)	0.004 (−0.28)	<0.001	0.003 (−0.25)	<0.001
Migration networks						
Family members who were international migrants in *t* − 1						
Number of females agriculture	8.514 (−0.01)	8.071 (−0.01)	−3.627 (−0.26)	−0.031	−3.705 (−0.25)	−0.03
Number of females nonagriculture	1.818 (2.04)**	1.783 (2.09)**	1.362 (4.08)***	0.043	1.352 (4.05)***	0.04
Number of males agriculture	0.728 (−0.74)	0.675 (−0.7)	0.322 (−0.84)	0.01	0.302 (−0.79)	0.0089
Number of males nonagriculture	2.123 (5.34)***	2.118 (5.33)***	1.319 (9.23)***	0.042	1.324 (9.23)***	0.039
Family members who were internal migrants in *t* − 1						
Number of females agriculture	11.12 (−0.01)	11.289 (−0.01)	0.77 (0.57)	0.024	0.749 (−0.55)	0.022
Number of females nonagriculture	0.032 (−0.05)	0.076 (−0.13)	−0.207 (−0.53)	−0.0065	−0.221 (−0.56)	−0.007
Number of males agriculture	0.286 (−0.34)	0.273 (−0.33)	0.744 (−1.64)	0.024	0.744 (−1.64)	0.022
Number of males nonagriculture	2.368 (3.18)***	2.326 (3.20)***	−0.007 (−0.03)	<0.001	−0.019 (−0.07)	<0.001

(Table continues on the following page)

Table 3.10. Logit Results for Female International Migration to Nonagricultural Jobs (Continued)

Variable	Fixed-effects (FE) model		Random-effects (RE) model			
	Estimated coefficients (1)	Estimated coefficients (2)	Estimated coefficients (3)	Marginal effect[a] (4)	Marginal coefficients (5)	Marginal effect[a] (6)
Macroeconomic and policy variables						
Percent change in exchange rates	n.a.	0.719 (−0.79)	n.a.	n.a.	0.357 (−0.52)	0.011
Lagged Mexican GDP	n.a.	−0.003 (−0.52)	n.a.	n.a.	−0.001 (−0.18)	<0.001
Lagged U.S. GDP	n.a.	0 (−0.4)	n.a.	n.a.	0 (0)	<0.001
Percent change in border control	n.a.	−2.966 (2.27)**	n.a.	n.a.	−2.529 (2.51)**	−0.075
NAFTA	n.a.	−0.083 (−0.18)	n.a.	n.a.	−0.341 (−0.79)	−0.01
IRCA	n.a.	−0.119 (0.17)	n.a.	n.a.	−0.886 (−1.5)	−0.04
Joint test of policy variables (χ^2)	774.1***	5.76	n.a.	n.a.	10.63	n.a.
Overall goodness of fit (χ^2)		780.29***	823.55***	n.a.	822.22***	n.a.
Hausman χ^2	20.78**	14.24	n.a.	n.a.	n.a.	n.a.
Number of observations	1,565	1,565	49,828	n.a.	49,828	n.a.
Number of id	102	102	3,249	n.a.	3,249	n.a.

Source: 2003 ENHRUM.

Note: Absolute value of z statistics in parentheses.

*** Significant at 1 percent.

** Significant at 5 percent.

* Significant at 10 percent.

n.a. Not applicable.

a. Marginal effects presented as percentage points.

Table 3.11. Logit Results for Male International Migration to Nonagricultural Jobs

Variable	Fixed-effects (FE) model		Random-effects (RE) model			
	Estimated coefficients (1)	Estimated coefficients (2)	Estimated coefficients (3)	Marginal effect[a] (4)	Marginal coefficients (5)	Marginal effect[a] (6)
Time-invariant variables						
Constant	n.a.	n.a.	-2.873 (12.55)**	n.a.	-5.857 (5.38)**	n.a.
Trend	n.a.	n.a.	-0.019 (2.32)**	-0.0067	-0.136 (2.13)**	-0.047
Age	n.a.	n.a.	-0.091 (14.68)***	-0.032	-0.091 (14.67)***	-0.032
Years of schooling	n.a.	n.a.	-0.003 (-0.14)	<0.001	-0.002 (-0.12)	<0.001
Work experience						
International agriculture	0.229 (-1.22)	0.29 (-1.48)	0.098 (-1.19)	0.035	0.099 (-1.21)	0.034
International agriculture squared	0 (0)	0 (-0.04)	-0.003 (-0.65)	-0.001	-0.003 (-0.65)	-0.001
International nonagriculture	1.542 (26.81)***	1.698 (23.00)***	2.042 (44.22)***	0.716	2.045 (44.15)***	0.709
International nonagriculture squared	-0.089 (23.88)***	-0.096 (22.72)***	-0.081 (38.97)***	-0.029	-0.082 (38.94)***	-0.028
National agriculture	-0.433 (1.72)*	-0.375 (-1.48)	-0.156 (-1.62)	-0.055	-0.148 (-1.55)	-0.051
National agriculture squared	0.016 (-1.4)	0.015 (-1.32)	0.009 (-1.52)	0.0032	0.009 (-1.46)	0.003

(Table continues on the following page)

Table 3.11. Logit Results for Male International Migration to Nonagricultural Jobs (Continued)

	Fixed-effects (FE) model			Random-effects (RE) model		
Variable	Estimated coefficients (1)	Estimated coefficients (2)	Estimated coefficients (3)	Marginal effect[a] (4)	Marginal coefficients (5)	Marginal effect[a] (6)
National nonagriculture	−0.21 (2.25)**	−0.165 (1.73)*	−0.173 (3.20)***	−0.061	−0.172 (3.19)***	−0.060
National nonagriculture squared	0.011 (2.00)**	0.01 (−1.89)	0.011 (3.23)***	0.0038	0.011 (3.22)***	0.004
Migration networks						
Family members who were international migrants in $t − 1$						
Number of females agriculture	−0.44 (−0.08)	−0.373 (−0.06)	0.427 (−0.38)	0.186	0.475 (−0.43)	0.210
Number of females nonagriculture	1.434 (4.65)***	1.436 (4.67)***	1.096 (5.03)***	0.38	1.067 (4.87)***	0.37
Number of males agriculture	0.013 (−0.03)	−0.114 (−0.22)	0.036 (−0.14)	0.0125	0.019 (−0.08)	0.007
Number of males nonagriculture	0.575 (3.11)***	0.679 (3.52)***	1.336 (12.65)***	0.468	1.32 (12.47)***	0.458
Family members who were internal migrants in $t − 1$						
Number of females agriculture	0.258 (−0.33)	0.174 (−0.22)	0.039 (−0.05)	0.014	0.067 (−0.09)	0.023
Number of females nonagriculture	0.006 (−0.02)	0.064 (−0.26)	0.113 (−0.66)	0.039	0.116 (−0.68)	0.04

Number of males agriculture	−0.694	−0.81	−0.495	−1.412	−1.423	−0.493
	(−0.58)	(−0.68)		(−1.34)	(−1.35)	
Number of males nonagriculture	−0.312	−0.24	−0.018	−0.052	−0.046	−0.016
	(−1.11)	(−0.83)		(−0.29)	(−0.26)	
Macroeconomic and policy variables						
Percent change in exchange rates	n.a.	−0.182	n.a.	n.a.	−0.4	−0.139
		(−0.5)			(−1.35)	
Lagged Mexican GDP	n.a.	0.003	n.a.	n.a.	0.005	0.002
		(−1.39)			(2.05)**	
Lagged U.S. GDP	n.a.	0	n.a.	n.a.	0	<0.001
		(1.66)*			(−0.26)	
Percent change in border control	n.a.	0.335	n.a.	n.a.	0.383	0.133
		(−0.82)			(−0.26)	
NAFTA	n.a.	−0.486	n.a.	n.a.	−0.252	−0.087
		(2.61)***			(−1.06)	
IRCA	n.a.	0.802	n.a.	n.a.	0.483	0.144
		(2.88)***			(−1.23)	
					(1.77)*	
Joint test of policy variables (χ^2)	n.a.	32.99	n.a.	n.a.	15.59**	n.a.
Overall goodness of fit (χ^2)	2,048.7***	2,081.8***	n.a.	2,400.32***	2,415.75***	n.a.
Hausman χ^2	0	836.99***	n.a.	n.a.	n.a.	n.a.
Number of observations	6,494	6,494	n.a.	48,535	48,535	n.a.
Number of id	410	410	n.a.	3,153	3,153	n.a.

Source: 2003 ENHRUM.

Note: Absolute value of *z* statistics in parentheses.

*** Significant at 1 percent.

**Significant at 5 percent.

* Significant at 10 percent.

n.a. Not applicable.

a. Marginal effects presented as percentage points.

Table 3.12. Odds Ratio for Select Variables for International Nonagricultural Migration, by Gender

Variable	Fixed effects		Random effects	
	Female (1)	Male (2)	Female (3)	Male (4)
Work experience				
International agriculture	0.05	1.34	0.43	1.10
International agriculture squared	1.83	1.00	1.05	1.00
International nonagriculture	10.43	5.46	15.85	7.73
International nonagriculture squared	0.86	0.91	0.89	0.92
National agriculture	0.00	0.69	1.18	0.86
National agriculture squared	6.17	1.02	0.98	1.01
National nonagriculture	0.52	0.85	0.90	0.84
National nonagriculture squared	1.04	1.01	1.00	1.01
Family members who were international migrants in $t - 1$				
Female agriculture	3,200.28	0.69	0.02	1.61
Female nonagriculture	5.95	4.20	3.86	2.91
Male agriculture	1.96	0.89	1.35	1.02
Male nonagriculture	8.31	1.97	3.76	3.74
Family members who were internal migrants in $t - 1$				
Female agriculture	79,924.36	1.19	2.12	1.07
Female nonagriculture	1.08	1.07	0.80	1.12
Male agriculture	1.31	0.44	2.10	0.24
Male nonagriculture	10.24	0.79	0.98	0.95
Macroeconomic and policy variables				
Percent change in border control	0.05	1.40	0.08	1.47

Source: 2003 ENHRUM.

women (significant in the second FE model; see table 3.10). This observation contrasts with the findings for female migration to agricultural jobs presented in table 3.7, for which the cross-sector experience effect is positive. For male migration to U.S. nonfarm jobs, previous migration to nonfarm jobs abroad has a significant positive effect. In contrast, past migration to agriculture does not have a significant effect. These findings suggest limited migrant mobility from farm to nonfarm jobs. In a few cases, past experience as an internal nonfarm labor migrant decreases the probability of international nonfarm migration. This cross-destination effect is generally more significant for males than for females and suggests that there may be competition between U.S. and Mexican nonfarm sectors for rural migrants' labor.

Network effects clearly are sector specific for nonagricultural labor migration by both genders. Both male and female nonfarm networks raise the likelihood of migration to nonfarm jobs by males and females. In contrast, the cross-effects of agricultural networks on nonfarm migration are not significant for either gender. The effect of internal migration networks on nonfarm international migration is insignificant in all cases for males. However, for females there is some evidence that internal nonfarm networks increase the likelihood of international nonfarm migration.

When we evaluate odds ratios (table 3.12), the importance of male networks becomes more apparent. For females, the cross-gender effect of male networks on the odds of migrating to nonagricultural jobs is greater than the own-gender network effect. The cross-gender network effect is more important than the own-gender effect for males as well, but the difference is not as large as it is for females.

For males, the effect of NAFTA on nonagricultural labor migration is significant and negative. The effect of the IRCA is significant and positive. Border control expenditures have a significant negative effect on the probability of international migration to nonfarm jobs for females, but not for males.

In the RE models, age negatively affects international migration to nonfarm jobs by both males and females. Schooling has a significant positive effect on female but not male international migration to nonfarm jobs. For females, the positive effect of schooling on nonfarm migration stands in contrast to the insignificant (negative) effect on farm migration. Schooling appears to have sector-specific effects on international migration by females, but no effect on international migration by males.

Conclusions

Our analysis of gender dynamics in international migration using a panel data set constructed from retrospective migration histories takes a step toward filling a lacuna in the social sciences literature on how the determinants of international migration as well as the migration impacts of policy and macroeconomic shocks differ between men and women. This study is unique in its ability to apply panel-data econometric methods to control for unobservable individual and household characteristics, which may confound and bias findings in cross-sectional studies, and in considering migrants' choice of economic sector in which to work as well as their decision to migrate abroad.

Fixed-effects estimation using panel data makes it possible to test the robustness of many of these results to unobserved individual and household variables. In general, we obtain qualitatively similar results using FE and RE estimation. This is reassuring, because the RE specification makes it possible to test for effects on international migration that cannot be considered in a FE model, including individual characteristics like human capital that do not vary significantly over the time period covered by our panel. However, for the majority of the models estimated we reject the null hypothesis that the RE model produces consistent and efficient coefficients. Thus when there are conflicting results from the two models, it is advisable to rely more heavily on the results obtained from the FE model.

A surprising result from our econometric analysis is that most policy and macroeconomic variables are insignificant in explaining international migration from rural Mexico by both genders, under both model specifications. U.S. border enforcement expenditures are the exception; however, their effect is not the same for men and for women. We find evidence that increased border expenditures significantly deter migration by women, but not by men. This may suggest that females are more risk averse than males or, alternatively, that cultural norms discourage women from attempting the border crossing under heightened security. A positive effect of border control expenditures on male migration raises new questions, including the likelihood that enforcement deters return migration. Are males more willing than females to play a "cat and mouse" game, in which border officials catch migrants and release them back into Mexico, whereupon they again try to cross the border and eventually succeed (see Donato and Patterson 2004)? Or does increased border enforcement raise the sunk cost of migration and thus increase the amount of time that migrants must stay in the United States in order to recoup their investment in crossing the border in ways that differ between genders?

Other key findings on the determinants of migration from rural Mexico include the following:

- The dynamics of international migration differ significantly between men and women. We easily reject the null hypothesis that the determinants of Mexico-to-U.S. migration and their changes over time are gender neutral. International migration selects differently on men than on women. This finding offers important panel-data support to findings of other studies that use cross-sectional data (see chapter 2).
- Overall, women are significantly less likely than men to migrate abroad. However, international migration selects differently on the human capital of men and women. Schooling is positively associated with international migration by females, but not by males. For females, the effect of schooling is significant only for international migration to nonagricultural jobs. This suggests that the economic returns to female education are higher in those jobs than in agriculture. It indicates that the effect of education is not simply to raise women's willingness

to migrate, as suggested by the social norms argument advanced by Hondagneu-Sotelo (1994) and others. It contradicts the finding by Curran and Rivero-Fuentes (2003) that education is insignificant in explaining migration. That study does not control for sector of employment, which could have confounded the empirical results. We find that, in order for schooling to significantly increase women's likelihood of migrating abroad, the migration must be linked specifically to nonfarm jobs.

- The gross international migration time trend is steeper for males than for females (figure 3.1). Age deters international migration slightly more for men than for women. The finding that females may migrate at an older age than males is supported by Kanaiaupuni (2000).

- Family migration networks, or contacts with family members who are already abroad, have a more important effect on migration decisions than do macroeconomic and policy variables, and these network effects are both gender and sector specific. Own-gender and sector network effects are always positive, but not always greater than cross-gender network effects. It appears incorrect to conclude that women are more dependent on female than on male networks (as concluded in Hondagneu-Sotelo 1994; Kossoudji and Ranney 1984). Our results reveal that male migration networks are not more influential than female migration networks, but they nevertheless are highly significant in explaining both male and female international migration. Males may provide critical information and assistance in crossing the border, and social norms may discourage female migration without male assistance. However, we also find that female networks are significant in explaining male migration, and in some cases they are more significant than own-gender male network effects. This lends support to studies suggesting that female networks are deeper and more extensive than male networks and may provide services that male networks cannot (Curran and Rivero-Fuentes 2003; Menjivar 2000).

- Migration network effects are sector as well as gender specific. Agricultural own-gender migrant networks are not significant in explaining migration to nonagricultural jobs for either males or females, which suggests that the contacts made by agricultural migrants do not help males or females to secure information or contacts necessary to migrate to nonagricultural jobs.

- Finally, nonagricultural employment dominates agricultural employment for international migrants of both genders, but especially for females.

Overall, our findings highlight the importance of incorporating gender into international migration models, since there sometimes are striking differences in the determinants of international migration for men and women.

Endnotes

1. See chapter 2 for a discussion of how these four categories of variables may affect the costs and benefits of migration differently for men and women.

2. Most human capital studies estimate experience as age minus education minus five. Strictly speaking, this is accurate if children enter school at age five and are fully employed when not in school. Including both age and experience thus derived in a migration regression results in a problem of multicolinearity. The only way that both variables can be included is if there is not full employment outside of school and detailed data are available on time worked, which is rarely the case.

3. Joint migration is migration by the entire household unit; that is, the household's location changes, either all at once or via sequential moves in which other household members follow the initial migrant. See chapter 2 for a discussion of split versus joint migration models.

4. When whole households migrate, the estimated trend is biased downward because the household members are not counted as migrants in 2002.

5. It also may reflect households' perceptions of whether or not female migrants work while abroad or perhaps even their reluctance to admit that female migrants are working.

6. For purposes of this analysis, "nonmigrants" refer to those who did not migrate abroad and may include internal migrants.

7. Complete results are available from the authors.

8. An odds ratio of more than 1 indicates an increased chance of international migration, while an odds ratio of less than 1 indicates a decreased chance. The odds ratio for male international migration networks, equal to 1.81 for females, means that having a male international migrant in the household increases a female's chance of migrating by 81 percent.

9. Results on macroeconomic variables should be interpreted with some caution. We assume that the time trend and macroeconomic variables capture the effects of any omitted variables. Nonetheless, the existence of any such omitted variables common across individuals at a given point in time could reduce the precision of the estimation and bias the standard errors in either the random-effects or fixed-effects model. Our estimation assumes that any omitted variables common across time periods are not correlated with the policy variables. See Moulton (1986) for a discussion.

10. For male migration we can reject the null hypothesis that the random-effects model is both consistent and efficient.

11. In order to estimate a FE model, there needs to be variation in all variables. Variables that have no variation are dropped from the model.

References

Aguilera, Michael, and Douglas S. Massey. 2003. "Social Capital and the Wages of Mexican Migrants: New Hypotheses and Tests." *Social Forces* 82 (2): 671–701.

Cackley, Alicia Puente. 1993. "The Role of Wage Differentials in Determining Migration Selectivity by Sex: The Case of Brazil." In *Internal Migration of Women in Developing Countries.* New York: United Nations, Department for Economic and Social Information and Policy Analysis.

Cerrutti, Marcela, and Douglas S. Massey. 2001. "On the Auspices of Female Migration from Mexico to the United States." *Demography* 38 (2): 187–200.

Corts, Kenneth S., and Jasjit Singh. 2002. "The Effect of Relationships on Contract Choice: Evidence from Offshore Drilling." Unpublished mss. University of Toronto, J. L. Rotman School of Management.

Curran, Sara R., and Estela Rivero-Fuentes. 2003. "Engendering Migrant Networks: The Case of Mexican Migration." *Demography* 40 (2): 289–307.

Davis, Benjamin, and Paul Winters. 2001. "Gender, Networks, and Mexico-U.S.-Migration." *Journal of Development Studies* 38 (2): 1–26.

de la Brière, Bénédicte, Alain de Janvry, Elisabeth Sadoulet, and Sylvie Lambert. 2002. "The Roles of Destination, Gender, and Household Composition in Explaining Remittances: An Analysis for the Dominican Sierra." *Journal of Development Economics* 68 (2): 309–28.

Donato, Katharine M. 1993. "Current Trends and Patterns of Female Migration: Evidence from Mexico." *International Migration Review* 27 (4): 748–71.

Donato, Katharine M., and Evelyn Patterson. 2004. "Women and Men on the Move: Undocumented Border Crossing." In *Crossing the Border: Research from the Mexican Migration Project*, ed. Jorge Durand and Douglas Massey. New York: Russell Sage Foundation.

Hondagneu-Sotelo, Pierrette. 1994. *Gendered Transitions: Mexican Experiences of Immigration*. Berkeley: University of California Press.

Kanaiaupuni, Shawn M. 2000. "Reframing the Migration Question: An Analysis of Men, Women, and Gender in Mexico." *Social Forces* 78 (4): 1311–47.

Kossoudji, Sherrie A., and Susan I. Ranney. 1984. "The Labor Market Experience of Female Migrants: The Case of Temporary Mexican Migration to the U.S." *International Migration Review* 18 (4): 1120–43.

Levy, Santiago, and Sweder van Wijnbergen. 1994. "Labor Markets, Migration, and Welfare: Agriculture in the North American Free Trade Agreement." *Journal of Development Economics* 43 (2): 263–78.

Maume, David J. 2004. "Is the Glass Ceiling a Unique Form of Inequality?" *Work and Occupations* 31 (2): 250–74.

Menjívar, Cecilia. 2000. "The Intersection of Work and Gender: Central American Immigrant Women and Employment in California." *American Behavioral Scientist* 42 (4): 601–27.

Mincer, Jacob. 1974. *Schooling, Experience, and Earnings*. New York: Columbia University Press.

Mora, Jorge, and J. Edward Taylor. 2006. "Determinants of Migration, Destination, and Sector Choice: Disentangling Individual, Household, and Community Effects." In *International Migration, Remittances, and the Brain Drain*, ed. Çaglar Özden and Maurice Schiff. New York: Palgrave Macmillan.

Moulton, Brent R. 1986. "Random Group Effects and the Precision of Regression Estimates." *Journal of Econometrics* 32 (3): 385–97.

Munshi, Kaivan. 2003. "Networks in the Modern Economy: Mexican Migrants in the U.S. Labor Market." *Quarterly Journal of Economics* 118 (2): 549–99.

Richter, Susan, J. Edward Taylor, and Antonio Yúnez-Naude. 2005. "Policy Reforms and the Gender Dynamics of Rural Mexico-to-U.S. Migration." Paper prepared for presentation at the American Agricultural Economics Association Annual Meeting, Providence, RI, July 24–27.

Robinson, Sherman, Mary Burfisher, Raul Hinojosa-Ojeda, and Karen Thierfelder. 1993. "Agricultural Policies and Migration in a U.S.-Mexico Free Trade Area." *Journal of Policy Modeling* 15 (5–6): 673–701.

Sjaastad, Larry A. 1962. "The Costs and Returns of Human Migration." *Journal of Political Economy* 70 (5): 80–93.

Smith, James P., and Duncan Thomas. 2003. "Remembrances of Things Past: Test-Retest Reliability of Retrospective Migration Histories." *Journal of the Royal Statistics Society Series A* 166 (1): 23–49.

Taylor, J. Edward. 1987. "Undocumented Mexico-U.S. Migration and the Returns to Households in Rural Mexico." *American Journal of Agricultural Economics* 69 (3): 626–38.

Taylor, J. Edward, and Irma Adelman. 1996. *Village Economies: The Design, Estimation, and Use of Villagewide Economic Models*. Cambridge, U.K.: Cambridge University Press.

Taylor, J. Edward, Antonio Yúnez-Naude, Fernando Barceinas, and George Dyer. 2005. "Transition Policy and the Structure of the Agriculture of Mexico." In *North American Agrifood Market Integration: Situation and Perspectives*, ed. Karen M. Huff, Karl Meilke, Ronald D. Knuston, Rene F. Ochoa, James Rude, and Antonio Yúnez-Naude, 86-118. Altona, Manitoba: Friesen Printers.

Wolf, Diane. 1992. *Factory Daughters: Gender, Household Dynamics, and Rural Industrialization in Java*. Berkeley: University of California Press.

Wooldridge, Jeffrey. 2002. *Econometric Analysis of Cross Section and Panel Data*. Cambridge, MA: MIT Press.

4

GENDER AND THE IMPACTS OF INTERNATIONAL MIGRATION: EVIDENCE FROM RURAL MEXICO

Lisa Pfeiffer and J. Edward Taylor

The impacts of international migration are often thought of as effects on labor markets in destination countries. Given that more than 175 million people live outside their country of birth, destination-country impacts are, indeed, important (O'Neil 2003). However, migrants also leave family, friends, businesses, and communities behind. The impacts of international migration on households and communities of origin have been the subject of a growing literature in economics and the other social sciences. Despite a growing awareness that gender shapes the *determinants* of international migration, almost no economic research has focused on gender-specific *impacts* of migration in migrant-sending areas.

This chapter takes a step toward filling the void in research on the gender impacts of international migration. It addresses two critical questions. First, how does the gender of migrants affect the impacts of international migration on the economic activities of household members left behind? We specifically investigate households' participation in cropping and nonagricultural activities. Second, what impact does female and male migration have on household investments in education and health?

Theoretically, if a household is welfare maximizing, it would only choose to have migrants if that decision increased welfare. However, increases in welfare may come at the expense of some or all nonmigration activities, and the impact of migration on these activities may differ depending on the gender of the migrants.

99

In an effort to address these questions, we construct and estimate an econometric model of migration and its impacts and estimate this model using data from the 2003 Mexico National Rural Household Survey (Encuesta Nacional a Hogares Rurales de México—ENHRUM). We begin by briefly discussing hypothesized impacts of migration and remittances in existing migration models. We then present our econometric model, describe and summarize the data, and report the econometric results. A final section summarizes our conclusions.

Review of Literature on the Impacts of Migration in Economic Models

International migration potentially produces both direct and indirect impacts on households in migrant-sending areas.

The most visible direct impact is the lost-labor effect of migration on household production and income activities. Family labor invariably decreases when a family member migrates away from the farm, and household production and other income-generating activities adjust. In addition, migrant remittances add directly to the receiving household's income.

Indirect effects are more complex. They are associated with the role of migrants as financial and risk intermediaries, providing households with liquidity to invest in new production activities or technologies and income security, as well as the income effect that migration and remittances may have on the supply of family labor for production activities, highlighted by research on what has become known as the new economics of labor migration (NELM; for example, see articles reprinted in Stark 1991).

A household perspective provides a useful basis for considering both the direct lost-labor and remittance effects and the indirect influences of migration on rural households. In an agricultural household model with perfect markets, as in the basic model presented by Singh et al. (1986), neither the loss of family labor to migration nor the receipt of remittances is hypothesized to influence household production activities. This is because, as a wage taker in local labor markets, the household can simply hire laborers to take the place of those who migrate, and remittances, while adding to the household's budget, do not affect any of the conditions for profit maximization. In such a model the only impacts of migration and remittances are on the consumption side. These effects include an increased demand for leisure and other normal goods. A finding that migration significantly affects farm-household production would not be consistent with the perfect-markets model.

In the past two decades, as the emphasis of development economics shifted toward the study of market imperfections, new perspectives emerged stressing the complexity of migration as an economic institution, interrelationships between migration's determinants and impacts, and the household's role in migration decision making (Stark 1991; Taylor and Martin 2001). Migrant-sending households, particularly in rural areas, typically find themselves in a context of missing or imperfect markets. The presence of market imperfections vastly increases the potential scope for migration impacts on sending households.

In a context of market imperfections, migration can produce both positive and negative effects. For example, if migrant remittances enable households to overcome credit and risk constraints on production, migration may increase incomes in migrant-sending households by more than the dollar amount that migrants remit, creating an income multiplier of remittances *within* households.[1] However, if households cannot hire perfect substitutes for the labor of family members who migrate, there may be negative lost-labor effects on production. Remittances also can have a negative effect on production if they increase incomes in migrant-sending households, leisure is a normal good, and households cannot hire perfect substitutes for their labor in family production activities. These negative impacts of migration on production activities are not necessarily inconsistent with a positive impact on welfare. However, they may dampen or even reverse positive effects of remittances on household income, production, and expenditures on education, health, and other items. Econometric studies find evidence of negative lost-labor effects of migration in migrant-sending households, but positive remittance effects (León-Ledesma and Priacha 2004; Rapoport and Docquier 2005; Rozelle et al. 1999; Taylor et al. 2003), particularly in the long run (Taylor 1992).

Chapter 2 of this volume presents some compelling reasons to expect that the impacts of migration and remittances on production, incomes, and expenditures are shaped by the gender of both those who migrate and those who stay behind. Rural household surveys and ethnographic research reveal that men and women often are engaged in different household production activities. If male and female workers are not perfect substitutes in these activities, then migration may have different opportunity costs for men and women. For example, suppose that prior to migration women are employed largely in unpaid household work, while men work the fields. In this case, it is possible that migration by women would not reduce crop production, while migration by men would. However, if female migration pulls male labor out of the fields and into household activities traditionally occupied by women, then female migration could reduce crop production via a labor substitution effect.

Migrants' remittances may either mitigate this lost-labor effect by loosening capital and risk constraints on production or reinforce it by increasing the household's demand for leisure. There is very little empirical evidence available on gender differences in remittance behavior, but the evidence that does exist suggests that both the magnitude and motives for remitting may be different for men and women. A study in the Dominican Republic finds that female migrants send home more remittances, on average, than male migrants, and they are more likely to send money when there are income shocks due, say, to a parent's illness (de la Brière et al. 2002). That is, in addition to being more committed remitters, female migrants seem to play more of an "insurance" role for their household than do male migrants. Another study finds that Philippine male migrants abroad are more likely to remit than females (Semyonov and Gorodzeisky 2005). Differences in remittance behavior create the potential for gender disparities in the economic returns to households from migration as well as in the investment and insurance effects of remittances. A burgeoning literature examining intra-household resource allocation suggests that the person who controls resources within a household can influence the way in which these resources are allocated, with important implications for efficiency (for example, see Udry 1996; Schultz 1990). In the case of migration, who receives the remittances (or monitors their use) could shape the effects of remittances on a household's expenditures on production inputs, education, health, and other items. The gender of both the migrants and those remaining in the household could matter (for more details on these issues, see chapter 5 in this volume).

Migration networks have become central to most models of international migration behavior, and there are compelling reasons to expect that the effects of networks are gender specific. Migrant networks convey information and provide assistance to prospective migrants, thus reducing the costs and risks and increasing the benefits of future migration. As a result, they can positively influence the probability of migration and also the economic returns from migrating (Munshi 2003; Winters et al. 1999). Networks are thus a form of social capital, which together with human and physical capital creates disparities in the costs and benefits of migration across households and individuals. Network formation may be endogenous from a household perspective; households may strategically invest in establishing networks that influence their future economic returns from migration. If the information and assistance value of family networks is gender specific, then a family's optimal choice may be to invest in the gender network that maximizes future net benefits—for example, keeping the only son at home to work on the farm, which minimizes the negative direct lost-labor effects of migration, while sending off the oldest daughter, who can constitute a network that will facilitate future migration by her younger female siblings. While no empirical study has attempted to test this specific hypothesis, it is well accepted that past migration directly influences future migration, and recent studies support the notion that the gender of migrant networks matters (chapter 3 of this volume; Curran and Rivero-Fuentes 2003).

Econometric Model

Our econometric model is designed to test for gender-specific migration impacts on migrant-sending households. Consider a "thought experiment" in which a set of rural households is randomly selected to participate in migration. Specifically, from a population of identical households, a random sample of households is chosen to receive a female migration treatment (by having one or more female members plucked out and sent to the United States), a male migration treatment, or no migration treatment at all. If such an experiment were possible, one could test whether participating in international migration significantly affects household production activities and expenditures and, if so, whether this migration effect differed depending on the gender of the migrants. One could do this simply by comparing production activities and expenditures between households that did and did not have male or female migrants.

This thought experiment is unrealistic for at least two reasons. First, households are not identical. Thus it is necessary to use statistical methods to control for variables that influence household participation in different production activities, expenditures, and other outcomes, independent of migration. Second, households and individuals are not randomly selected to participate in international migration. If the selection bias of migration choices is ignored, estimated effects of migration on household production, expenditure, and income outcomes may be biased. Table 4.1 shows that migrant and nonmigrant households are in fact quite different with respect to many demographic variables. Instruments for migration are needed to address this endogeneity problem.

Let M_{gi} denote migration by gender g in household i; let Y_i denote an outcome of interest in household i—for example, income from crop production or investment in schooling; and let X_{Mgi} and X_{Yi} denote exogenous variables that explain migration by gender and the outcomes in household i, respectively. Finally, let ε_{Mgi} and ε_{Yi} denote stochastic errors. The core equation of interest in our model is for the production, remittance, or expenditure outcome, Y_i:

$$Y_i = \gamma_0 + \gamma_{1g}M_{gi} + \gamma_2 X_{Yi} + \varepsilon_{Yi}. \tag{4.1}$$

The parameter γ_0 is an intercept, and γ_{1g} and γ_2 are parameter vectors representing, respectively, the effects of male and female migration and other variables on the outcome being modeled.

Equation 4.1 has a number of interesting implications. For production outcomes (for example, Y_i = the quantity or value of crop or noncrop production), a perfect-markets household-farm model would predict that the elements of γ_{1g} are all zero; that is, neither gender's migration affects production. An imperfect labor market that results in a household's inability to obtain a perfect substitute

Table 4.1. Summary Statistics, by Household Migration Status

Variable	No migrants in household	Migrants in household	T-test of difference in the means
Household head age	47.25	55.33	−8.96**
Household head experience	37.58	46.75	−9.01**
Household head education	4.67	3.59	5.21**
Male average education	4.98	5.58	−3.67**
Female average education	4.88	5.37	−3.11**
Household size	5.85	8.13	−13.27**
Number of children (<16 years of age)	1.80	1.38	4.39**
Percent of males who are married in household	0.44	0.53	−4.67**
Percent of females who are married in household	0.45	0.57	−6.27**
Speak indigenous language	0.22	0.07	6.73**
Number of hectares farmed	3.89	8.48	−3.16**
Hectares of good-quality land	1.60	1.38	0.29
Average number of days sick of members of household	7.07	9.14	−1.36
Household experienced natural disaster	0.33	0.39	−2.12*
Number of observations	1,388	377	

Source: 2003 ENHRUM.

**Significant at 5 percent.

*Significant at 10 percent.

for migrants' lost labor, other things equal, would imply $\gamma_{1g} < 0$ for the gender for which the labor market constraint is binding. A positive insurance effect of migration (that is, a promise by migrants to remit in the case of crop failure that encourages crop investments), other things being equal, would imply the opposite. If remittances by male or female migrants (or both) loosen the liquidity constraints on production, this could counteract the negative lost-labor effect, possibly making $\gamma_{1g} > 0$ for at least one of the genders. However, if remittances increase the household's demand for leisure, we expect the opposite effect. In light of this, the sign of this coefficient is ambiguous a priori; it must be determined econometrically.

The variables X_{Yi} include household assets that influence production, including physical capital (land, machinery) and human capital (education of the household head and other family members at home). The parameter vector γ_2 denotes the returns to these assets in the production activity.[2]

For Y_i = expenditures on schooling or health, the variables X_{Yi} include determinants of total income or expenditures. They may also include household characteristics and demographic variables that influence marginal utilities (Deaton and Muellbauer 1980) and variables that permit one to test for gender influences described earlier. If migration by either gender does not influence expenditure on a given item, controlling for total expenditures, then $\gamma_{1g} = 0$. A finding to the contrary would imply that migration influences the marginal utility of expenditures in some fashion.

The vector of variables X_{Yi} controls for the fact that households are not identical. Nevertheless, econometric estimation of equation 4.1 is complicated by the fact that migration by both genders is endogenous. To correct for this endogeneity problem, instruments for the participation of household members in international migration are needed. These migration instruments are obtained by estimating a probit equation for participation in international migration of the following form:

$$\Pr[M_{gi} = 1 | X_{Mgi}, \beta_g] = F(X'_{Mgi}\beta_g), \tag{4.2}$$

where X_{Mgi} is a vector of variables used to obtain an instrument for household i's participation in male or female international migration, β_g is a vector of parameters, and $F(\cdot)$ is the normal cumulative distribution function. Thus we estimate two separate probit regressions: one for male international migration and one for female international migration.

The elements of the vector X_{Mgi} include human capital variables, assets, and migration network variables typically included in a household migration model. The human capital and migration network variables are defined separately for the two genders. In order for equations 4.1 and 4.2 to be identified, at least one element of the vector X_{Mgi} for each gender equation must be excluded from X_{Yi}. Our identification strategy entails the use of five such variables. These include two dummy variables, one for the presence of household female international migrants and the other for the presence of male international migrants in 1980, the first year covered by the migration life histories in our data (described in detail in chapter 3); a pair of similar dummy variables for 1980 participation in internal (within Mexico) migration, by gender; and historic state-level migration rates for the period 1955–59. The justification for these instruments is that they are clearly predetermined variables, sufficiently far back in time to be unlikely to influence production and other outcomes in 2002, the last year of the ENHRUM survey. However, because of the importance of migration networks in aiding migration and migrant's earnings, they are likely to be correlated with migration in 2002. The historic state-level migration rates were taken from González Navarro (1974); they have been used as an instrument for household migration in other studies,

Table 4.2. Hausman-Wu Test of the Instruments

Variable	Test results	Critical value
Dependent variable	χ^2 *test that instruments have no effect on the residuals*	*(5 percent)* = 16.92
Staple crops	1.117	Fail to reject
Nonstaple crops	0.438	Fail to reject
Agricultural income	0.158	Fail to reject
Livestock income	0.174	Fail to reject
Wage income	0.283	Fail to reject
Education spending	20.66	Reject
Health spending	2.199	Fail to reject
Poverty	0.096	Fail to reject
Instrumented variable	*F(5,1755) tests of insignificant IVs*	*(5 percent)* = 2.21
Male U.S. migration	193.145	Reject
Female U.S. migration	50.822	Reject

Source: 2003 ENHRUM.

including Woodruff and Zenteno (2001) and McKenzie and Rapoport (2004).[3] It has been suggested that these historic international migration rates were the result of the pattern of arrival of railroads in Mexico (Massey et al. 2002; McKenzie and Rapoport 2004). One can argue that households in communities with high levels of early twentieth-century migration will have a higher likelihood of having a migrant member than an otherwise identical household living in a community with low initial migration rates. Our identifying assumption is that these historic state migration rates and historic, gender-specific household migration do not affect income outcomes 23 to 43 years later. Our instrumental variables (IV) estimation relies on this exogeneity assumption. The results of a series of Hausman-Wu tests are presented in table 4.2.

The stochastic terms ε_{Yi} and ε_{Mgi} are assumed to be normally and independently distributed with variance σ_i^2. The right-hand-side gender-specific migration instruments in equation 4.1 are predictions from the binomial probits, in which the dependent migration variable equals 1 if the household is observed with an international migrant of the corresponding gender in 2002, and zero otherwise.

The vectors X_{Yi} and X_{Mgi} include household demographic and human and physical capital variables. An extensive literature explores the returns to schooling and other human capital in production (Jamison and Lau 1982) and in migration (Taylor and Martin 2001). Human capital measures include the education level, in years, and experience level of the household head. Other variables hypothesized to affect farm and nonfarm production include the availability and quality of land, household physical capital and demographic variables, and wealth.

Some type of two-step approach is needed to estimate the migration equation 4.2, which will be used to identify the outcome equation 4.1. However, the consistency and efficiency of simply estimating a probit model and using predicted probabilities in the outcome model are limited when multiple instruments are obtained from separate probit regressions and the outcome equation is also a probit or tobit model (Bhattacharya et al. 2006; Newey 1987). A more efficient estimation method is to use a maximum-likelihood estimation of Amemiya's generalized least squares estimator (see Newey 1987), which is referred to as IV probit. Alternatively, Angrist (2000) demonstrates that an instrumental variables linear probability model will produce a "best linear estimate" of average treatment effects in the case of binary endogenous variables. These alternative estimation methods are shown to produce qualitatively similar results.

Data

Our empirical analysis is based on data from the Mexico National Rural Household Survey (Encuesta Nacional a Hogares Rurales de México, or ENHRUM). This survey and the data are described in detail in chapter 3 of this volume.

Rural Mexico is an ideal laboratory for studying the impacts of migration on the rural economy. Figure 3.1 of chapter 3, constructed from retrospective migration data gathered in the survey, shows that the percentage of Mexico's village populations working at international migrant destinations increased sharply at the end of the twentieth century.[4] Throughout this time period, migration propensities were lower for women than for men, and the rate of growth of male immigration was higher. Villagers' propensity to migrate to U.S. jobs more than doubled from 1990 to 2002. This surge in migration mirrors an unexpectedly large increase in the number of Mexico-born persons living in the United States, as revealed by the U.S. 2000 census.[5] During this period, there was a sharp upward trend in the percentage of international migrants working in nonfarm jobs and a mildly upward trend of the percentage working in U.S. farm jobs.

Table 4.3 defines and summarizes the variables used in our econometric analysis. The top panel summarizes activity participation and migration variables; the bottom panel, exogenous variables. A substantial percentage of households participate in each income activity, implying that income diversification is common. (To be classified as participating in a production activity, a household had to produce the good or service; it did not necessarily have to sell it or make a profit.) Almost a third (30 percent) of all rural households participated in staple crop production, 34 percent in nonstaple crop production, 29 percent in livestock production, and 64 percent in wage work. Of all households, 19 percent had one or more male international migrants, and 8 percent had at least one female international migrant. A slightly smaller percentage received remittances from

Table 4.3. Summary Statistics

Variable	Mean	Standard error	Minimum	Maximum
Endogenous variables				
Male international migrants (indicator)	0.188	0.009	0	1
Female international migrants (indicator)	0.083	0.007	0	1
Remittances from male international migrants (indicator)	0.165	0.009	0	1
Remittances from female international migrants (indicator)	0.039	0.005	0	1
Staple production (indicator)	0.298	0.009	0	1
Nonstaple production (indicator)	0.343	0.010	0	1
Agricultural income (indicator)	0.363	0.010	0	1
Livestock income (indicator)	0.291	0.011	0	1
Wage income (indicator)	0.637	0.012	0	1
Below poverty level	0.812	0.010	0	1
Education expenditures[1]	3,923.81	206.629	0	83,400
Health expenditures[1]	2,595.02	173.416	0	85,000
Exogenous variables				
Household head age	49.222	0.417	15	95
Household head experience	39.623	0.478	1	90
Household head education	4.599	0.096	0	20
Male average education	5.240	0.074	0	15
Female average education	5.105	0.069	0	15
Household size	6.270	0.078	1	21
Number of children (<16 years of age)	1.646	0.040	0	12
Percent of males who are married in household	0.469	0.009	0	1
Percent of females who are married in household	0.483	0.009	0	1
Speak indigenous language	0.155	0.006	0	1
Number of hectares farmed	4.912	0.685	0	537.5
Hectares of good-quality land	1.744	0.538	0	500
Average number of days sick of members of household	7.452	0.633	0	360
Household experienced natural disaster in 2002	0.314	0.010	0	1

Source: 2003 ENHRUM.

Note: Sample size is 1,765. Corrected for survey design.

[1] In Mexican pesos.

each. Households spent an average of 3,924 pesos (roughly $392) on education and 2,595 pesos ($259) on health. Based on the income data obtained from the survey, 81 percent of rural households had per capita daily incomes that put them below the official poverty line set by the Mexican government (Secretaría de

Desarrollo Social) at 28.1 pesos a day, including 15.4 pesos for food, 3.5 for basic health and education, and 9.8 for clothing, shelter, utilities, and transportation.[6] Household heads in the sample averaged 49 years of age and 4.6 years of completed schooling. However, average schooling of other household members was slightly higher, around five years for both males and females. Households in the sample had an average size of 6.3 persons, including 1.6 children younger than 16 years. They had 4.9 hectares of land, including 1.7 hectares that they considered to be of good quality. On average, household members were sick 7.5 days in 2002. Just over a third of all households suffered some kind of natural disaster that affected their production activities. An indigenous language was spoken by at least one household member in 6 percent of the households.

Econometric Findings

We now turn to the econometric results of the study.

Migration

The gender-specific international migration probit results appear in the first two columns of table 4.4. The error terms are clustered by village, and the reported coefficients are marginal effects on the migration probability. The instruments all have the expected signs. Both same-gender 1980 household network variables are significant and have positive coefficients in the respective international migration regressions. Same-gender national migration networks are negatively but insignificantly related to the probability of international migration. The state historic migration variable is positive and significant for both genders, but larger and more significant for males. Inasmuch as migration from rural Mexico in the 1950s consisted overwhelmingly of males, often aided by the Bracero program, which targeted single men for agricultural jobs, it is not surprising that this variable is more important in explaining male migration. Taken together, these historic migration variables appear to be good instruments with which to explain household participation in international migration in 2002. The cross-gender network effects are insignificant in the probit regressions.

Family size increases the probability of both male and female migration, while the number of children in the household decreases it, especially for migration by women. Household international migration has a quadratic relationship with the age of the household, proxied by the age of the household head; the probability of participating in migration first increases and then flattens out with the households age.[7] Higher education of household heads significantly discourages participation in international migration by both genders, consistent with a positive productivity effect of the household head's schooling on family labor at home. Higher average

Table 4.4. First-Stage Prediction of Migration

Variable	Probit		Ordinary least squares	
	Female migration (1)	Male migration (2)	Female migration (3)	Male migration (4)
Household head age (×10)	0.045	0.053	0.031	0.070
	(2.30)**	(1.42)	(0.86)	(1.10)
Household head age squared (×100)	−0.004	−0.007	−0.006	−0.013
	(2.51)**	(1.97)**	(1.57)	(1.98)**
Household head education (×10)	−0.035	−0.097	−0.084	−0.158
	(2.83)***	(2.56)**	(2.75)***	(2.10)**
Household size	0.010	0.036	0.051	0.119
	(8.69)***	(8.47)***	(6.15)***	(9.16)***
Number of children	−0.014	−0.029	−0.060	−0.130
	(5.96)***	(3.60)***	(5.52)***	(6.49)***
Female education (×10)	0.024	n.a.	0.006	n.a.
	(1.87)*		(0.16)	
Male education (×10)	n.a.	0.090	n.a.	0.045
		(1.70)*		(0.57)
Percent of females in household married	0.017	n.a.	0.060	n.a.
	(1.11)		(1.83)*	
Percent of males in household married	n.a.	−0.002	n.a.	0.009
	.	(0.07)		(0.16)
Indigenous	−0.033	−0.098	−0.049	−0.147
	(3.58)***	(3.03)***	(2.19)**	(3.57)***
Asset index	0.016	0.032	0.055	0.071
	(4.60)***	(4.16)***	(4.94)***	(3.96)***
Female international migrants, 1980	0.145	−0.002	0.787	0.156
	(3.11)***	(0.03)	(2.42)**	(0.58)
Female national migrants, 1980	−0.053	0.020	−0.122	0.081
	(1.51)	(0.49)	(3.51)***	(0.47)
Male international migrants, 1980	−0.007	0.160	0.060	0.802
	(0.37)	(5.25)***	(0.62)	(5.37)***
Male national migrants, 1980	−0.009	−0.036	−0.065	−0.135
	(0.69)	(0.88)	(2.19)**	(1.98)**
State migration rate, 1955–59	0.386	2.565	2.063	4.599
	(1.82)*	(2.79)***	(2.87)***	(4.19)***
Constant	n.a.	n.a.	−0.122	−0.242
			(1.37)	(1.51)
R^2	n.a.	n.a.	0.18	0.27

Source: 2003 ENHRUM.

Note: Sample size is 1,765. Regression is corrected for survey design where possible; where impossible regression is weighted to correct for the survey design and errors are clustered by village. Dprobit option is specified, so parameters are marginal effects and robust z statistics are in parentheses. dF/dx is for discrete change of dummy variable from 0 to 1.

***Significant at 1 percent.

**Significant at 5 percent.

*Significant at 10 percent.

n.a. Not applicable.

schooling of females increases the likelihood of female migration, and the average schooling of males has the same effect on male migration.[8] Households with larger asset holdings have a significantly higher probability of participating in international migration.[9] Households in which an indigenous language is spoken at home, other things being equal, have a significantly lower likelihood of having a male or a female international migrant.

Household Activity Participation

The two migration probits were used to construct an instrument for 2002 migration by each gender for each household in the sample. These, together with the other explanatory variables in table 4.3, were included in the probit regressions for household participation in each of five activities: crop production, staple production, nonstaple crop production, livestock production, and local wage work. The probit specification corresponding to equation 4.1 is

$$\Pr[Y_i > 0 | Z_i, \gamma] = F(Z_i'\gamma), \tag{4.3}$$

where $Z_i = [X_{Yi}, M_{gi}]$, $\gamma = [\gamma_0, \gamma_1, \gamma_2]$, and $F(\cdot)$, as before, is the normal cumulative distribution function.

A limitation of the two-step probit model is the inability to correct standard errors when multiple migration instruments are obtained from separate probit regressions. Alternative estimation methods alluded to previously have other limitations but provide a check on the robustness of our estimates. We estimate each activity-participation equation in four ways, the results of which are reported in columns 1 through 4 in each table: a two-stage probit; an IV probit; an IV linear probability model; and a three-stage least squares linear probability model. In the two linear probability models for activity choice, the migration instruments are obtained from an ordinary least squares (OLS) migration probability model. Columns 3 and 4 of table 4.4 report the results of the OLS migration probability estimation, which are similar to the probit results in columns 1 and 2. The methods employed correct the standard errors for the IV procedure, and the three-stage least squares method corrects for correlation between equations.

Tables 4.5 through 4.9 present results of the activity-participation probits. The tables report marginal effects of the explanatory variables on the probability of participating in each activity. Errors are clustered by village. Our findings are reasonably robust with respect to the estimation method used.

The results reveal strikingly different impacts of male and female migration on participation in some household production activities. Table 4.5 indicates that the impacts of male migration on crop production are significant and negative, while those of female migration are less clear cut. More clarity is attained when crop production is decomposed into staples and other crops.[10] Neither female nor male

Table 4.5. Second-Stage Activity Choice Regressions: Agricultural (Crop) Income

Variable	Two-stage probit[a] (1)	IV probit[b] (2)	IV linear probability[c] (3)	Three-stage least squares linear probability[d] (4)
Household head experience (×10)	0.103	0.092	0.097	0.077
	(2.53)**	(2.31)**	(2.87)***	(2.47)**
Household head experience squared (×100)	−0.014	−0.012	−0.013	−0.009
	(3.18)***	(2.86)***	(3.36)***	(2.64)***
Household head education (×10)	−0.235	−0.240	−0.215	−0.177
	(3.71)***	(3.52)***	(3.74)***	(3.48)***
Male education (×10)	0.126	0.126	0.067	0.096
	(1.93)*	(1.62)	(1.14)	(1.68)*
Female education (×10)	−0.051	−0.089	−0.032	−0.001
	(0.82)	(1.23)	(0.55)	(0.01)
Household size	0.029	0.046	0.044	0.032
	(2.38)**	(3.36)***	(4.39)***	(4.31)***
Number of children	−0.012	−0.023	−0.036	−0.012
	(0.74)	(1.15)	(2.61)***	(1.01)
Land (hectares)	0.012	0.014	0.003	0.003
	(2.73)***	(7.38)***	(2.96)***	(4.87)***
Hectares of good-quality land	0.014	0.012	−0.001	0.001
	(2.08)**	(3.27)***	(0.49)	(0.81)
Average number of days sick	−0.000	0.000	0.000	0.000
	(0.19)	(0.78)	(0.94)	(0.33)
Percent of household married	−0.017	0.033	0.046	0.019
	(0.30)	(0.53)	(0.87)	(0.41)
Indigenous	0.310	0.313	0.279	0.340
	(3.06)***	(7.15)***	(7.18)***	(10.06)***
Female migration	0.597	0.028	−0.334	0.110
	(2.83)***	(0.05)	(2.06)**	(0.41)
Male migration	−0.541	−0.444	−0.439	−0.394
	(2.10)**	(2.10)**	(2.83)***	(2.39)**

Source: 2003 ENHRUM.

Note: Sample size is 1,765. Errors are clustered by village. Probit option is specified, so parameters are marginal effects and robust z statistics are in parentheses.

***Significant at 1 percent.

**Significant at 5 percent.

*Significant at 10 percent.

a. Probit assuming that migration is endogenous, using predictions from first-stage probit in table 4.4, weighted and clustered for survey correction.

b. Maximum likelihood estimations of Amemiya's generalized least squares estimator (see Newey 1987). Not possible to weight or cluster errors.

c. Survey-corrected instrumental variables linear probability model.

d. Three-stage least squares linear probability model; not possible to weight or cluster errors.

Table 4.6. Second-Stage Activity Choice Regressions: Staple Crop Production

Variable	Two-stage probit[a] (1)	IV probit[b] (2)	IV linear probability[c] (3)	Three-stage least squares linear probability[d] (4)
Household head experience (×10)	0.118	0.108	0.105	0.077
	(3.32)***	(3.00)***	(3.57)***	(2.52)**
Household head experience squared (×100)	−0.013	−0.012	−0.012	−0.009
	(3.70)***	(3.14)***	(3.61)***	(2.76)***
Household head education (×10)	−0.160	−0.159	−0.121	−0.168
	(2.84)***	(2.65)***	(2.38)**	(3.42)***
Male education (×10)	0.075	0.085	0.053	0.073
	(1.13)	(1.24)	(1.04)	(1.34)
Female education (×10)	−0.070	−0.059	−0.034	−0.019
	(1.27)	(0.94)	(0.68)	(0.39)
Household size	0.020	0.029	0.023	0.035
	(1.67)*	(2.44)**	(2.66)***	(4.86)***
Number of children	−0.001	−0.001	−0.007	−0.010
	(0.09)	(0.06)	(0.60)	(0.84)
Land (hectares)	0.001	0.002	0.002	0.001
	(1.26)	(2.65)***	(2.00)**	(2.80)***
Hectares of good-quality land	0.011	0.013	0.000	0.001
	(2.56)**	(4.79)***	(0.33)	(1.46)
Average number of days sick	−0.000	0.000	−0.000	0.000
	(0.47)	(0.54)	(0.10)	(0.30)
Percent of household married	0.032	0.063	0.056	0.044
	(0.61)	(1.17)	(1.19)	(0.98)
Indigenous	0.302	0.334	0.297	0.325
	(3.44)***	(8.36)***	(8.07)***	(9.87)***
Female migration	0.104	−0.070	−0.205	−0.245
	(0.57)	(0.15)	(1.47)	(0.94)
Male migration	−0.278	−0.210	−0.176	−0.348
	(1.17)	(1.01)	(1.31)	(2.16)**

Source: 2003 ENHRUM.

Note: Sample size is 1,765. Errors are clustered by village. Probit option is specified, so parameters are marginal effects and robust *z* statistics are in parentheses.

***Significant at 1 percent.

**Significant at 5 percent.

*Significant at 10 percent.

a. Probit assuming that migration is endogenous, using predictions from first-stage probit in table 4.4, weighted and clustered for survey correction.

b. Maximum likelihood estimations of Amemiya's generalized least squares estimator (see Newey 1987). Not possible to weight or cluster errors.

c. Survey-corrected instrumental variables linear probability model.

d. Three-stage least squares linear probability model; not possible to weight or cluster errors.

Table 4.7. Second-Stage Activity Choice Regressions: Nonstaple Crop Production

Variable	Two-stage probit[a] (1)	IV probit[b] (2)	IV linear probability[c] (3)	Three-stage least squares linear probability[d] (4)
Household head experience (×10)	0.099	0.089	0.091	0.067
	(2.55)**	(2.27)**	(2.79)***	(2.11)**
Household head experience squared (×100)	−0.014	−0.012	−0.013	−0.009
	(3.44)***	(2.86)***	(3.48)***	(2.58)***
Household head education (×10)	−0.273	−0.265	−0.241	−0.225
	(4.62)***	(3.96)***	(4.29)***	(4.40)***
Male education (×10)	0.114	0.126	0.078	0.105
	(1.79)*	(1.67)*	(1.38)	(1.84)*
Female education (×10)	−0.025	−0.055	−0.013	0.013
	(0.40)	(0.79)	(0.23)	(0.26)
Household size	0.028	0.044	0.040	0.037
	(2.26)**	(3.30)***	(4.24)***	(4.93)***
Number of children	−0.015	−0.024	−0.033	−0.019
	(0.97)	(1.26)	(2.48)**	(1.59)
Land (hectares)	0.002	0.003	0.002	0.002
	(1.14)	(3.16)***	(2.10)**	(4.00)***
Hectares of good-quality land	0.015	0.017	−0.000	0.001
	(2.78)***	(5.33)***	(0.28)	(1.02)
Average number of days sick	−0.000	0.001	0.000	0.000
	(0.43)	(0.88)	(0.53)	(0.34)
Percent of household married	−0.001	0.032	0.040	0.009
	(0.03)	(0.54)	(0.77)	(0.19)
Indigenous	0.322	0.327	0.286	0.331
	(3.29)***	(7.50)***	(7.52)***	(9.73)***
Female migration	0.466	0.005	−0.317	−0.066
	(2.34)**	(0.01)	(2.03)**	(0.24)
Male migration	−0.515	−0.419	−0.388	−0.437
	(1.98)**	(2.10)**	(2.71)***	(2.63)***

Source: 2003 ENHRUM.

Note: Sample size is 1,765. Errors are clustered by village. Probit option is specified, so parameters are marginal effects and robust z statistics are in parentheses.

***Significant at 1 percent.

**Significant at 5 percent.

*Significant at 10 percent.

a. Probit assuming that migration is endogenous, using predictions from first-stage probit in table 4.4, weighted and clustered for survey correction.

b. Maximum likelihood estimations of Amemiya's generalized least squares estimator (see Newey 1987). Not possible to weight or cluster errors.

c. Survey-corrected instrumental variables linear probability model.

d. Three-stage least squares linear probability model; not possible to weight or cluster errors.

Table 4.8. Second-Stage Activity Choice Regressions: Livestock Production

Variable	Two-stage probit[a] (1)	IV probit[b] (2)	IV linear probability[c] (3)	Three-stage least squares linear probability[d] (4)
Household head experience (×10)	0.082	0.096	0.093	0.089
	(1.95)*	(2.65)***	(2.30)**	(2.71)***
Household head experience squared (×100)	−0.010	−0.011	−0.012	−0.009
	(2.31)**	(2.62)***	(2.67)***	(2.65)***
Household head education (×10)	−0.153	−0.138	−0.169	−0.134
	(2.15)**	(2.19)**	(2.58)**	(2.53)**
Male education (×10)	0.014	0.003	−0.016	0.002
	(0.22)	(0.04)	(0.24)	(0.04)
Female education (×10)	−0.038	−0.027	−0.042	0.029
	(0.66)	(0.35)	(0.66)	(0.53)
Household size	0.033	0.036	0.048	0.031
	(2.92)***	(2.38)**	(4.20)***	(3.91)***
Number of children	0.008	0.009	−0.017	0.007
	(0.54)	(0.39)	(1.09)	(0.55)
Land (hectares)	0.003	0.002	0.003	0.002
	(0.96)	(2.42)**	(2.31)**	(3.13)***
Hectares of good-quality land	0.013	0.010	−0.001	0.000
	(3.12)***	(2.91)***	(0.89)	(0.41)
Average number of days sick	0.000	0.000	0.001	0.000
	(0.45)	(0.86)	(1.47)	(0.40)
Percent of household married	0.067	0.079	0.101	0.062
	(1.09)	(1.33)	(1.73)*	(1.26)
Indigenous	0.186	0.174	0.141	0.176
	(3.42)***	(4.26)***	(3.31)***	(4.96)***
Female migration	0.100	−0.312	−0.623	−0.471
	(0.47)	(0.39)	(2.79)***	(1.67)*
Male migration	−0.419	−0.249	−0.393	−0.083
	(1.62)	(0.82)	(2.08)**	(0.48)

Source: 2003 ENHRUM.

Note: Sample size is 1,765. Errors are clustered by village. Probit option is specified, so parameters are marginal effects and robust *z* statistics are in parentheses.

***Significant at 1 percent.

**Significant at 5 percent.

*Significant at 10 percent.

a. Probit assuming that migration is endogenous, using predictions from first-stage probit in table 4.4, weighted and clustered for survey correction.

b. Maximum likelihood estimations of Amemiya's generalized least squares estimator (see Newey 1987). Not possible to weight or cluster errors.

c. Survey-corrected instrumental variables linear probability model.

d. Three-stage least squares linear probability model; not possible to weight or cluster errors.

Table 4.9. Second-Stage Activity Choice Regressions: Wage Income

Variable	Two-stage probit[a] (1)	IV probit[b] (2)	IV linear probability[c] (3)	Three-stage least squares linear probability[d] (4)
Household head experience (×10)	−0.056 (1.49)	−0.052 (1.41)	−0.029 (0.76)	−0.056 (1.70)*
Household head experience squared (×10)	−0.002 (0.62)	−0.004 (0.96)	−0.005 (1.27)	−0.003 (0.83)
Household head education (×10)	−0.197 (3.57)***	−0.175 (2.81)***	−0.169 (2.45)**	−0.190 (3.53)***
Male education (×10)	0.150 (2.28)**	0.141 (2.12)**	0.156 (2.23)**	0.129 (2.16)**
Female education (×10)	−0.052 (1.18)	−0.106 (1.69)*	−0.100 (1.49)	−0.033 (0.63)
Household size	0.049 (4.09)***	0.051 (4.36)***	0.054 (4.74)***	0.050 (6.37)***
Number of children	−0.022 (1.32)	−0.035 (2.13)**	−0.029 (1.79)*	−0.035 (2.82)***
Average number of days sick	−0.001 (1.36)	−0.001 (1.02)	−0.000 (0.37)	−0.001 (1.80)*
Percent of household married	−0.140 (2.58)***	−0.122 (2.20)**	−0.093 (1.60)	−0.131 (2.68)***
Indigenous	−0.156 (3.07)***	−0.182 (4.26)***	−0.168 (3.95)***	−0.161 (4.51)***
Female migration	−0.087 (0.35)	−0.010 (0.03)	−0.167 (0.47)	−0.186 (0.67)
Male migration	−0.674 (2.41)**	−0.674 (3.36)***	−0.730 (4.11)***	−0.667 (3.79)***

Source: 2003 ENHRUM.

Note: Sample size is 1,765. Errors are clustered by village. Probit option is specified, so parameters are marginal effects and robust z statistics are in parentheses.

***Significant at 1 percent.

**Significant at 5 percent.

*Significant at 10 percent.

a. Probit assuming that migration is endogenous, using predictions from first-stage probit in table 4.4, weighted and clustered for survey correction.

b. Maximum likelihood estimations of Amemiya's generalized least squares estimator (see Newey 1987). Not possible to weight or cluster errors.

c. Survey-corrected instrumental variables linear probability model.

d. Three-stage least squares linear probability model; not possible to weight or cluster errors.

migration has any effect on the propensity to produce staple crops. Other studies have suggested that staple crop production in rural Mexico resists decline despite strong economic incentives to the contrary (Preibisch et al. 2002; Dyer et al. 2006). If females are less likely to engage in crop production activities, the negative effect of their lost labor will be minimal. The production of maize and beans also is culturally important to rural households.[11] Nonstaple crop production, however, is less important to the subsistence of rural households and generally involves higher capital costs, more inputs, and substantially more intensive labor practices. In light of this finding, it is not surprising that participation in this activity responds negatively to male, but not female, migration (table 4.7). An alternative and possibly complementary explanation is that females are larger remitters than males and that remittances stimulate household production activities by loosening liquidity and risk constraints. It could also be the case that remittances from females are more likely to be channeled toward on-farm investments. Liquidity and risk constraints tend to be more binding for the production of nonstaple crops, with their relatively large input demands. Thus, it is possible that migration by males affects nonstaple crop production negatively, through the loss of labor, while female migration affects it mainly through a remittance effect that cancels out any lost-labor effects.

Livestock production (table 4.8) is not significantly affected by migration of either gender. In rural Mexico, small-scale livestock production requires little labor, and it is likely that substitute labor with the requisite skills to care for livestock can be found within the household (for example, children tending animals).

Wage income (table 4.9), in contrast, is significantly and negatively affected by male, but not female, migration. Males in rural Mexico are more likely to be involved in wage work prior to migrating, and there are often few opportunities for women to work outside of the household.

There is a quadratic relationship between the household head's experience and the probability of participation in all activities, as well as a negative (linear) relationship between the household head's age and wage income. As schooling of the household head increases, households significantly shift out of all household production activities. Schooling of male household members significantly increases household participation in nonstaple crop and wage activities, but the effect of female education on participation is insignificant for all of these activities. Other things being equal, larger households are more likely to participate in all activities. Landholdings, especially of high-quality land, increase participation in crop and livestock activities. Indigenous households are significantly more likely than others to participate in all activities except local wage labor.

Schooling and Health Expenditures

If all prices are fixed, migration by either gender can influence household expenditures via a simple income-transfer effect (increasing expenditures on "normal" goods if remittances increase household income). In this scenario, controlling for total expenditures and household demographics, one would expect migration by either gender to have no significant effect on expenditures for specific goods. Differential or negative effects of migration on expenditures would indicate other migration effects, independent of income, including influences of migration on household preferences or influences of migrants' preferences on household demands. For example, a female migrant might remit under the condition that funds be used for schooling or health, particularly if her own children are part of the sending household (as when grandparents raise children while parents are away). If preferences of male migrants are different, this will be reflected in a different impact of male migration on household expenditures, other things being equal.

A comprehensive analysis of the influence of international migration on household expenditures is beyond the scope of this chapter. As a first step toward doing this analysis, we tested for independent migration effects on household expenditures for two key items, health and education, using a tobit model similar to the probit model presented for other household outcomes. The tobit specification accounts for the fact that not all households have positive expenditures for health and education (64 and 60 percent, respectively). The results from a linear probability three-stage least squares regression are also presented, as before, to demonstrate the robustness of the estimates.

The results are reported in table 4.10. They show significant differences between the effects of female and male migration on household expenditures for education and health. Other things being equal, households with female migrants spend significantly less on education and more on health than otherwise similar households without female migrants. The negative effect of female migration on schooling investments stands in striking contrast to the finding that households with more educated females spend more on schooling (table 4.10) and that international migration selects positively on female education (table 4.4). This result could lend support to intra-household bargaining models that find that monitoring is important. If females are more likely than males to monitor their children's education and the household's educational expenditures, then female migration may cause a decrease in monitoring and thus in schooling expenditures.

The findings reveal a quadratic relationship between household head experience and schooling investments, similar to the effect of the household head's experience on participation in income activities. Inasmuch as the income effects of the household head's experience are implicit in total expenditures, this finding

Table 4.10. Effects of Migration on Education and Health Spending

Variable	Education spending		Health spending	
	Two-step tobit (1)	Three-stage least squares (2)	Two-step tobit (3)	Three-stage least squares (4)
Household head experience	462.373	180.511	−44.486	8.025
	(6.45)***	(4.21)***	(0.74)	(0.19)
Household head experience squared	−5.983	−1.971	0.500	0.104
	(7.41)***	(4.22)***	(0.78)	(0.22)
Household head education	0.463	97.213	60.924	100.792
	(0.00)	(1.38)	(0.61)	(1.43)
Male education	654.461	340.659	55.109	42.965
	(5.91)***	(4.38)***	(0.54)	(0.55)
Female education	801.937	405.733	−114.305	−112.200
	(7.97)***	(5.61)***	(1.24)	(1.55)
Household size	257.685	110.816	314.554	164.069
	(1.56)	(0.89)	(2.15)**	(1.31)
Number of children	1,795.464	647.661	−35.151	−56.131
	(7.52)***	(3.55)***	(0.16)	(0.31)
Asset index	783.403	415.245	411.517	377.947
	(3.17)***	(2.37)**	(1.82)*	(2.16)**
Total expenditures	0.020	0.016	0.019	0.015
	(6.00)***	(6.83)***	(6.11)***	(6.29)***
Average days sick	−15.634	−5.735	42.647	26.451
	(1.49)	(0.95)	(5.39)***	(4.40)***
Percent of household married	−6,888.555	−2,621.178	867.533	438.446
	(6.57)***	(4.06)***	(0.97)	(0.68)
Indigenous	−685.989	−522.696	−1,788.554	−639.133
	(1.01)	(1.21)	(2.79)***	(1.48)
Female migration	−8,428.056	−3,181.552	6,126.766	3,381.479
	(2.12)**	(1.63)	(1.97)**	(1.73)*
Male migration	−1,252.618	192.225	−1,755.249	−1,072.243
	(0.39)	(0.22)	(0.65)	(1.25)
Constant	−15,999.698	−4,906.693	−2,567.269	−174.157
	(9.00)***	(4.44)***	(1.65)*	(0.16)

Source: 2003 ENHRUM.

Note: Sample size is 1,754. Errors are clustered by village. Latent variable results $\delta E(y^*|x) / \delta x = \beta$ reported for tobit regressions. Robust z statistics are in parentheses.

***Significant at 1 percent.

**Significant at 5 percent.

*Significant at 10 percent.

almost certainly reflects household demographics: schooling expenditures are highest in the middle of a household's life cycle. Schooling investments also increase with household wealth and the number of children (controlling for household total size).

De la Brière et al. (2002) find that females remit more in response to family health shocks than do males, presumably in part to finance health care. Our findings are consistent with that result. Other things being equal, expenditures on health increase with household size, illness, and female (but not male) migration. The insignificant effect of male migration on health spending suggests that males have different motives to remit (also consistent with de la Brière et al.) or else that males return to work on the farm when other family members become ill—a labor response that would contrast with the remittance response of female migrants.

Conclusions

Our econometric findings offer strong evidence that the effects of migration on migrant-sending households depend significantly on migrants' gender. In some cases, a change in the gender of a household's migrants *reverses* the sign of migration's effect on production and wage income activities as well as on expenditures. Past studies report negative lost-labor effects of migration on household production. We find this only for migration by males, who are more likely than females to be engaged in household production activities such as nonstaple crop production and wage work prior to migrating. This result suggests that perfect hired substitutes for the male laborer who migrates are not available in rural Mexico or that remittance-induced demand for leisure increases significantly enough to decrease production. Positive migration effects, posited by NELM research, are evident only for female migration. This may be because females participate less than males in production activities prior to migrating or else work only in a subset of activities, such as the cultivation of maize and beans; thus the positive remittance and insurance effects of female migration counterbalance the negative lost-labor effects.

In a conventional demand analysis, one would not expect migration, let alone the gender of migrants, to independently affect household expenditures (that is, controlling for household total income and demographic variables). However, we find that, other things being equal, both migration and the gender of migrants significantly reshape expenditures on education and health. Female *education* has a larger positive and more significant effect on new schooling investments than male education. However, female *international migration* has a negative effect. Most migrants from rural Mexico enter the United States illegally, working in low-skill service jobs in which the returns to schooling are likely to be low. It is possible that international migrants send a signal to households not to invest in schooling. Alternatively, it is possible that females who have migrated lose the ability to monitor their household's schooling investments.

The overarching conclusion of this research is that the impacts, like the determinants, of international migration are gender specific. Studies that fail to differentiate between males and females produce findings that are likely to be both statistically biased and an unreliable basis for designing policies to enhance the positive and mitigate the negative effects of international migration in migrant-sending countries.

Endnotes

1. This is distinct from an income multiplier of remittances *among* households, as estimated by Adelman et al. (1988).

2. They also include market prices for inputs and outputs, which may vary over time but not across households at a given point in time, unless there are significant transaction and transportation costs. Because our analysis uses cross-sectional data, prices are not included as explanatory variables in the econometric model.

3. We are greatly indebted to David McKenzie for bringing González Navarro's data to our attention and for providing us with them.

4. The size of both villager and migrant populations in the synthetic cohorts created using retrospective data is biased downward as one goes back in time, because some individuals are removed from the population due to death and thus are not available to be counted in 2003. Permanent migration does not pose a problem, because information about migrants was provided by other family members in the village. In the relatively rare case where entire families migrated, overall migration estimates may be biased downward; however, it is not clear whether this would produce an upward or a downward bias in the *slope* of the migration trend.

5. The Mexico-born population in the United States increased from 6.7 million to 10.6 million between 1990 and 2000 (U.S. Census Bureau).

6. See http://www.sedesol.gob.mx/index/index.php.

7. The crossover point at which the age effect becomes negative is at a household head age of approximately 56 years for the female equation and 38 years for the male equation. These age variables are statistically significant only for female migration.

8. These average household-education effects do not necessarily imply that *individuals* with more schooling are more likely to migrate internationally; see Mora and Taylor (2006).

9. The asset index was created using principle components analysis; see Filmer and Pritchett (2001) for an overview. The asset index includes the value of land, business assets, and other assets owned by the household; the number of rooms in the house; whether the house has a kitchen, running water, drainage, electricity, or a telephone; and whether the house is owned by the household. Our index of assets is based on nonproductive asset holdings in the year prior to the survey year. Nevertheless, this predetermined variable may be correlated with past migration. To explore whether possible endogeneity of this variable confounds the effects of other variables in the model, we reestimated this and all other regressions in the chapter without the wealth variable, and none of the conclusions of this chapter changed.

10. Staple crops are defined as corn and beans. All other crops are included in the category of non-staple crops.

11. Small maize farmers in Mexico value maize for traditional, ceremonial, ritual values, as well as for their taste and cooking quality (Salvador 1997; Dyer-Leal 2006; Perales et al. 2003; Brush and Chauvet 2004).

References

Adelman, Irma, J. Edward Taylor, and Stephen Vogel. 1988. "Life in a Mexican Village: A SAM Perspective." *Journal of Development Studies* 25 (5): 5–24.

Angrist, Joshua. 2000. "Estimation of Limited-Dependent Variable Models with Dummy Endogenous Regressors: Simple Strategies for Empirical Practice." NBER Technical Working Paper 248. National Bureau of Economic Research, Cambridge, MA. (http://www.nber.org/papers/T0248).

Bhattacharya, Jay, Dana Goldman, and Daniel McCaffrey. 2006. "Estimating Probit Models with Self-Selected Treatments." *Statistics in Medicine* 25 (3): 389–413.

Brush, Stephen, and Michelle Chauvet. 2004. "Assessment of Social and Cultural Effects Associated with Transgenic Maize Production." In *Maize and Biodiversity: The Effects of Transgenic Maize in Mexico*, 1–55. Commission for Environmental Cooperation Secretariat.

Curran, Sara R., and Estela Rivero-Fuentes. 2003. "Engendering Migrant Networks: The Case of Mexican Migration." *Demography* 40 (2): 289–307.

Deaton, Angus, and John Muellbauer. 1980. *Economics and Consumer Behavior*. Cambridge, U.K.: Cambridge University Press.

de la Brière, Bénédicte, Alain de Janvry, Elisabeth Sadoulet, and Sylvie Lambert. 2002. "The Roles of Destination, Gender, and Household Composition in Explaining Remittances: An Analysis for the Dominican Sierra." *Journal of Development Economics* 68 (2): 309–28.

Dyer, George, Steve Boucher, and J. Edward Taylor. 2006. "Subsistence Response to Market Shocks." *American Journal of Agricultural Economics* 88 (2): 279–91.

Dyer-Leal, George A. 2006. "Crop Valuation and Farmer Response to Change: Implications for In-situ Conservation of Maize in Mexico." In *Valuing Crop Biodiversity: On-Farm Genetic Resources and Economic Change*, ed. Melinda Smale, 17–32. Wallingford, U.K.: CABI Publishing.

Filmer, Deon, and Lant Pritchett. 2001. "Estimating Wealth Effects without Expenditure Data or Tears: An Application to Educational Enrollments in States of India." *Demography* 38 (1): 115–32.

González Navarro, Moises. 1974. *Población y sociedad en México, 1900–1970*. Mexico City: Universidad Autónoma de México Press.

Jamison, Dean T., and Lawrence J. Lau. 1982. *Farmer Education and Farm Efficiency*. Baltimore, MD: Johns Hopkins University Press.

León-Ledesma, Miguel, and Matloob Priacha. 2004. "International Migration and the Role of Remittances in Eastern Europe." *International Migration* 42 (4): 65–83.

Massey, Douglas S., Jorge Durand, and Nolan J. Malone. 2002. *Beyond Smoke and Mirrors: Mexican Immigration in an Era of Economic Integration*. New York: Russell Sage Foundation.

McKenzie, David, and Hillel Rapoport. 2004. "Network Effects and the Dynamics of Migration and Inequality: Theory and Evidence from Mexico." BREAD Working Paper 063. Harvard University, Kennedy School of Government, Bureau for Research and Economic Analysis of Development, Cambridge, MA.

Mora, Jorge, and J. Edward Taylor. 2006. "Determinants of Migration, Destination, and Sector Choice: Disentangling Individual, Household, and Community Effects." In *International Migration, Remittances, and the Brain Drain*, ed. Çağlar Özden and Maurice Schiff. New York: Palgrave Macmillan.

Munshi, Kaivan. 2003. "Networks in the Modern Economy: Mexican Migrants in the U.S. Labor Market." *Quarterly Journal of Economics* 118 (2): 549–99.

Newey, Whitney K. 1987. "Efficient Estimation of Limited Dependent Variable Models with Endogenous Explanatory Variables." *Journal of Econometrics* 36 (3, November): 231–50.

O'Neil, Kevin. 2003. "Remittances from the United States in Context." *Migration Information Source*. (http://www.migrationinformation.org/feature/display.cfm?ID=138).

Perales, Hugo R., Stephen B. Brush, and C. O. Qualset. 2003. "Landraces of Maize in Central Mexico: An Altitudinal Transect." *Economic Botany* 51 (1): 7–20.

Preibisch, Kerry, Gladys Rivera Herrejón, and Steve Wiggins. 2002. "Defending Food Security in a Free-Market Economy: The Gendered Dimensions of Restructuring in Rural Mexico." *Human Organization* 61 (1): 68–79.

Rapoport, Hillel, and Frédéric Docquier. 2005. *The Economics of Migrants' Remittances.* IZA Discussion Paper 1531. Bonn: Institute for the Study of Labor (IZA).

Rozelle, Scott, J. Edward Taylor, and Alan de Brauw. 1999. "Migration, Remittances, and Productivity in China." *American Economic Review* 89 (2): 287–91.

Salvador, Ricardo J. 1997. "Maize." In *The Encyclopedia of Mexico: History, Culture, and Society,* ed. Michael Werner. Filtzroy Dearborn Publishers.

Schultz, T. Paul. 1990. "Testing the Neoclassical Model of Family Labor Supply and Fertility." *Journal of Human Resources* 25 (4): 599–634.

Semyonov, Moshe, and Anastasia Gorodzeisky. 2005. "Labor, Migration, Remittances, and Household Income: A Comparison between Filipino and Filipina Overseas Workers." *International Migration Review* 39 (1): 45–68.

Singh, Inderjit, Lyn Squire, and John Strauss. 1986. "An Overview of Agricultural Household Models: The Basic Model; Theory, Empirical Results, and Policy Conclusions." In *Agricultural Household Models, Extensions, Applications, and Policy,* ed. Inderjit Singh, Lyn Squire, and John Strauss. Washington, DC: World Bank; Baltimore, MD: Johns Hopkins University Press.

Stark, Oded. 1991. *The Migration of Labor.* Cambridge, U.K.: Basil Blackwell.

Taylor, J. Edward. 1992. "Remittances and Inequality Reconsidered: Direct, Indirect, and Intertemporal Effects." *Journal of Policy Modeling* 14 (2): 187–208.

Taylor, J. Edward, and Philip L. Martin. 2001. "Human Capital: Migration and Rural Population Change." In *Handbook of Agricultural Economics,* vol. 1, ed. Bruce Gardener and Gordon Rausser, 457–511. Amsterdam: Elsevier.

Taylor, J. Edward, Scott Rozelle, and Alan de Brauw. 2003. "Migration and Income in Source Communities: A New Economics of Migration Perspective from China." *Economic Development and Cultural Change* 52 (1): 75–101.

Udry, Christopher. 1996. "Gender, Agricultural Production, and the Theory of the Household." *Journal of Political Economy* 104 (5): 1010–46.

Winters, Paul, Alain de Janvry, and Elisabeth Sadoulet. 1999. "Family and Community Networks in Mexico-U.S. Migration." ARE Working Paper 99-12. University of New England, Graduate School of Agricultural and Resource Economics.

Woodruff, Christopher, and Rene Zenteno. 2001. "Remittances and Microenterprises in Mexico." Working Paper. University of California, San Diego; Instituto Tecnológico y de Estudios Superiores de Monterrey, Guadalajara, December.

5

THE IMPACT OF REMITTANCES AND GENDER ON HOUSEHOLD EXPENDITURE PATTERNS: EVIDENCE FROM GHANA

Juan Carlos Guzmán, Andrew R. Morrison,
and Mirja Sjöblom

In recent decades international migration and remittance flows from migrants have increased substantially. In 2005 the recorded remittances sent home by migrants originating from developing countries reached $188 billion, and this number is expected to increase to $199 billion in 2006 (World Bank 2006b). Remittances represent an important category of capital transfers from North to South and have proven to be a crucial tool for poverty alleviation (for review of the impact of remittances on poverty at the household level, see World Bank 2006a). Women form an increasing part of the migratory movements—almost half of today's migrant population is female (UNDP 2005)—and there are indications that the character of female migration is changing: more women are migrating for employment reasons instead of following their male relatives (United Nations 2005).

The authors would like to thank Richard H. Adams Jr., David McKenzie, Pierella Paci, and Maurice Schiff of the World Bank, two anonymous reviewers, and participants at the nineteenth Villa Mondragone conference, held on June 25–26, 2007, for their helpful comments and suggestions.

Migrants who remit to their origin households may have a greater say over the allocation of origin-household spending than if they had stayed at home, by virtue of their increased financial contribution to the household. However, since migrants are not physically present in the origin household, typical principal-agent problems may limit the extent to which they can influence or monitor household spending. The same arguments apply to the individuals who remain in households where a principal earner has migrated: these individuals may enjoy greater independence and influence in decisions on household expenditures, or the migrants may have a greater say in household expenditure decisions because of a greater financial contribution to the household, subject to the principal-agent issues mentioned above. In sum, it is expected that migration and remittances alter intra-household bargaining patterns and, in turn, affect household expenditure allocations.

This chapter pulls together the strands of literature on intra-household allocation and remittances to examine, using data from Ghana, how household budget allocations are affected by the sex of the individual who sends remittances and by the sex of the household head who receives remittances.

The remainder of the chapter is organized as follows. The following section presents relevant research on the determinants of and motivations for remittances, with particular emphasis on the differences between men and women. It also examines the most salient results from the intra-household expenditure literature. The second section describes the data that are employed. The third section describes the econometric approach used, and the fourth presents the results of the regression analysis. A final section concludes.

Motivations to Remit and Intra-Household Models of Expenditures: A Quick Review of Research

The literature on the determinants of remittances is particularly important for the purpose of this chapter, because there is growing consensus that remittance flows are not driven solely by individual motives, but rather are explained as part of familial intertemporal contracts between the migrant and the remittance receivers (Lucas and Stark 1985; Stark and Lucas 1988; Rapoport and Docquier 2005).

The major focus of literature examining the motivation for remittances is whether individuals remit because of altruistic motives or because of self-interest. Only a subset of these studies disaggregates by the gender of the remitter. One of the earliest studies to do so was Hoddinott (1994), who shows, using data from western Kenya, that the remittances of sons respond to their parents' inheritable assets, while those of daughters do not. Using data from the Dominican highlands, de la Brière et al. (2002) document that remittances from female migrants respond strongly to the number of lost working days by parents (consistent with altruistic motives for remitting), while remittances from male migrants are unaffected by this variable—unless a male migrant is the sole migrant in the household. However, their results also indicate that remittances sent as an investment to increase future inheritance are gender neutral. They conclude that insurance is the main motive to remit for international female migrants. These results are in line with the findings from a study on financial support to parents that was conducted in Taiwan (China), which shows that daughters respond to parents' special needs rather than ordinary needs and function as an insurer of last resort, while sons do not (Lee et al. 1994). Finally, a study by Vanwey (2004) investigates gender differences in remittance motives in Thailand. She concludes that female remitters are more motivated by altruism than are male remitters.

Beyond the motivation for remittances, male and female remitters potentially may have different preferences about the type of expenditures that their remittances should support. In her Mexican case study, de La Cruz (1995) finds that male migrants, to a greater degree than female migrants, intend to return to Mexico to live permanently in the future; for this reason, their remittances are directed toward personal investments such as land, housing, agricultural production, and cattle. Female migrants also remit for investment purposes, but it appears that their investments are more targeted to support origin households with education and business opportunities rather than personal educational and business investments to facilitate a future return.

Along the lines of these findings, a descriptive study by the International Organization for Migration (IOM), using data from Moldova, finds that substantially more women than men remit funds to pay for education, health, furniture, and loans. Female migrants from Moldova state that they intend their remittances to be spent on current expenses (food, clothes, commodities, and household equipment) and special expenses (education, health, furniture, and loans); male migrants prefer to direct their remittances to investment in housing, cars, and consumer durables (IOM 2005).[1]

In sum, the tentative conclusion emerging from the literature is that female remitters function as insurers for the receiving families and prefer their remittances to be spent on education and health, while male remitters tend to prefer investments in housing and other assets.

An important question, then, is whether migrants' preferences for the use of their remittances are respected by origin households. If male and female remitters have systematically different preferences for the use of remittances, it is reasonable to expect that the identity of the individual receiving the remittances—and, more broadly, the demographic composition of the household receiving the remittance and male-female power relations in the household—may also influence how remittances are spent.

Thus the findings of the large literature on intra-household expenditure patterns are quite relevant. In general, this research rejects the traditional *unitary household model*, which assumes that a household has a single preference function and fully pools resources; instead, it suggests that there are differences in preferences among household members and that distribution of resources depends on individuals' bargaining power within the household (Quisumbing 2003; for reviews, see Haddad, Hoddinott, and Alderman 1997; Strauss and Thomas 1995). A key finding of the intra-household expenditure literature is that allocations toward education, health, and nutrition increase with the number of resources controlled by women (Quisumbing 2003).

Quisumbing and Maluccio (2000), using data from Bangladesh, Ethiopia, Indonesia, and South Africa, conclude that the most consistent effect across countries of an increased percentage of resources controlled by women at the time of marriage is an increase in expenditure shares for education.[2] This finding holds for all countries except for Ethiopia. Similar studies in rural Bangladesh find that an increase in women's assets has a positive effect on expenditures for children's clothing and education (Hallman 2000; Quisumbing and de la Brière 2000).[3]

This behavior by women may be eminently rational. Since women often marry at an earlier age than men and also have longer life expectancies, on average they outlive their husband. Consequently, they choose to invest in education of their children, as they rely on them for old-age support to a greater extent than men (Quisumbing and Maluccio 2000). Moreover, Guyer (1997) claims that, in societies where assets that enable consumption smoothing are controlled by men, investments in human capital may be an attempt by females to smooth consumption over time.

Regarding health expenditures and outcomes, various studies published during the 1980s and 1990s conclude that, on average, women spend a greater part of their income on health care for children than men (see Dwyer and Bruce 1988; García 1991; Guyer 1997; Katz 1992; Kennedy 1991; Thomas 1990, 1994; Thomas and Chen 1994). For example, Thomas (1994) finds that control of nonlabor income by women is associated with increased expenditures on health care in Brazil, Ghana, and the United States. In the case of Brazil, Thomas (1990) finds that the marginal impact of female-controlled income on child survival is 20 times that of male-controlled income. A more recent study by Hallman (2000) uses data from Bangladesh and finds that assets controlled by women are associated with better health outcomes for girls. A more recent study by Duflo (2003) shows that pensions received by women in South Africa have a larger impact on measures of weight-for-height and height-for-age of girls, but little effect on those of boys. She finds no effect for pensions received by men.

With respect to expenditure on nutrition, Haddad and Hoddinott (1995), using the Côte d'Ivoire Living Standards Survey, show that share of income controlled by females has a positive and significant effect on the budget share spent on food. Drawing on Demographic and Health Survey data from Bangladesh, India, Nepal, and Pakistan, Smith and Byron (2005) conclude that increases in women's decision-making power relative to that of men are associated with improved nutritional well-being of children.

To our knowledge, only one study has examined whether the impact of remittances on health and education outcomes of children in the receiving household depends on the bargaining power of women in the household. De and Ratha (2005), using female head of household as a proxy for bargaining power, show that remittances in Sri Lanka have a positive impact on health and education of the children when the household head is female, but not when the household head is male. If the household head is male, remittances have a positive impact on asset accumulation.

Data

This chapter uses data from the Ghana Living Standards Survey round four (GLSS 4), collected nationwide by the Republic of Ghana Statistical Service between April 1998 and March 1999. The data set comprises 5,998 households and is representative both at the national level and for urban and rural areas. Although the survey is comprehensive in character and includes detailed information on households' expenditure patterns, it is not a specialized survey of remittances or migration. As such, it collects only basic information on current remitters' characteristics: sex, relationship to household head, and place of residence. Neither does it contain comprehensive data on migrants; only migrants who remit (and whose remittances are declared by the receiving household) are captured by the survey. The lack of data on migrants implies that we cannot observe the effect of migration on expenditure patterns. However, we can observe the impact of remittances,[4] since the data set does contain relatively good data on remittances, including amount remitted in cash and in kind and frequency with which remittances are received. Furthermore, the expenditure data included in the survey are of high quality (for more information on the data set, see Republic of Ghana Statistical Service 1999).

Studies on Ghana show that both cash and in-kind remittances are important (Quartey 2005). For this reason, the definition used in this chapter for remittances includes cash, food, and other goods (nonfood items). Remittance-receiving households are defined as households receiving remittances from within Ghana, from abroad, or from both. We make a distinction between remittances received from Ghana (internal remittances) and remittances received from abroad (international remittances), since previous literature suggests that internal and international remittances differ both in frequency and amount (see López Córdoba 2005; Mora and Taylor 2004; Adams 2006a, 2006b).

Of the 5,998 households included in the sample, 41 percent of households receive remittances: 35 percent of households receive remittances from Ghana, 8 percent receive remittances from abroad, and 3 percent receive both international and internal remittances. In terms of gender, 32 percent of households in the sample are female headed.

Table 5.1 shows descriptive statistics from the Ghana household survey, disaggregated by the six groups of interest for the study: female-headed households not receiving remittances (14.3 percent), female-headed households receiving remittances from Ghana (17.1 percent), female-headed households receiving remittances from abroad (2.2 percent), male-headed households not receiving remittances (44 percent), male-headed households receiving remittances from Ghana (18.6 percent), and male-headed households receiving remittances from abroad (3.5 percent).

Methodology

The purpose of this chapter is to test whether remittance-receiving households in which women have stronger bargaining power have different expenditure patterns than households in which women have less bargaining power, and whether the sex of the individual sending the remittances matters as well.

The first challenge is to find a variable that captures intra-household decision-making power. GLSS 4 lacks the type of predetermined, exogenous variables typically used to measure decision-making power and women's empowerment (for example, wealth upon marriage). The best proxy available is the sex of the household head; since the household head is defined as the person who provides most of the needs of the household, we expect him or her to be in a strong bargaining position within the household (Republic of Ghana Statistical Service 1999).[5]

A general methodological issue well recognized in the literature on remittances is that comparisons of remittance-receiving and nonreceiving households are likely to produce biased estimates if receivers of remittances differ systematically from nonreceivers along observable and nonobservable dimensions (see Acosta 2006;

Table 5.1. Descriptive Statistics

Variable	Female-headed households			Male-headed households		
	Not receiving remittances	Receiving remittances from Ghana	Receiving remittances from abroad	Not receiving remittances	Receiving remittances from Ghana	Receiving remittances from abroad
Household size	3.808	3.558	4.032	4.727	4.356	4.284
Age of household head (years)	44.886	48.693	47.960	42.857	46.602	44.077
Number of males >15	0.518	0.428	0.652	1.406	1.342	1.415
Number of females >15	1.573	1.502	1.854	1.177	1.098	1.161
Girls < 5	0.277	0.282	0.280	0.419	0.377	0.313
Boys < 5	0.274	0.258	0.124	0.420	0.355	0.286
Number of members >15 with primary education	0.298	0.266	0.412	0.329	0.322	0.247
Number of members >15 with junior secondary school	0.613	0.554	0.793	0.802	0.789	0.862
Number of members >15 with secondary school	0.078	0.069	0.114	0.060	0.052	0.112
Number of members >15 with university education	0.005	0.004	0.010	0.014	0.010	0.051
Head of household is of Asante ethnicity (1 = yes)	0.200	0.257	0.280	0.139	0.172	0.205
Head of household is married (1 = yes)	0.338	0.354	0.437	0.842	0.784	0.841
Total household expenditure (GHC millions)	1.395	1.456	1.854	1.433	1.332	1.860
Number of observations	857	1,026	134	2,660	1,113	208

Source: Authors' calculations based on Ghana Living Standards Survey (GLSS) round four.

Note: N = 5,998 households; 146 households receive both internal and international remittances. These are counted as receiving internal remittances. In 1999, US$1.00 = 2,394 Ghanaian cedis (GHC).

Adams 2006a; De and Ratha 2005; Yang and Martínez 2005). There are multiple ways to correct for nonrandom selection, including difference-in-difference estimation (DID), an instrumental variable (IV) approach, and propensity score matching (PSM). McKenzie et al. (2006) use the point estimates of the impact of migration on income from a natural experiment in New Zealand as a benchmark to compare how well these three correction approaches perform; they find that the IV approach with a good IV is the best method, followed by PSM and DID. Using a poor IV approach proved to generate substantially more biased results than those produced by ordinary least squares (OLS).

For purposes of this chapter, feasible methods are restricted by data availability. In the absence of panel data, the DID approach is not possible. As an alternative, the IV approach was used initially, with the age of the household head, an indicator for previous migration experience by any household member (returned migrant), and whether or not the household head was of Asante ethnicity as IVs.[6] Jointly, these three variables were partially correlated with the instrumented variable—that is, receiving remittances from within Ghana or from abroad. It is difficult to guarantee, however, that these variables are not directly correlated with the dependent variable—that is, household budget allocations. In fact, there are several plausible reasons why we might expect these IVs to be highly correlated with budget allocations.[7] For this reason, we cannot use these IVs and therefore do not report the results using them. Other IVs commonly used in the remittances literature, such as distance that separates remitters and receiving households or average income of the remitter's place of residence, are not available in the data set.[8] In sum, given that the data set does not include any good IVs and based on the conclusions of McKenzie, Gibson, and Stillman (2006), we fear that the use of the available IVs may do more harm than good for the analysis.

The remaining option is to use PSM, but this methodology also proved infeasible for several reasons. As mentioned, there are six comparison groups in this study. Thus we cannot proceed with the standard approach of matching one group that receives treatment with another group that does not. In the case of multiple treatments, PSM requires using a multinomial approach, but Imbens (1999) shows that, in such instances, the effect of the treatments cannot be identified unless an instrument is used. In other words, since we are lacking a good IV, the PSM approach is not feasible either. As a consequence of the limitations imposed by data availability, our preferred specification is a standard fractional logit model without instruments.

The choice of functional form to model expenditure shares depends on the degree of emphasis placed on various properties that one desires the function to possess. For purposes of this chapter, the functional form needs to meet the following criteria: (a) it must be suitable for multiple types of goods; (b) it should allow for increasing, decreasing, and constant marginal propensities to spend over a wide range of expenditure levels; and (c) it should satisfy the additivity criterion—that is, the sum of the marginal propensities for all goods should equal unity (Adams 2006a). In the light of these considerations, we use an adjusted Working-Leser curve as specified in Case and Deaton (2002) and Bhalotra and Attfield (1998).

Our six dependent variables reflect the six categories of household expenditure collected in GLSS 4. Those are the fraction of total expenditure spent on food, consumer and durable goods, housing, education, health, and other items (for more information on the dependent variables included in the study, see table 5.2). The study uses an approach similar to that used in Adams (2006a) to estimate the determinants of expenditure shares among Ghanaian households.

We specify the model of the form:

$$w_{ih} = \alpha_i + \beta_i \log \frac{x_h}{n_h} + \varepsilon_i \log n_h + \theta_i z_h + u_{ih}, \qquad (5.1)$$

where w_{ih} is the share of the budget devoted to expenditure category i by household h, x_h is total household expenditure, n_h is household size (that is, x_h/n_h is per capita expenditure), z_h is a vector of household characteristics that may affect expenditure behavior, and u_{ih} is an error term.

Since our dependent variables are bound between 0 and 1 (being the percentage of total expenditure spent on good i), we model E $(w_{ih}|X)$ as a logistic function: E $(w_{ih}|X) = \exp(X\beta)/[1 + \exp(X\beta)]$, where w_{ih} represents the fraction of total expenditure spent on each of our six expenditure categories, and X is a

Table 5.2. Description of Dependent Variables

Variable	Description	Examples
Food	Purchased food	Maize, bread, cassava, meat
	Nonpurchased food	Food from own production, gifts, donations
Consumer and durable goods	Consumer goods	Clothing and footwear, fabric
	Household durables	Annual use value of stove, refrigerator, furniture
Housing	Annual use value	Estimated from rental payments or imputed values
Education	Educational expenses	Books, school supplies, uniforms, registration fees
Health	Health expenses	Doctor and dentist fees, medicine, hospitalization
Other	Utilities	Water, gas, electricity, telephone
	Transport	Bus and taxi fees, gasoline, postage, fax
	Remittance expenses	Expenses on remittances

Source: Authors' calculations based on GLSS 4.

matrix of independent and control variables. This model guarantees that predicted values of w_{ih} fall between 0 and 1 (for more details on the rationale for using the fractional logit model, see Papke and Wooldridge 1996; Wooldridge 2002).

The following basic equation serves as a point of departure for the analysis:

$$w_{ijh} = \alpha_{ij} + \beta_{0ij} RR\_INT_{jh} + \beta_{1ij} RR\_EXT_{jh} + \beta_{ik} \log \frac{x_{jh}}{n_{jh}}$$
$$+ \varepsilon_{ij} \log n_{jh} + \theta_{ij} z_{jh} + u_{jih}, \qquad (5.2)$$

where j defines the gender of the household head (male or female), w_{ih} is defined as above, RR_INT is a dummy variable that equals unity for those households receiving internal remittances (from Ghana) and zero for households not receiving internal remittances, and RR_EXT represents a dummy variable that equals unity for households receiving remittances from abroad and zero for households not receiving international remittances.

To analyze the impact of the gender of the household head on expenditure patterns in remittance-receiving households, we run separate regressions for female-headed households and male-headed households.

The second part of our analysis asks whether or not the sex of the remitter is associated with differences in household expenditure allocations. In this analysis, we use the remitter as the unit of analysis instead of the household, and thus we focus only on households receiving remittances. In the data set, 4,011 individuals are identified as sending remittances to 2,481 households. The advantage of this approach is that we do not have to create multiple summary variables that classify the different cases that would be present in households that receive remittances from multiple individuals. By using remitters as the unit of analysis, we examine whether or not, on average, the households to which women send remittances allocate their expenditures differently than the households to which men send remittances.

The dependent variables, as above, are household expenditure shares of the household receiving remittances from the individual remitter. Household characteristics of the receiving household are included in the analysis; because these characteristics will be common across all individuals remitting to the same household, we cluster by household and calculate robust standard errors. We divide each weight by the number of remitters to the household so that the weights add up to the original population size. The final sample of remitters is 4,011 individuals, of which 1,617 (40 percent) are female and 2,394 (60 percent) are male.

Assuming that the remitter has a specific preference for how the remittances should be spent, the relation between the remitter and the receiving household could be framed as a classical *principal-agent problem,* where the remitter (the principal) desires effective use of the remittances, and the receiver of the remittances (the agent) actually allocates the remittances. Through this lens, the extent to which the remitter is able to enforce his or her contract with the receiver of the remittances becomes important for the analysis (for a detailed discussion and noncooperative decision making and migration, see Chen 2006). In other words, even if male and female remitters have different preferences for the use of remittances, those preferences may not be realized because of principal-agent problems.

In order to deal with this issue, we introduce new variables into the analysis to capture the severity of principal-agent problems: the remitter's relationship to the household head, the country of residence of the remitter, and the frequency of remitting.[9] (See the next section for a more detailed discussion of these proxies for ability to monitor and control the origin household's use of expenditures.) The sex of the remitter may matter as well; thus we also interact the sex of the remitter with the relationship to the head of the household and the location of the remitter.[10]

Results

Initially the budget allocation among the different expenditure categories shows little difference among the various types of households. Table 5.3 shows descriptive statistics on average budget shares allocated to the six expenditure categories for the six comparison groups described in the previous section. Overall, the share of expenditure allocated to each category is surprisingly similar for the different groups. Households receiving remittances from abroad (both female and male), however, seem to have a somewhat different expenditure pattern—with smaller expenditure shares allocated to food. Comparing female-headed households in each group with their male counterparts, we observe that female-headed households, on average, allocate greater resources than male-headed households to education and health, while male-headed households allocate greater resources to consumer and durable goods. These findings coincide with those in the literature on intra-household bargaining.

Table 5.4 shows descriptive statistics on average budget shares by the sex of remitter in remittances-receiving households allocated to the six expenditure categories by sex of the remitter. As indicated in the table, the differences in expenditure shares between households that receive remittances from female and male remitters, respectively, seem to be extremely small.

Impact of Remittances on Expenditures in Female- and Male-Headed Households

Table 5.5 shows coefficients from the fractional logit regression for the determinants of expenditure shares, with the coefficients expressed in odds ratios. A coefficient larger (smaller) than 1 indicates that the corresponding variable is associated

Table 5.3. Average Budget Shares by Sex of the Household Head and Status of Receiving Households in Ghana, 1998–99

Expenditure Category	FHH[1] not receiving remittances	FHH[1] receiving remittances from Ghana	FHH[1] receiving remittances from abroad	MHH[1] not receiving remittances	MHH[1] receiving remittances from Ghana	MHH[1] receiving remittances from abroad
Food	0.6100	0.6080	0.5330	0.5900	0.6000	0.5550
Consumer and durable goods	0.1810	0.1730	0.2170	0.2080	0.2030	0.2200
Housing	0.0240	0.0270	0.0250	0.0240	0.0250	0.0260
Education	0.0420	0.0430	0.0600	0.0350	0.0330	0.0440
Health	0.0360	0.0430	0.0400	0.0350	0.0370	0.0350
Other	0.1070	0.1060	0.1250	0.1080	0.1020	0.1200
Total	1.00	1.00	1.00	1.00	1.00	1.00
Number of observations	857	1,026	134	2,660	1,113	208

Source: Authors' calculations based on GLSS 4.

Note: 1. FHH = female-headed households, MHH = male-headed households.

Robust standard errors are used to account for the primary sample unit (PSU) of the survey methodology.

Table 5.4. Average Budget Shares, by Sex of Remitter in Remittance-Receiving Households in Ghana, 1998–99

Expenditure category	Female remitter	Male remitter
Food	0.6090	0.6069
Consumer and durable goods	0.1786	0.1847
Housing	0.0297	0.0270
Education	0.0362	0.0394
Health	0.0429	0.0402
Other	0.1036	0.1019
Total	1.00	1.00
Number of observations	1,671	2,340

Source: Authors' calculations based on GLSS 4.

with an increase (decrease) in the share of expenditure for each type of consumption good.

The expenditure equations perform reasonably well for both male- and female-headed households. In general, there are strong impacts of the log of total expenditure and its square on the expenditures on food, consumer and durable goods, and housing (the income elasticities for per capita income for the six categories of expenditure by sex of the household head are presented table 5.6). Household size also matters: larger households tend to spend a larger share on education and consumer or durable goods and a smaller share on food and housing.

As expected, having a larger proportion of girls and boys under age five increases the share of expenditures devoted to food and health, while decreasing the share of expenditures on education. The proportion of household members who have completed junior secondary school and senior secondary school also affects expenditure patterns: it decreases expenditure allocations to food, while increasing the share to consumer durables and education. The proportion of household members who have completed university has similar effects, but there is no impact on the share of expenditures going to education. The location dummies are consistently significant, as indicated in table 5.5.

The coefficients discussed above by and large have quite similar values for male- and female-headed households. The central question motivating this analysis, however, is whether remittances have a differential impact on expenditure patterns in male- and female-headed households. The evidence reported in table 5.5 suggests that international remittances consistently affect household expenditure shares in female-headed households, but have no such effect in male-headed households. In female-headed households, international remittances lower the

Table 5.5. Fractional Logit Odds Ratio Coefficients, by Expenditure Type and Gender of Household Head

Variable	Food		Consumer and durable goods		Housing	
	Male-headed household	Female-headed household	Male-headed household	Female-headed household	Male-headed household	Female-headed household
Receive internal remittances	0.987 (0.020)	0.965 (0.027)	1.019 (0.024)	0.978 (0.029)	1.016 (0.023)	0.972 (0.022)
Receive international remittances	0.96 (0.044)	0.774 (0.033)***	1.053 (0.049)	1.223 (0.055)***	1.028 (0.050)	1.173 (0.049)***
log_total expenditure per capita	5.312 (2.487)***	2.719 (1.583)*	0.181 (0.095)***	0.797 (0.478)	0.055 (0.026)***	0.053 (0.028)***
log_total expenditure per capita squared	0.938 (0.016)***	0.964 (0.020)*	1.07 (0.020)***	1.013 (0.022)	1.082 (0.020)***	1.079 (0.020)***
log_household size	0.849 (0.029)***	0.778 (0.030)***	1.057 (0.033)*	1.251 (0.055)***	0.551 (0.018)***	0.48 (0.017)***
Age of household head	1.006 (0.001)***	1.011 (0.001)***	0.99 (0.001)***	0.986 (0.001)***	1 (0.001)	1.002 (0.001)**
Proportion of males >15 years	1.118 (0.083)	1.025 (0.088)	0.845 (0.061)**	1.085 (0.111)	1.195 (0.088)**	1.167 (0.093)*
Proportion of females >15 years	0.994 (0.062)	0.824 (0.070)**	1.04 (0.079)	1.248 (0.093)***	1.126 (0.070)*	1.308 (0.096)***
Proportion of girls <5 years	1.242 (0.111)**	1.287 (0.151)**	1.073 (0.102)	1.137 (0.114)	0.739 (0.084)***	0.908 (0.059)
Proportion of boys <5 years	1.206 (0.103)**	1.319 (0.148)**	1.053 (0.087)	1.261 (0.152)*	0.718 (0.057)***	0.967 (0.098)

Proportion of family members who have completed primary school	1.008 (0.059)	0.936 (0.078)	0.995 (0.055)	1.087 (0.107)	0.874 (0.064)*	0.946 (0.061)
Proportion of family members who have completed junior secondary school	0.885 (0.042)**	0.835 (0.049)***	1.117 (0.060)**	1.262 (0.076)***	1.026 (0.043)	1.071 (0.060)
Proportion of family members who have completed senior secondary school	0.671 (0.053)***	0.515 (0.096)***	1.236 (0.128)**	1.739 (0.275)***	1.14 (0.069)**	1.092 (0.132)
Proportion of family members who have completed university	0.402 (0.115)***	0.098 (0.049)***	1.357 (0.250)*	6.068 (4.731)**	3.019 (1.212)***	1.641 (1.596)
Head of household is married (1 = yes)	0.862 (0.033)***	1.082 (0.036)**	1.212 (0.054)***	0.913 (0.032)***	0.984 (0.043)	0.986 (0.027)
Location 2 (urban coastal)	1.063 (0.087)	1.15 (0.101)	1.024 (0.061)	0.973 (0.077)	0.483 (0.048)***	0.372 (0.027)***
Location 3 (urban forest)	1.11 (0.084)	1.21 (0.102)**	1.262 (0.083)***	1.151 (0.088)*	0.463 (0.030)***	0.46 (0.029)***
Location 4 (urban savannah)	1.381 (0.142)***	1.564 (0.210)***	1.075 (0.088)	0.978 (0.123)	0.591 (0.056)***	0.484 (0.037)***
Location 5 (rural coastal)	1.368 (0.119)***	1.314 (0.119)***	1.122 (0.074)*	1.009 (0.078)	0.367 (0.026)***	0.363 (0.022)***
Location 6 (rural forest)	1.396 (0.101)***	1.409 (0.114)***	1.21 (0.065)***	1.226 (0.091)***	0.3 (0.020)***	0.299 (0.018)***
Location 7 (rural savannah)	1.757 (0.148)***	1.644 (0.167)***	1.089 (0.081)	1.119 (0.098)	0.303 (0.020)***	0.253 (0.017)***
Head of household is of Asante ethnicity	0.94 (0.039)	1.055 (0.049)	1.014 (0.042)	0.899 (0.036)***	1.06 (0.040)	1.011 (0.044)
Number of observations	3,981	2,017	3,981	2,017	3,981	2,017
Deviance	272.11	115.47	196.73	75.3	22.29	7.92

(Table continues on the following page)

Table 5.5. Fractional Logit Odds Ratio Coefficients, by Expenditure Type and Gender of Household Head (Continued)

Variable	Health		Education		Other	
	Male-headed household	Female-headed household	Male-headed household	Female-headed household	Male-headed household	Female-headed household
Receive internal remittances	1.046 (0.050)	1.173 (0.066)***	1.01 (0.065)	1.115 (0.067)*	0.975 (0.036)	0.984 (0.042)
Receive international remittances	1.076 (0.111)	1.211 (0.130)*	1.122 (0.119)	1.137 (0.105)	0.965 (0.045)	1.145 (0.075)**
log_total expenditure per capita	1.062 (1.073)	4.004 (4.319)	1.55 (2.135)	0.683 (1.355)	1.114 (0.617)	0.53 (0.427)
log_total expenditure per capita squared	1.000 (0.036)	0.956 (0.037)	0.981 (0.049)	1.015 (0.074)	1.001 (0.020)	1.025 (0.030)
log_household size	0.988 (0.068)	0.983 (0.082)	3.411 (0.268)***	2.484 (0.202)***	1.017 (0.046)	1.166 (0.063)***
Age of household head	1.004 (0.002)**	1.001 (0.002)	1.002 (0.002)	0.996 (0.003)	0.999 (0.001)	0.994 (0.002)***
Proportion of males >15 years	0.821 (0.151)	0.923 (0.221)	0.259 (0.059)***	0.448 (0.124)***	0.985 (0.140)	1.049 (0.140)
Proportion of females >15 years	1.321 (0.267)	0.919 (0.170)	0.259 (0.077)***	0.147 (0.038)***	1.07 (0.100)	1.649 (0.184)***
Proportion of girls <5 years	1.593 (0.281)***	1.112 (0.230)	0.046 (0.012)***	0.112 (0.030)***	1.078 (0.155)	1.025 (0.214)
Proportion of boys <5 years	2.05 (0.370)***	1.617 (0.361)**	0.062 (0.017)***	0.056 (0.016)***	0.942 (0.105)	0.782 (0.167)
Proportion of family members who have completed primary school	1.135 (0.187)	0.745 (0.117)*	1.029 (0.276)	1.589 (0.379)*	1.036 (0.091)	1.103 (0.137)

Proportion of family members who have completed junior secondary school	1.003 (0.089)	0.992 (0.137)	2.065 (0.421)***	2.1 (0.419)***	1.014 (0.053)	0.94 (0.078)
Proportion of family members who have completed senior secondary school	0.494 (0.110)***	0.675 (0.200)	11.297 (4.211)***	4.369 (1.612)***	1.112 (0.146)	1.41 (0.390)
Proportion of family members who have completed university	0.672 (0.424)	0.214 (0.289)	2.959 (2.481)	2.871 (3.918)	2.036 (0.719)**	6.477 (3.224)***
Head of household is married (1 = yes)	1.025 (0.087)	0.996 (0.080)	0.912 (0.121)	0.982 (0.068)	1.101 (0.059)*	0.958 (0.044)
Location 2 (urban coastal)	1.132 (0.185)	1.016 (0.213)	0.734 (0.102)**	0.689 (0.100)**	1.048 (0.081)	1.182 (0.112)*
Location 3 (urban forest)	1.117 (0.166)	0.966 (0.173)	0.522 (0.070)***	0.646 (0.082)***	0.832 (0.064)**	0.83 (0.063)**
Location 4 (urban savannah)	0.787 (0.115)	0.714 (0.183)	0.379 (0.056)***	0.354 (0.059)***	0.738 (0.082)***	0.846 (0.085)*
Location 5 (rural coastal)	1.249 (0.185)	1.093 (0.205)	0.435 (0.057)***	0.529 (0.072)***	0.669 (0.055)***	0.94 (0.106)
Location 6 (rural forest)	1.183 (0.158)	1.127 (0.204)	0.437 (0.061)***	0.434 (0.057)***	0.589 (0.043)***	0.639 (0.060)***
Location 7 (rural savannah)	0.933 (0.142)	0.93 (0.172)	0.237 (0.034)***	0.419 (0.078)***	0.512 (0.043)***	0.592 (0.086)***
Head of household is of Asante ethnicity	0.936 (0.062)	0.954 (0.074)	1.171 (0.122)	0.996 (0.113)	1.071 (0.075)	1.075 (0.073)
Number of observations	3,981	2,017	3,981	2,017	3,981	2,017
Deviance	146.66	64.83	171.53	89.12	192.88	93.44

Source: Authors' calculations based on GLSS 4.

Note: Robust standard errors are in parentheses. Robust standard errors are used to account for the primary sample unit of the survey methodology.

***Significant at 1 percent.

**Significant at 5 percent.

*Significant at 10 percent.

Table 5.6. Income Elasticities (for Per Capita Income), by Expenditure Category

Expenditure category	Male-headed household	Female-headed household
Food	−0.022642	−0.006248
Consumer and durables	0.025495	0.019449
Housing	−0.015062	−0.017299
Health	0.001937	0.004653
Education	−0.002026	0.001191
Other	0.013221	0.004172

Source: Authors' calculations based on GLSS 4.

expenditure share for food and increase the expenditure share for all other categories except education, where the effect is not statistically significant. In the case of internal remittances, the expenditure share for health and education is increased in female-headed households, but there is no effect at all on expenditure shares in male-headed households.

The findings with respect to the impact of internal remittances are consistent with the results from the intra-household bargaining literature—that is, women prefer to spend more on health and education. Although female-headed households receiving international remittances also have higher expenditures on health, there are other more nuanced effects as well: they spend significantly less on food and more on consumer and durable goods, housing, and other goods. The increase in allocations to consumer durables and housing is consistent with the emerging findings about the preferences of male migrants for the allocation of remittances. Because we control for the level of per capita expenditures in the household, those impacts are net of any income effects.

The fact that female-headed households that receive remittances do not behave in the simple way predicted by the intra-household bargaining literature—allocating a larger percentage of expenditures to health and education (and possibly food) and reducing expenditures on consumer and durable goods—suggests that the preferences of the remitter also influence the outcome. We now turn to that topic.

Impact of Sex of the Remitter on Household Budget Allocation

In this section, we use the remitter as the unit of analysis rather than the household in Ghana. As expected, most of the results from the previous analysis carry over to this analysis. Results for per capita expenditure, household size, proportion of girls and boys under age five, proportion of household members who have completed junior secondary school, senior secondary school, and university, and the location dummies are quite consistent with those in the previous section.

The central purpose of this analysis is to determine whether the sex of the remitter has any impact on the allocation of household expenditures. In an initial specification of the model, we found that the sex of the remitter does not have a significant impact on household expenditure allocations. As mentioned, this may be due to principal-agent issues: the remitter cannot enforce his or her preferences about how remittances should be spent because he or she is absent from the household.

To control for the ability of the individual remitter to monitor and control how remittances are spent in the receiving household, we introduce new variables into the analysis in table 5.7. We include the remitter's relation to the household head, the frequency of remitting, and the remitter's place of residence. A remitter has a close relationship to the household head if s/he is the spouse, the child, or the sibling of the household head. We suspect that with a remitter with a close relationship to the household head will have more say over how remittances are spent. Similarly, a remitter who sends remittances more frequently has closer contact with his or her origin household and therefore more control over how his or her remittances are being spent. Categories of frequency are weekly or monthly, quarterly, and annually; the omitted category is irregularly. Finally, the place of residence is incorporated as a dummy variable; remitters who are located close to the receiver of the remittances (defined as within Ghana) are presumed to have more ability to monitor and control expenditures.

Once these variables are included in the regression, the sex of the remitter significantly influences the patterns of expenditure. Controlling for the remitter's ability to supervise how the household spends the remittances, the dummy for female remitter is statistically significant for the expenditure shares for food, health, and other goods. The expenditure share for food is lower, while the expenditure shares for health and other goods are higher, than for male remitters.

The location of the remitter also affects the composition of the household expenditure. If the remitter lives in Ghana, the budget share for food is higher, while the shares for housing and for consumer and durable goods are lower than when the remitter lives outside Ghana. If the remitter lives in Ghana *and* is female, the budget share for food is even higher, while the expenditure shares for health and other goods are lower than they are in other households.

The remitter's relationship to the household head also influences expenditure shares. If the remitter is a child of the household head, the health share increases and the education share decreases. If the remitter is the spouse of the household head, the share for education increases. Finally, if the remitter is the sibling of the household head, the share for consumer and durable goods decreases. This finding

Table 5.7. Fractional Logit Odds Ratio Coefficients, by Expenditure Type, Controlling for Principal-Agent Problem

Variable	Food	Consumer and durable goods	Housing	Health	Education	Other
Remitter is female	0.836	1.054	1.013	1.328	1.078	1.237
	(0.054)***	(0.070)	(0.071)	(0.184)**	(0.164)	(0.121)**
Remitter is child of head of household	1.045	0.965	0.954	1.217	0.845	1.005
	(0.047)	(0.046)	(0.035)	(0.113)**	(0.087)*	(0.070)
Remitter is spouse of head of household	0.972	1.001	0.942	1.044	1.333	0.925
	(0.043)	(0.047)	(0.045)	(0.118)	(0.154)**	(0.065)
Remitter is sibling of head of household	1.051	0.930	1.014	1.038	1.047	0.981
	(0.037)	(0.036)*	(0.048)	(0.073)	(0.098)	(0.050)
Remitter lives in Ghana	1.112	0.882	0.910	1.036	0.981	0.957
	(0.047)**	(0.040)***	(0.048)	(0.099)	(0.102)	(0.049)
Remitter is female and child of head of household	1.122	0.926	0.997	0.806	1.188	0.869
	(0.060)**	(0.051)	(0.048)	(0.106)*	(0.157)	(0.072)*
Remitter is female and spouse of head of household	1.158	1.006	0.972	0.587	0.457	1.191
	(0.255)	(0.317)	(0.143)	(0.265)	(0.174)**	(0.294)
Remitter is female and sibling of head of household	1.133	0.952	0.958	0.942	0.819	0.881
	(0.055)**	(0.049)	(0.068)	(0.108)	(0.111)	(0.072)
Remitter is female and lives in Ghana	1.122	0.978	0.975	0.799	0.952	0.860
	(0.065)**	(0.060)	(0.061)	(0.108)*	(0.135)	(0.072)*
Household receives remittances weekly or monthly	0.985	0.965	1.110	1.164	0.918	1.030
	(0.038)	(0.037)	(0.037)***	(0.089)**	(0.077)	(0.069)
Household receives remittances quarterly	1.017	0.918	1.029	1.028	1.265	0.975
	(0.041)	(0.033)**	(0.036)	(0.085)	(0.128)**	(0.063)
Household receives remittances annually	1.044	0.950	1.020	0.942	1.043	0.989
	(0.037)	(0.033)	(0.035)	(0.065)	(0.115)	(0.060)

log_total expenditure per capita	4.348 (2.310)***	0.420 (0.225)	0.052 (0.026)***	3.789 (3.879)	1.001 (1.586)	0.452 (0.292)
log_total expenditure per capita squared	0.948 (0.018)***	1.037 (0.020)*	1.081 (0.020)***	0.956 (0.035)	1.000 (0.057)	1.032 (0.024)
Remitter's share in total remittances received by household	1.044 (0.035)	1.000 (0.035)	0.980 (0.036)	0.929 (0.080)	1.093 (0.089)	0.929 (0.050)
Female-headed household	1.024 (0.038)	0.858 (0.038)***	0.904 (0.031)***	1.063 (0.083)	1.497 (0.127)***	0.985 (0.047)
log_household size	0.800 (0.023)***	1.239 (0.045)***	0.486 (0.013)***	1.063 (0.059)	3.082 (0.219)***	1.026 (0.040)
Age of household head	1.007 (0.001)***	0.989 (0.001)***	1.003 (0.001)***	1.000 (0.002)	1.001 (0.004)	0.997 (0.002)*
Proportion of males >15 years	0.959 (0.061)	1.058 (0.094)	1.052 (0.080)	1.205 (0.214)	0.366 (0.090)***	1.026 (0.095)
Proportion of females >15 years	0.863 (0.057)**	1.277 (0.082)***	1.202 (0.070)***	1.418 (0.235)**	0.215 (0.054)***	1.122 (0.117)
Proportion of girls <5 years	1.223 (0.129)*	1.075 (0.083)	0.945 (0.090)	1.383 (0.268)*	0.091 (0.025)***	1.193 (0.257)
Proportion of boys <5 years	1.301 (0.138)**	1.188 (0.129)	0.733 (0.071)***	2.521 (0.464)***	0.058 (0.019)***	0.756 (0.130)
Proportion of family members who have completed primary school	1.069 (0.070)	0.929 (0.064)	0.992 (0.060)	1.015 (0.209)	0.949 (0.213)	1.040 (0.100)
Proportion of family members who have completed junior secondary school	0.925 (0.049)	1.158 (0.059)***	1.056 (0.051)	0.995 (0.133)	1.599 (0.383)*	0.911 (0.076)

(Table continues on the following page)

Table 5.7. Fractional Logit Odds Ratio Coefficients, by Expenditure Type, Controlling for Principal-Agent Problem (Continued)

Variable	Food	Consumer and durable goods	Housing	Health	Education	Other
Proportion of family members who have completed senior secondary school	0.686 (0.085)***	1.313 (0.165)**	1.097 (0.076)	0.611 (0.150)**	4.968 (1.747)***	1.196 (0.252)
Proportion of family members who have completed university	0.228 (0.088)***	1.925 (0.676)*	5.369 (3.426)***	2.708 (1.846)	1.152 (1.021)	2.573 (1.014)**
Location 2 (urban coastal)	1.248 (0.114)**	0.950 (0.074)	0.397 (0.028)***	1.105 (0.205)	0.583 (0.072)***	1.049 (0.086)
Location 3 (urban forest)	1.279 (0.114)***	1.092 (0.081)	0.467 (0.028)***	1.057 (0.191)	0.538 (0.072)***	0.817 (0.066)**
Location 4 (urban savannah)	1.644 (0.196)***	0.889 (0.082)	0.487 (0.054)***	0.785 (0.180)	0.418 (0.126)***	0.761 (0.095)**
Location 5 (rural coastal)	1.449 (0.138)***	1.012 (0.071)	0.374 (0.026)***	1.146 (0.224)	0.448 (0.057)***	0.766 (0.073)***
Location 6 (rural forest)	1.474 (0.133)***	1.188 (0.082)**	0.303 (0.020)***	1.099 (0.188)	0.382 (0.046)***	0.635 (0.055)***
Location 7 (rural savannah)	1.710 (0.154)***	1.177 (0.089)**	0.280 (0.017)***	0.941 (0.172)	0.278 (0.057)***	0.558 (0.054)***
Head of household is of Asante ethnicity	1.000 (0.044)	0.955 (0.038)	1.024 (0.042)	0.969 (0.071)	1.157 (0.119)	1.050 (0.074)
Number of observations	4,011	4,011	4,011	4,011	4,011	4,011

Source: Authors' calculations based on GLSS 4.

Note: Robust standard errors are in parentheses. Robust standard errors are used to account for the primary sample unit of the survey methodology.

***Significant at 1 percent.

**Significant at 5 percent.

*Significant at 10 percent.

indicates that remitters have different impacts on household budgets depending on their relation to the receiving household.

Female remitters with a close relationship to the head of the household also influence certain groups of expenditure, but in a different way than male remitters do. Households receiving remittances from female children allocate a higher share to food and education and a lower share to health and other goods than other households. Households receiving remittances from female siblings allocate more of their budget to food. Households receiving remittances from a wife allocate much less of their budget to education than households receiving remittances from a husband. There are two likely explanations for this result. First, according to the intra-household bargaining literature, males tend to spend less on education than other commodities; in households where the wife is absent, it is likely that the head of the household is a man who has relatively more say over household decisions. Second, when the wife leaves the household, it is plausible that children leave with her or that she leaves when the children are out of school age; in either case, the expenditure share on education in the household left behind would decrease.

The results obtained in this section, in which we include the remitter's relationship to the household head, the remitter's location, and the frequency of remitting, have two possible interpretations. The first is that we are capturing the principal-agent monitoring problem and thus are controlling better for this aspect of the unobserved heterogeneity of migrant households. The second interpretation is that these variables are in fact identifying unobserved preferences that make households with internal and international migrants allocate their budget differently.

We favor the first interpretation because the results are consistent with previous research on intra-household bargaining. First, the intra-household bargaining literature predicts that increasing the amount of resources controlled by women raises the allocation of resources toward education, health, and nutrition. The results show that when the remitter is the husband, the share of expenditure on education increases, since the wife is staying behind. In contrast, when the wife is the remitter, the share of education decreases, since the male is staying behind. This might be the result of the increase in control of expenditure that a wife experiences when she is the household head or the lack of ability to control and monitor expenditures when she is away.

Conclusions

In this chapter, we examine two research questions regarding remittances and gender: first, how the sex of the household head and remittances affect household budget allocations and, second, how the sex of the remitter shapes these allocations. We find that female-headed households receiving remittances (both internal and international) seem to have different expenditure patterns than their male counterparts. We observe an interesting difference between female-headed households receiving remittances from within Ghana and female-headed households receiving remittances from abroad. The former group has larger expenditure shares for health and education, thus confirming conclusions from a host of intra-household models. While the latter group has higher expenditure shares for health, they spend significantly less on food and more on consumer and durable goods, housing, and other goods, patterns that are consistent with the emerging findings about the preferences of male migrants for the allocation of remittances. Thus we observe heterogeneity in expenditure patterns within the group of female-headed households receiving remittances.

At first blush, the sex of the remitter has no impact on expenditure patterns. Once we control for the remitters' relation to the household head, the frequency of sending remittances, and whether funds are remitted from inside or outside of Ghana, however, significant differences emerge. These variables serve as a proxy for the capacity of the remitter to follow up on the intended use of the remittances. Our results indicate that households with female remitters in Ghana devote a relatively lower share of their budget to food expenditure and a relatively higher share to health and other goods compared to households with male remitters. Our results also show that the remitter's relationship to the household head changes the expenditure shares in different directions. For instance, households with a remitter who is the husband of the household head, on average, have a higher expenditure share on education, while the opposite holds for households whose remitters are the wife of the household head. We presume that these changes in expenditure patterns can be attributed to shifts in power on the intra-household level that occur when a substantial part of the household budget relies on a household member abroad. Overall, the results of this exercise are evidence that the sex of the remitter can matter for budget allocations.

This chapter is one of the first pieces of evidence that the sex of both the sender and the receiver of remittances should be taken into account when analyzing the impact of remittances on household expenditure patterns. The chapter also shows that changes in intra-household bargaining that occur in the context of migration may influence the net impact of migration in the country of origin. In addition, we show that it is important to control for the ability of remitters to monitor and control expenditures when examining the determinants of household expenditure shares. In sum, we believe that the literature on remittances would benefit from including a gender perspective in order to further our understanding of the relationships between migration and its development impacts.

Future research should use data sets that contain information on absent household members, whether or not they send remittances. Such data would permit researchers to disentangle the effects of remittances and migration per se. This type of analysis is important, because migration will change household size and may affect the composition of expenditure, whether or not the migrants remit (Schiff 2006).

In addition, it is necessary to develop better data that can provide more precise measurement of intra-household bargaining power, thus obviating the need to use imperfect proxy variables such as the sex of the household head. Future research should also work to solidify the links between the intra-household allocation literature and the migration literature by measuring not only the impact of migration on expenditure shares, but also its impact on important developmental outcomes such as children's nutritional and educational outcomes.

Endnotes

1. Intentional data on the use of remittances may not give an accurate indication on how remittances actually will be used unless there are mechanisms of monitoring available for the remitter to control how the receivers of the remittances spend the money they receive.

2. The importance of measuring resources controlled at time of marriage—rather than resources currently controlled—is that it is exogenous to any bargaining process during the marriage process itself.

3. Current asset is defined as all assets owned by the household at the time of the survey. For more information, see Quisumbing and de la Brière (2000).

4. This implies that we risk conflating remittance effects with other impacts of migration on the household level. For a more detailed discussion, see McKenzie (2006).

5. While this is a less-than-perfect proxy, there is precedent for using it in a study of remittances to measure bargaining power (see De and Ratha 2005).

6. The variables age of the household head and Asante ethnicity of the household head are used as instrumental variables by Adams (2006b) in his study on the impact of remittances on expenditures in Ghana.

7. Specifically, the household budget allocation might be influenced by the age of the household head (for example, the number and age of children are related to the age of the household head, and the number and age of children, in turn, are an important determinant of the composition of household expenditures). Similarly, migration experience may exert a direct effect on the composition of household expenditures because of a change in consumption preferences that results from the experience of living elsewhere, either within Ghana or abroad.

8. Data on the exact location of the remitter are only available for half of the sample (only for remitters inside Ghana). Without exact location, we cannot calculate neither distance nor average incomes.

9. The data set includes six categories of the remitter's relationship to the household head: (1) parent, (2) spouse, (3) child, (4) sibling, (5) other relative, and (6) nonrelative. The frequency of remitting is captured by three dummy variables that capture whether or not the remittances are sent monthly or weekly, quarterly, or annually. The main assumption here is that remitters might have more contact with their household if they remit on a regular basis, and consequently, they might have more control over how their remittances are being spent.

10. We do not interact the sex of the remitter with the frequency of the remittances sent because we do not have reasons to believe that the effect of one type of frequency might have a different impact on household expenditure if sent by a man or a woman, other things being equal.

References

Acosta, Pablo. 2006. "Labor Supply, School Attendance, and Remittances from International Migration: The Case of El Salvador." Policy Research Working Paper WPS3903. World Bank, Washington, DC.

Adams, Richard H. Jr. 2006a. "Remittances, Consumption, and Investments in Ghana." Unpublished mss. World Bank, Washington, DC.

————. 2006b. "Remittances, Poverty, and Investments in Guatemala." In *International Migration, Remittances, and the Brain Drain,* ed. Çağlar Özden and Maurice Schiff. New York: Palgrave Macmillan.

Bhalotra, Sonia, and Cliff Attfield. 1998. "Intrahousehold Resource Allocation in Rural Pakistan: A Semiparametric Analysis." *Journal of Applied Econometrics* 13 (5): 463–80.

Case, Anne C., and Angus Deaton. 2002. "Consumption, Health, Gender, and Poverty." Research Program in Development Studies 212. Princeton University, Princeton, NJ.

Chen, Joyce J. 2006. "Migration and Imperfect Monitoring: Implications for Intra-Household Allocation." *American Economic Review* 96 (2): 227–31.

De, Prabal, and Dilip Ratha. 2005. "Remittance Income and Household Welfare: Evidence from Sri Lanka Integrated Household Survey." Unpublished mss. World Bank, Washington, DC.

de la Brière, Bénédicte, Alain de Janvry, Elisabeth Sadoulet, and Sylvie Lambert. 2002. "The Roles of Destination, Gender, and Household Composition in Explaining Remittances: An Analysis for the Dominican Sierra." *Journal of Development Economics* 68 (2): 309–28.

de la Cruz, Blanca E. 1995. "The Socioeconomic Dimensions of Remittances: A Case Study of Five Mexican Families." *Berkeley McNair Journal* 3: 1–10.

Duflo, Esther. 2003. "Grandmothers and Granddaughters: Old-Age Pensions and Intrahousehold Allocation in South Africa." *World Bank Economic Review* 17 (1): 1–25.

Dwyer, Daisy H., and Judith Bruce, eds. 1988. *A Home Divided: Women and Income in the Third World.* Palo Alto, CA: Stanford University Press.

García, Marito. 1991. "Impact of Female Sources of Income on Food Demand among Rural Households in the Philippines." *Quarterly Journal of International Agriculture* 30 (2): 109–24.

Guyer, Jane I. 1997. "Endowments and Assets: The Anthropology of Wealth and the Economics of Intrahousehold Allocation." In *Intrahousehold Resource Allocation in Developing Countries: Models, Methods, and Policy,* ed. Lawrence Haddad, John Hoddinott, and Harold E. Alderman. Food Policy Statement 24. Washington, DC: International Food Policy Research Institute.

Haddad, Lawrence, and John Hoddinott. 1995. "Does Female Income Share Influence Household Expenditures? Evidence from Côte d'Ivoire." *Oxford Bulletin of Economics and Statistics* 57 (1): 77–96.

Haddad, Lawrence, John Hoddinott, and Harold Alderman, eds. 1997. *Intrahousehold Resource Allocation in Developing Countries: Models, Methods, and Policy.* Baltimore, MD: Johns Hopkins University Press.

Hallman, Kelly K. 2000. *Mother-Father Resource Control, Marriage Payments, and Girl-Boy Health in Rural Bangladesh.* FCND Discussion Paper 93. Washington, DC: International Food Policy Research Institute.

Hoddinott, John. 1994. "A Model of Migration and Remittances Applied to Western Kenya." *Oxford Economic Papers* 46 (3): 459–76.

Imbens, Guido W. 1999. "The Role of the Propensity Score in Estimating Dose-Response Functions." NBER Technical Working Paper 0237. National Bureau of Economic Research, Cambridge, MA.

IOM (International Organization for Migration). 2005. *Migration and Remittances in Moldova.* Moldova: IOM.

Katz, Elizabeth G. 1992. *Intrahousehold Resource Allocation in the Guatemalan Central Highlands: The Impact of Nontraditional Agricultural Exports.* Ph.D. diss., University of Wisconsin, Madison.

Kennedy, Eileen. 1991. "Income Sources of the Rural Poor in Southwestern Kenya." In *Income Sources of Malnourished People in Rural Areas: Microlevel Information and Policy Implications,* ed. Joachim von Braun and Rajul Pandya-Lorch. Washington, DC: International Food Policy Research Institute.

Lee, Yean-Ju, William L. Parish, and Robert J. Willis. 1994. "Sons, Daughters, and Intergenerational Support in Taiwan." *American Journal of Sociology* 99 (4): 1010–41.

López Córdoba, Ernesto. 2005. "Globalization, Migration, and Development: The Role of Mexican Migrant Remittances." Unpublished mss. Inter-American Development Bank, Washington, DC.

Lucas, Robert E. B., and Oded Stark. 1985. "Motivations to Remit: Evidence from Botswana." *Journal of Political Economy* 93 (5): 901–18.

McKenzie, David. 2006. "Beyond Remittances: The Effects of Migration on Mexican Households." In *International Migration, Remittances, and the Brain Drain,* ed. Çağlar Özden and Maurice Schiff. New York: Palgrave Macmillan.

McKenzie, David, John Gibson, and Steven Stillman. 2006. "How Important Is Selection? Experimental Versus Non-experimental Measures of the Income Gains from Migration." Policy Research Working Paper 3906. World Bank, Development Research Group, Washington, DC.

Mora, Jorge, and J. Edward Taylor. 2004. "Remittances, Inequality, and Poverty: Evidence from Rural Mexico." Unpublished mss. World Bank, Development Research Group, International Migration and Development Research Program, Washington, DC.

Papke, Leslie E., and Jeffrey M. Wooldridge. 1996. "Econometric Methods for Fractional Response Variables with an Application to 401(K) Plan Participation Rates." *Journal of Applied Econometrics* 11 (6): 619–32.

Quartey, Peter. 2005. "Shared Growth in Ghana: Do Migrant Remittances Have a Role?" Paper presented at the international conference "Shared Growth in Africa," Cornell University, Institute of Statistical, Social, and Economic Research (University of Ghana), and the World Bank, Accra, July 21–22.

Quisumbing, Agnes R., ed. 2003. *Household Decisions, Gender, and Development: A Synthesis of Recent Research.* Baltimore, MD: Johns Hopkins University Press for the International Food Policy Research Institute.

Quisumbing, Agnes R., and Bénédicte de la Brière. 2000. *Women's Assets and Intrahousehold Allocation in Rural Bangladesh: Testing Measures of Bargaining Power.* FCND Discussion Paper 86. Washington, DC: International Food Policy Research Institute, Food Consumption and Nutrition Division.

Quisumbing, Agnes R., and John A. Maluccio. 2000. *Intrahousehold Allocation and Gender Relations: New Empirical Evidence from Four Developing Countries.* FCND Discussion Paper 84. Washington, DC: International Food Policy Research Institute, Food Consumption and Nutrition Division.

Rapoport, Hillel, and Frédéric Docquier. 2005. *The Economics of Migrants' Remittances.* IZA Discussion Paper 1531. Bonn: Institute for the Study of Labor (IZA).

Republic of Ghana Statistical Service. 1999. Ghana Living Standards Survey Round Four (GLSS 4) 1998/99. Data User's Guide. Accra.

Schiff, Maurice. 2006. "Poverty Impact of Migration and Remittances: Household Size, Policy-Related Reference Groups, and Informational Content of Poverty Measures." Unpublished mss. World Bank, Washington, DC.

Smith, Lisa C., and Elizabeth M. Byron. 2005. *Is Greater Decisionmaking Power of Women Associated with Reduced Gender Discrimination in South Asia?* IFPRI Discussion Paper 200. Washington, DC: International Food Policy Research Institute.

Stark, Oded, and Robert E. B. Lucas. 1988. "Migration, Remittances, and the Family." *Economic Development and Cultural Change* 36 (3): 465–81.

Strauss, John, and Duncan Thomas. 1995. "Human Resources: Empirical Modeling of Household and Family Decisions." In *Handbook of Development Economics,* vol. 3A, ed. Jere Behrman and T. N. Srinivasan. Amsterdam: North-Holland Elsevier.

Thomas, Duncan. 1990. "Intrahousehold Resource Allocation: An Inferential Approach." *Journal of Human Resources* 25 (4): 635–64.

———. 1994. "Like Father, Like Son; Like Mother, Like Daughter: Parental Resources and Child Height." *Journal of Human Resources* 29 (4): 950–88.

Thomas, Duncan, and Chien-Liang Chen. 1994. "Income Shares and Shares of Income: Empirical Tests of Models of Household Resource Allocations." Labor and Population Working Paper Series 94-08. RAND Corporation, Santa Monica, CA.

United Nations. 2005. *2004 World Survey on the Role of Women in Development: Women and International Migration.* New York: United Nations, Department of Economic and Social Affairs (DESA).

UNDP (United Nations Development Programme). 2005. *Trends in Total Migrant Stock 1960–2005.* POP/DB/MIG/Rev. 2005. New York: UNDP.

Vanwey, Leah K. 2004. "Altruistic and Contractual Remittances between Male and Female Migrants and Households in Rural Thailand." *Demography* 41 (4): 739–56.

Wooldridge, Jeffrey M. 2002. *Econometric Analysis of Cross Section and Panel Data.* Cambridge, MA: MIT Press.

World Bank. 2006a. *Global Economic Prospects 2006: Economic Implications of Remittances and Migration.* Washington, DC: World Bank, Development Prospects Group.

———. 2006b. "Migration and Development Brief 2." World Bank, Development Prospects Group, Migration and Remittances Team, Washington, DC. (http://siteresources.worldbank.org/INTPROSPECTS/Resources/334934-1110315015165/MigrationDevelopmentBriefingNov2006.pdf).

Yang, Dean, and Claudia A. Martínez. 2006. "Remittances and Poverty in Migrants' Home Areas: Evidence from the Philippines." In *International Migration, Remittances, and the Brain Drain,* ed. Çağlar Özden and Maurice Schiff, 81–121. New York: Palgrave Macmillan.

6

IMMIGRANT WOMEN'S PARTICIPATION AND PERFORMANCE IN THE U.S. LABOR MARKET

Çağlar Özden and Ileana Cristina Neagu

Approximately half of all immigrants to the United States are women, yet previous research on the labor market assimilation and performance of migrants has focused mostly on men. Given the increasing education levels of migrant women and their higher participation in the labor market, there are no excuses for the absence of the gender dimension in policy debates and research on migration and labor markets. Analysis of women's labor market participation and performance levels is becoming especially important as many women are migrating individually for employment purposes, while their families stay at home. Furthermore, the educational gaps between women and men are rapidly eroding in many migrant-sending developing countries, and we are observing higher levels of brain drain among educated women. Thus there is greater urgency for migration, development, and gender issues to be explored jointly.

We address several interrelated questions in this chapter. As the vast literature on labor economics has shown in the context of women's labor market outcomes, performance and participation levels need to be analyzed jointly, as employed women are not chosen from a random sample. Using empirical methods that control for such sample selection biases, we analyze the determinants of migrant

This chapter is part of the World Bank's Research Program on International Migration and Development. The idea for it resulted from a conversation with Maurice Schiff. The chapter has benefited from the insightful comments of David McKenzie, Andrew R. Morrison, Mirja Sjöblom, and L. Alan Winters.

women's participation and performance levels, which are measured via two separate variables. In addition to wages—the standard performance variable used in the literature—we look at the average skill level of the occupation obtained by the migrant as a measure of her relative placement in the labor market. The occupational placement of migrants relative to their education and skill levels is a relatively underexplored, yet very important, issue in the brain drain debate.[1]

Our results indicate striking differences in the labor market participation and placement levels of female migrants with similar educational backgrounds but from different countries. Even after we control for age, education, experience, and various family characteristics such as marital status and number of children, we find that migrant women from different countries have widely different labor market experiences. For example, a hypothetical 35-year-old college-educated Nigerian migrant has a 68 percent probability of labor market participation, while a Mexican migrant of identical age, education, experience, and family structure has only a 46 percent probability. In terms of labor market outcomes, the most successful migrants come from Western Europe or English-speaking developing countries. Latin American migrants have lower levels of participation and performance. We find that a large portion of the low performance levels of Latin American migrants is simply due to low levels of education. Once we control for education, the gaps in labor market performance among migrant women from most developing countries disappear.[2] African and Eastern European female migrants have higher levels of participation, but lower levels of performance. Asian and Middle Eastern women have low levels of participation and high levels of performance. Personal and family characteristics, such as marital status, number of children, age, and experience, have the expected effects on migrant women. One key variable is education; an extra year of education increases labor market participation levels by 2.3 percent and annual wages by $3,000 to $4,000, depending on the home country of the migrant.

Some of these variations are due to factors that affect the quality of the human capital accumulated at home prior to migration. Among these factors are the resources spent on education as well as the prevalence of English in daily life. That is why migrants from ex-British colonies, such as South Africa, Nigeria, and India, perform remarkably well in the U.S. labor market. There are obviously other social and cultural factors that affect the trade-offs made by women between labor market participation and household responsibilities. This issue is closely related to the reasons why women migrate. We can broadly classify migrant women into two main categories: those who migrate to follow a husband or another family member and those who migrate alone for educational or occupational reasons. The labor market participation and performance levels of these two groups are likely to be rather different, even though education levels and other human capital characteristics are the same. We try to control for the factors that differentiate "economic migrants" from "accompanying migrants" through the selection model as well as other variables such as marital status, nationality of the husband, number of children, and location of education, among others. However, there are still substantial differences among migrants with different nationalities, even though they might have similar marital and demographic characteristics. This is another indication of the need for further research, especially identifying the impact of differences in migration decisions.

Our results have many implications, especially in terms of development policies and migration issues. One aspect is the relatively low level of employment of educated migrant women from many developing countries, which implies that their skills are being underutilized. Obviously, we need to compare these to employment levels at home to see if there is a global misallocation of human capital. If the employment levels are similar, then the low participation levels in the United States are likely to be due to cultural and personal preferences rather than to labor market constraints or discrimination. The second issue is the large variation in performance among migrant women from different countries, whether the differences are measured through wages or types of jobs obtained. Part of the variation is obviously due to the quality of the education received at home and other factors influencing the level of human capital acquired before migration. However, we still face the question of whether the positive social externalities generated by educated women would have been higher in their home country even if the private returns are likely to be higher in the United States. This question lies at the heart of the brain drain debate and is hard to explore empirically.

Our work is related to two strands in the literature on migration. The "assimilation" literature comprises a wide range of rigorous empirical analyses focusing on the performance of migrants in the host country (surveyed in Borjas 1994). The "brain drain" literature consists of sophisticated theoretical, but rather limited empirical work focusing on the effects of skilled migration, mostly on the home country (surveyed in Commander et al. 2003).

The existing "assimilation" literature focuses primarily on earnings as a measure of performance. Earnings do not reveal what immigrants actually do, even though they are likely to be correlated with occupational choices. If the global creation and allocation of human capital are a concern, then it is of interest what kind of jobs the highly educated immigrants obtain. Early studies note that the degree of similarity of the home country to the United States and immigration laws may influence the quality distribution of immigrants (Chiswick 1978, 1985). But this empirical research does not focus on the links between the characteristics of the home country and immigration behavior (Borjas 1985; Chiswick 1985). Borjas's (1987) influential paper emphasizes the importance of selection biases in migration patterns that are due to differences in the patterns of income distribution in the home and destination countries. His empirical analysis shows that earnings differences of immigrants with the same measured education levels are attributable to variations in political and economic conditions in the home countries. In particular, migrants from Western European countries do quite well compared with migrants from less-developed countries. Methodologically, our chapter is most closely related to Green (1999). Using the 1981, 1986, and 1991 censuses of Canada, he finds little evidence of immigrants being underrepresented in more skilled occupations relative to native-born workers with similar education and experience characteristics. One reason is Canadian immigration policy, which is characterized by a point system that screens migrants for their skill and education levels. Furthermore, differences in occupational attainment are linked to linguistic fluency-based differences, and the study does not relate outcomes to the differences in home-country attributes. Using detailed data from Israel, another country that has experienced a large influx of skilled migrants, Friedberg (2000) focuses on the source of the immigrants' human capital. She finds that human capital is imperfectly portable, and the national origin of an individual's education and experience is a crucial determinant of his or her value in the labor market.

Among the few papers on women migrants, Long (1980) finds that earnings of U.S. immigrant women are higher than those of native women (in the United States) around the time of migration and decrease over time. The author's explanation of this finding is the so-called "family investment strategy" in which women work harder at the beginning to support their husband's investment in human capital and other marketable skills. Later, as men assimilate to the U.S. labor market and earn higher wages, women work less. Baker and Benjamin (1994, 1997) build on the work of Long (1980) and confirm his findings. Some of our findings with respect to lower earnings of migrant women are consistent with this explanation. Duleep and Sanders (1993) and Schoeni (1998) use U.S. data and examine female labor force participation mainly focusing on assimilation. The former focuses on family characteristics, and the latter differentiates cohort effects. Both papers find that there are significant assimilation effects via higher participation rates, especially within the first decade of arrival, and that these are stronger among Asian migrants. Duleep and Sanders (1994) analyze the impact of children on the labor supply of migrants and natives. They find that the gaps are rather narrow and that similar child-status-work relations are present among migrants and natives. Schoeni (1998) uses data from three censuses to evaluate the assimilation effect purged of the cohort effect for female immigrants, using the procedure introduced by Borjas (1985) for male immigrants. Labor force participation and wage determinants are explored in the same paper; however, these are estimated separately, rather than jointly, even though the latter is the economically and empirically appropriate method. Cobb-Clark (1993) writes one of the few papers that examine the selectivity issue for women migrants. She finds that, as is the case with men, women from richer countries perform better in the United States. There has, however, been little investigation of joint labor market participation and performance decisions, especially when the participation decision is endogenous. This complication is relatively less important for men but creates significant selection biases for women—hence the importance of the empirical methodology we employ in this chapter.

The other strand of literature relevant to our study is on the brain drain. The main focus has been the negative impact on the sending developing countries, due to the decline in positive externalities that an educated labor force generates within the economy and lost investments in education and potential tax revenue (see Bhagwati and Hamada 1974; Bhagwati 1976). More recent work has pointed to benefits for source countries of return migration, resource repatriation, migrant networks, and the flow of information and knowledge (for example, Puri and Ritzema 2000). The magnitude of such benefits is likely to depend on how emigrants perform in the host-country labor market; substantial underachievement abroad could diminish the potential benefits. Recent work by Docquier and Marfouk (2006) provide the much needed and widely cited data on bilateral migrant flows by education levels. Our results imply that it might not be adequate to measure brain drain in terms of numbers of educated migrants; rather, the quality of their human capital needs to enter the analysis.

Data

Empirical research on the performance of migrants in destination labor markets, especially with respect to issues regarding education, skill level, and brain drain, suffers from the absence of high-quality and detailed data. One exceptional source is the U.S. census, which includes detailed information on the social and economic status of foreign-born people who are living in the United States. The data in this chapter are from the 5 percent sample of the 2000 census.[3] We restrict our analysis to female migrants who were between 16 and 64 years old at the time of the census and arrived in the United States between 1980 and 1999. We distinguish between migrants who completed their education in the United States and those who obtained their final degree before arrival, by their decade of entering the United States. Each individual observation in the census has a population weight attached to it, which is that representative observation's proportion in the overall U.S. population. We end up with close to 400,000 observations in our data set, which corresponds to more than 8.8 million migrants.

Among the most important variables influencing labor market participation and performance of a migrant is her education level. Each individual in the census declares an education level and a profession. For the education levels in our analysis, we simply take the years of education completed that are appropriate for the level declared by the individual. In terms of occupation, there are more than 500 separate categories in the census. In order to create a metric that would capture differences among occupations, we calculate the average education level of all people, including native-born Americans, who are employed in each category. Thus we arrive at an "average educational attainment" variable for each occupation, which reflects the skill level in that category. For example, the average educational attainment in the census is 17.2 years for all physicians, whereas it is 10.1 for restaurant workers.

We divide the data by the decade of arrival—1980s and 1990s—in order to separate cohort effects (Borjas 1987). Table 6.1 provides the distribution of the observations in each cohort across education levels and geographic regions. For example, we have close to 225,000 observations (corresponding to almost 5 million people) for female migrants who arrived in the 1990s. Of these, 8.2 percent have graduate degrees (master's, professional, and doctorate), 32.3 percent have

Table 6.1. Description of Data: All Female Migrants, Age 16–64 as of 2000, by Decade of Arrival
(percent unless otherwise noted)

Indicator	1990s	1980s
Total sample (number)	224,931	177,409
Corresponding population (number)	4,952,706	3,830,151
Education category		
Less than 9 years	25.2	24.8
High school	34.3	33.8
College	32.3	35.2
Graduate degree	8.2	6.2
Continent		
Latin America	51.1	54.5
Asia	27.0	28.9
Western Europe	7.7	8.0
Eastern Europe	8.2	3.8
Middle East	2.8	2.9
Africa	3.2	1.9

Source: U.S. 2000 census data.

college studies, and 34.3 percent have attended high school. In terms of place of origin, 27 percent came from Asian countries and 51.1 percent came from Latin American countries. When we examine the changes across cohorts, we see that average education levels of female migrants, especially for those with a graduate degree, increased in the 1990s, but the ratio of immigrants from most geographic regions stayed relatively stable. The only exception is the jump in the level of female migrants from Eastern Europe after the Berlin Wall collapsed. The decline in Latin American migrants is due to people who entered as children in the 1990s but had not entered employment age as of 2000.

Figure 6.1 presents the number of migrant women who arrived in the 1990s from the main source countries in each geographic region. Mexico dominates the sample, with close to 1.4 million migrants, but only 50,000 (around 4 percent) have tertiary education. Several Asian countries, such as the Philippines, Vietnam, India, and China, are the home countries for more than 200,000 migrants each. More than 60 percent of Indian women have tertiary education, compared with around 50 percent of women in the Philippines and China and only around 15 percent of women in Vietnam. Education levels of migrant women show large variation across countries, as seen in this figure. As is the case with male migrants, European, Asian, Middle Eastern, and African migrant women are more educated than migrant women from the Caribbean and Latin American countries.

The location where the education is obtained is one of the key issues in the brain drain and assimilation literature. Unfortunately, the census asks the respondents only their level of education, not where they obtained it. However, we know the age at which an immigrant entered the United States. Based on this information, we designate a person as "U.S. educated" if she arrived in the United States before she normally would have finished her declared education level. For example, if a university graduate arrived at the age of 23 or older, then she is considered "foreign educated." Figure 6.2 presents the share of female migrants from various countries who completed their education at home for the 1990s cohort. For example, more than 80 percent of all female Mexican migrants completed their education at home, compared with less than 60 percent of the tertiary-educated Mexican women. The figure reveals that a larger portion of tertiary-educated migrants from Central America and the Caribbean (along with various Asian countries) actually completed their education after migration, compared with the migrants from Europe. This finding reflects the higher level of migration of children who come with their parents (as is the case with many Latin American migrants) and of high school- and college-age students who complete their higher education in the United States (as is more common among Asian migrants).

The differences in underlying education levels—whether completed at home or in the United States—can be due to several reasons. First, the average education

Figure 6.1. Number of Female Migrants from Select Countries and Their Education Levels: 1990s Arrivals

(in thousands)

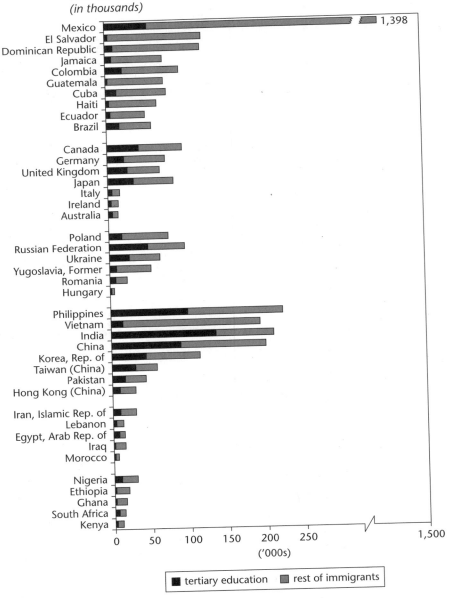

Source: U.S. 2000 census data.

Figure 6.2. Share of Female Migrants Who Completed Their Education Prior to Migration: 1990s Arrivals

Source: U.S. 2000 census data.

Figure 6.3. Tertiary School Enrollment Rates for Migrants and Native Populations

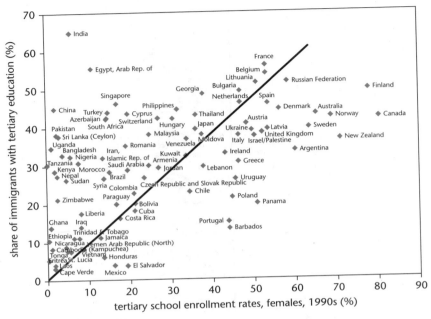

Source: U.S. 2000 census data.

levels, especially for women, might vary in their home country. Second, the migrants might be disproportionately drawn from different segments of the education spectrum of their home country. Figure 6.3 depicts the distribution of select countries along these two dimensions: the proportion of *all* immigrants to the United States with tertiary education against the proportion of tertiary education enrollment in the home country. The education levels among Latin American and developed-country migrants are lower than the average levels in their home country (that is, they are below the 45 degree line in figure 6.3). In contrast, immigrants from Africa, Middle East, and Asia, on average, are highly educated, even though education levels are lower in their home country. This evidence is an example of the fact that migrants do not form a random sample of the population of their home country. Furthermore, women migrants have several other selection issues. A large portion migrates with the family and has no plans to participate in the labor market but rather intends to take care of the household responsibilities. As a result, higher education is not an important asset and does not affect migration eligibility. However, highly educated women from developing countries might be more inclined to migrate individually if they face discrimination in their domestic labor market. These are complicated questions that are not easily answered with the existing data.

As is the case with native-born American women, labor market participation rates of immigrant women are lower than those of the comparable male population. This differential is one of the most important and well-researched areas in labor economics, and we borrow tools developed in this area in the empirical section. In our sample, around 35 percent of the migrant women in the 1990s cohort are in the labor force; for the 1980s cohort, the percentage is around 45 percent.[4] This relatively large gap might be due to differences in cohort characteristics as well as time needed to learn English and raise children until they reach a certain age. In the empirical estimation, we try to determine the causes of these differences. Table 6.2 presents the distribution of employed women along several dimensions: different cohorts, education levels, geographic regions, and professions.

Table 6.2. Description of Data: All Employed Female Migrants, Age 16–64 as of 2000

(percent unless otherwise noted)

Indicator	1990s	1980s
Total sample (number)	77,397	79,847
Corresponding population (number)	1,722,300	1,739,254
Education category		
Less than 9 years	17.2	16.5
High school	30.0	29.2
College	40.2	44.9
Graduate degree	12.6	9.4
Continent		
Latin America	42.7	48.2
Asia	30.5	33.4
Western Europe	10.2	8.9
Eastern Europe	10.2	4.3
Middle East	2.2	2.6
Africa	4.1	2.5
Job category		
Unskilled (less than 10 years)	44.1	37.7
Semiskilled (10–12 years)	29.8	36.0
Skilled (12–14 years)	19.6	20.8
Professional (14+years)	6.6	5.5

Source: U.S. 2000 census data.

It is best to compare tables 6.1 and 6.2 in order to identify overall differences in labor market participation levels. For example, women migrants with less than nine years of education form 25.2 percent of the overall sample for the 1990 arrivals, as seen in table 6.1. However, they form only 17.2 percent of the employed female migrants. Migrants with at least some college education are 40.2 percent of the 1990s migrants, but they represent 52.8 percent of the employed among them. These numbers imply that only around 25 percent of migrant women with less than a high school degree are in the labor force, compared with about 50 percent of women with some college. And it reaches 70 percent for those with a doctorate. Thus education level is among the most important determinants of employment for migrant women, as is the case for all other segments of the population.

The next issue to consider is the geographic dispersion of employment. Latin American migrants form more than 50 percent of the overall sample, but they are only 42.7 percent of the employed group. Western European women are 7.7 percent of the migrant population, but 10.2 percent of the employed. These figures indicate that the employment level is around 30 percent of Latin American and Middle Eastern, around 40 percent of Asian, and more than 45 percent of European and African migrant women.

Finally, we need to look at the occupational distribution of migrant women. We divide the occupational categories according to the average education levels of *all* people (migrant and nonmigrant) employed in that category, as explained earlier. Categories for which the average education level is less than 10 years are denoted as unskilled; semiskilled categories have between 10 and 12 years, and skilled have between 12 and 14 years of average education. Finally, professional categories have more than 14 years. As the last section of table 6.2 presents, 44.1 percent of migrant women who arrived in the 1990s are employed in unskilled occupations, whereas 26.2 percent are in skilled and professional categories.

Similar data are presented in figure 6.4 for the 1990s cohort from various countries. For example, 24 percent of all Mexican migrants are in the labor force, compared with around 36 percent of tertiary-educated Mexican women migrants. Labor market participation levels are higher for educated women regardless of the country of origin. However, overall participation levels are higher for European and African migrants and are significantly lower for tertiary-educated migrants from the Middle Eastern countries (such as Lebanon, Iraq, and Egypt) and the East and South Asian countries (such as Japan, Republic of Korea, Pakistan, and Taiwan, China).

The following section empirically analyzes these patterns in the data. There is wide variation in the education and employment levels of migrants from different countries. First, we seek to identify the personal determinants of labor market participation, such as education and experience, as well as country-specific

Figure 6.4. Share of Female Migrants Who Are in the Labor Force, by Education Level: 1990s Arrivals

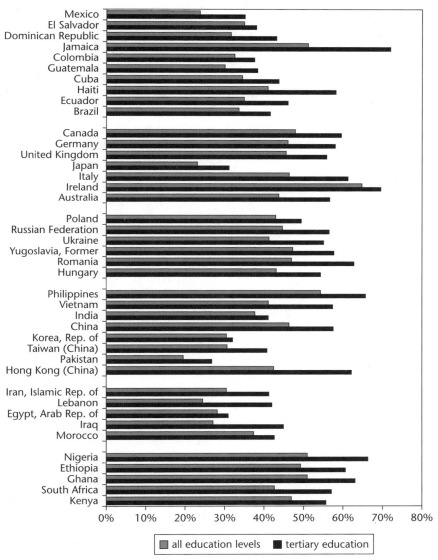

Source: U.S. 2000 census data.

variables. For example, it is very likely that the low levels of employment among Mexican women are due to low levels of education and that the differences with European migrants might disappear once the educational gap is taken into account. The second issue of interest is performance in the labor market—in terms of both wages and occupational placement. Mattoo et al. (2005) identify large differences in performance among male migrants from different countries with identical educational backgrounds and find similarly wide variation. The variation among women is more complicated, as the labor market participation decision of women is further influenced by other cultural and demographic factors. Whereas most men migrate for economic reasons, a large portion of women migrate to accompany their family and do not intend to participate actively in the labor market. These differences create certain biases and are controlled in the empirical estimation in this chapter.

This brain waste effect can be explained partially by country-specific factors that influence the quality of human capital, such as educational expenditures and dominance of English in the source country, and partially by factors that influence selection effects. For women, there is an additional empirical complication because their labor market participation rates are lower as they shoulder more of the household responsibilities. This leads to well-known sample selection biases, and, as such, we need to estimate labor market participation and performance levels simultaneously. This is the topic of the next section.

Empirical Framework

Our empirical analysis proceeds in several stages. For female migrants, labor market performance is critically related to the labor market participation decision. In other words, when identifying the determinants of labor market performance of female migrants (whether this is the wage level or the type of job obtained), there will be significant selection biases due to the employment decision. The seminal work of Heckman (1979) on sample selection bias was motivated by questions concerning the determinants of wages and labor supply behavior of women. Because employed women are unlikely to be chosen randomly from the underlying population of all migrant women, the employment decision and performance need to be estimated simultaneously.

The conventional sample selection model has the following form:

$$d_i^* = z_i'\gamma + \varepsilon_i, \qquad i = 1, \ldots N \tag{6.1}$$

$$y_i^* = x_i'\beta + v_i, \qquad i = 1, \ldots N, \tag{6.2}$$

where d^* is the latent labor market participation variable and y^* is the primary labor market performance variable. In our analysis, we use two endogenous performance variables: first is the wage earned by individual i, and second is the average educational attainment level, that is, the skill level of the occupation of the individual. This variable captures the quality of the labor market placement of the migrant, especially with respect to her education level. Naturally, we observe these performance variables only if the person is actually employed. The indicator variable d, which takes the value of 1 if y^* is observed and y is the observed counterpart of y^*. Thus we have the following relationships among these four variables:

$$d_i = 1 \quad \text{if} \quad d_i^* > 0 \quad \text{and} \quad d_i = 0 \quad \text{otherwise} \tag{6.3}$$

$$y_i = y_i^* * d_i. \tag{6.4}$$

Equation 6.1 captures sample selection, and equation 6.2 estimates the market performance, whether via the wage or the occupational placement variables. x and z are the exogenous variables, while β and γ are the vectors of parameters to be estimated. See Vella (1998) for the assumptions regarding the distributional properties of the error terms.

The explanatory variables that we use in the labor market performance equation (equation 6.2) are the following:

- *Years of education and years of education squared.* This is the number of years that corresponds to the education level declared by the individual.
- *Age and age squared.* These approximate the aggregate experience of the individual.
- *Years in the United States and years in the United States squared.* These approximate the experience of the individual in the U.S. labor market.
- *Country dummy variables.* These capture all of the relevant country-specific social and economic characteristics that influence an individual's performance. We use a dummy variable for each one of the 130 countries represented in the sample.

In the labor market participation equation (equation 6.1), we use the following variables in addition to the ones listed above:

- *Number of children.* This variable captures the extent of the household responsibilities placed on women.
- *Presence of a grandmother.* This is the number of women above the age of 65 who reside in the same household and measures the extent of domestic help available.
- *Marital status.* This is a set of eight dummy variables: never married, married to a husband of the same nationality, married to a husband of U.S. nationality, married to a husband of different nationality, married to an absent spouse, separated, divorced, and widowed.

We divide the data set along the following dimensions: cohorts (1990s and 1980s) and location of education (home country versus the United States). We perform the estimation separately for these four subsamples for each dependent variable (wage and occupational placement), for a total of eight estimated equations. The estimation is the standard Heckman selection model via maximum likelihood.

The coefficients estimated for the labor market participation equation are presented in table 6.3. The first four columns are for home-educated migrants, and the latter four are for migrants who completed their education in the United States. Columns 1–2 and 5–6 are for the 1990s cohort, whereas columns 3–4 and 7–8 are for the 1980s cohort. Finally, the odd-numbered columns are for the wage equation, and the even-numbered columns are for the labor market placement equations. Since the data are identical for this stage of the estimation for the wage and placement equations, the coefficients are also very similar for the same cohort and education location groups.

As the coefficients show, almost all of the coefficients are significant given the sample size, and they have the expected signs. Years of education, age, years in the United States, and the presence of a grandmother have a positive coefficient, whereas the number of children has a negative sign. Among the marital status dummy variables, "separated" was dropped from the estimation, and the coefficients for marital status variables should be interpreted as their impact relative to this dropped variable. Being married, especially to a husband with the same nationality, has the largest negative effect on the decision to enter the labor market. Being a widow, having a spouse who is absent from the household, or never being married also have negative effects compared to being separated. Only divorced women seem to have a higher likelihood of employment.

When we compare U.S.- and home-educated migrants, we see that education and age have stronger positive effects and the number of children has stronger negative effects on employment for U.S.-educated women. Years in the United States and marital status have similar effects. Finally, if we compare the 1980s and 1990s cohorts, education and age have similar effects, while years in the United States has weaker positive effects and number of children has weaker negative effects for U.S.-educated women. Marital status variables are again quite similar.

In order to assess the impact of the country-specific factors that operate through country dummy variables in the estimation, we calculate the predicted probability of employment for individuals with identical personal characteristics, but from different countries of origin. This artificial person is 35 years old, has been in the United States for six years (she arrived in 1994, hence she is in the 1990s cohort), has a college degree, has no children or a grandmother in the house, and is married to a spouse with the same nationality. Figure 6.5 presents the predicted

Table 6.3. First Stage of Heckman Selection Estimation

Variable	Home educated				U.S. educated			
	1990s arrivals		1980s arrivals		1990s arrivals		1980s arrivals	
	Wage (1)	Placement (2)	Wage (3)	Placement (4)	Wage (5)	Placement (6)	Wage (7)	Placement (8)
Years of education	0.024	0.024	0.023	0.023	0.151	0.134	0.056	0.049
	(6.10)***	(6.01)***	(4.94)***	(4.92)***	(6.45)***	(5.74)***	(3.87)***	(3.39)***
Years of education squared	0.001	0.001	0.002	0.002	−0.004	−0.003	0.003	0.003
	(5.36)***	(5.41)***	(7.95)***	(7.94)***	(3.75)***	(2.59)***	(3.83)***	(4.70)***
Age in 2000	0.112	0.112	0.13	0.13	0.426	0.398	0.288	0.289
	(44.77)***	(44.65)***	(25.67)***	(25.55)***	(27.14)***	(24.88)***	(40.69)***	(41.12)***
Age in 2000 squared	−0.001	−0.001	−0.002	−0.002	−0.007	−0.006	−0.004	−0.004
	(45.28)***	(45.09)***	(27.67)***	(27.45)***	(21.55)***	(19.55)***	(36.04)***	(36.32)***
Years in the United States	0.195	0.195	−0.01	−0.009	0.198	0.189	−0.036	−0.037
	(36.64)***	(36.70)***	(0.56)	(0.54)	(16.56)***	(15.70)***	(1.54)	(1.60)
Years in the United States squared	−0.013	−0.013	0.001	0.001	−0.012	−0.011	0.002	0.002
	(27.30)***	(27.32)***	(1.13)	(1.09)	(12.20)***	(11.61)***	(2.44)**	(2.46)**
Number of children	−0.093	−0.093	−0.058	−0.056	−0.2	−0.198	−0.135	−0.119
	(27.68)***	(27.72)***	(17.09)***	(16.47)***	(11.03)***	(15.33)***	(21.74)***	(19.12)***
Grandmother present	0.012	0.015	0.12	0.116	0.069	0.05	−0.035	−0.031
	(0.78)	(0.93)	(7.33)***	(7.04)***	(2.95)***	(2.37)**	(1.94)*	(1.76)*
Never married	0.003	0.001	−0.071	−0.077	−0.09	−0.118	−0.095	−0.074
	(0.13)	(0.03)	(3.16)***	(3.42)***	(1.58)	(2.27)**	(2.87)***	(2.19)**
Married with same nationality	−0.303	−0.304	−0.132	−0.135	−0.276	−0.256	−0.103	−0.122
	(16.14)***	(16.07)***	(6.83)***	(6.97)***	(4.81)***	(4.79)***	(3.08)***	(3.63)***

(Table continues on the following page)

Table 6.3. First Stage of Heckman Selection Estimation (Continued)

| | Home educated | | | | U.S. educated | | | |
| | 1990s arrivals | | 1980s arrivals | | 1990s arrivals | | 1980s arrivals | |
Variable	Wage (1)	Placement (2)	Wage (3)	Placement (4)	Wage (5)	Placement (6)	Wage (7)	Placement (8)
Married with U.S. citizen	−0.207 (9.53)***	−0.187 (8.33)***	−0.147 (6.30)***	−0.119 (4.92)***	−0.109 (1.82)*	−0.076 (1.34)	−0.039 (1.11)	−0.011 (0.31)
Married with other nationality	−0.338 (13.96)***	−0.338 (13.84)***	−0.145 (5.75)***	−0.144 (5.65)***	−0.252 (3.89)***	−0.215 (3.60)***	−0.074 (1.92)*	−0.092 (2.38)**
Married, spouse absent	−0.137 (5.91)***	−0.14 (6.06)***	−0.156 (5.42)***	−0.161 (5.55)***	−0.142 (2.22)**	−0.126 (2.14)**	−0.174 (4.11)***	−0.189 (4.47)***
Divorced	0.071 (3.06)***	0.064 (2.76)***	0.077 (3.40)***	0.064 (2.79)***	−0.081 (1.11)	−0.078 (1.13)	0.094 (2.33)**	0.072 (1.77)*
Widowed	−0.272 (9.23)***	−0.274 (9.22)***	−0.131 (4.45)***	−0.153 (5.23)***	−0.125 (0.69)	−0.081 (0.47)	−0.206 (2.09)**	−0.276 (3.02)***
Constant	−2.8 (9.26)***	−2.796 (9.25)***	−2.736 (6.02)***	−2.756 (6.18)***	−7.946 (11.99)***	−7.528 (11.88)***	−5.864 (11.28)***	−5.881 (11.46)***

Source: U.S. 2000 census data.

Note: Robust z statistics are in parentheses. Country dummies are included.

***Significant at 1 percent.

**Significant at 5 percent.

*Significant at 10 percent.

Figure 6.5. Predicted Probability of Employment for an Identical Person: 1990 Arrivals

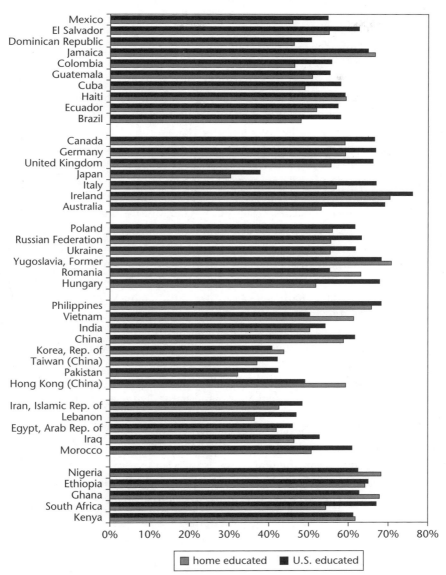

Source: U.S. 2000 census data.

probability of employment for this individual based on location of education and country of origin. The darker bars are for U.S.-educated migrants, and the lighter bars are for home-educated migrants. With few exceptions, such as Jamaica, Ghana, and Nigeria, U.S.-educated migrants are more likely to be employed. This is to be expected, since the quality of education is higher in the United States than in most developing countries. Furthermore, for many migrants, completing their education in the United States is the path to permanent migration.[5] However, we see significant variation between countries, especially for migrants who completed their education at home prior to migration. Migrants from Western and Eastern European countries as well as African countries have the highest levels of labor market participation. In contrast, East Asian countries, such as Japan, Taiwan (China), and Republic of Korea, and Middle Eastern countries have the lowest levels of employment. Earlier, we pointed out that migrants from Latin American and Caribbean countries have relatively low levels of employment compared to migrants from other regions, especially Europe and Africa. Moreover, there is a significant gap in the labor market participation rates of migrants from Latin America compared to migrants from other regions, as presented in table 6.2. It is now apparent that a large portion of the low level of employment is due to low levels of education. Even though there is still a considerable gap in the likelihood of employment for an identically educated Mexican and European migrant, the gap is much lower when education levels are taken into account.

Another interesting exercise is to consider how the predicted probability of employment changes over time. In order to accomplish this, we chose six source countries: Canada, China, India, Mexico, Nigeria, and the United Kingdom. We plotted the predicted probability of employment for the artificial individual by changing the years in the United States (and naturally the age of the migrant). Those predictions are presented in figure 6.6.

In year 0, the migrant, who was educated at home with a college degree, is assumed to be 29 years old; she has just arrived in the United States and has no child or grandmother in the house. She is married to a spouse with the same nationality. These variables do not change; the only variables to change are her age and years in the United States over time. The initial predicted probability of employment is highest for the Nigerian migrant, followed by the Canadian, Chinese, British, Indian, and, finally, Mexican migrants. The predicted probabilities are increasing at a decreasing rate; the assimilation effect is stronger at the beginning and declines over time. At the end of 10 years, our artificial Nigerian migrant has an 80 percent likelihood of employment, whereas the Mexican migrant has only a 60 percent likelihood of employment.

The final exercise we perform is to analyze the marginal effects of the other variables we have used. In table 6.4, we return to our artificial migrant: she is

Figure 6.6. Predicted Probability of Employment for an Identical Person over Time

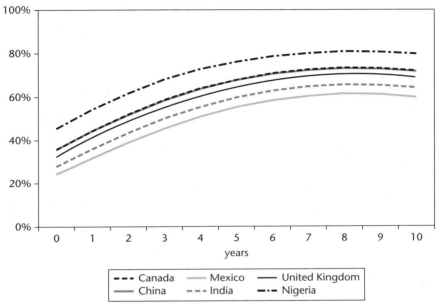

Predicted probability of employment versus years in the United States

Legend:
- --- Canada
- China
- Mexico
- --- India
- United Kingdom
- --- Nigeria

Source: U.S. 2000 census data.

35 years old, arrived in 1994, has a bachelor's degree obtained at home, is married to a husband with the same nationality, and has no children. This is our "base" case, and we take three home countries: Canada, China, and Mexico. The first column presents the predicted probability of employment. For our base case, the predicted probability of employment is 45.8 percent for the Mexican and 59 percent for the Canadian and Chinese migrants. Now we change one variable at a time. If we increase the age of the migrant by 1 (the second row for each country), the predicted probability of employment increases by around 0.50 percent. If we change the years in the United States by 1, the predicted probability increases by around 1.1 percent. Education has a larger effect, with an extra year of education increasing the probability by around 2.4 percent, whereas the first child decreases the probability of employment by around 3.6 percent. However, the largest effect arises from the marital status of the migrant. Never being married increases the employment probability by around 12 percent compared to a woman married to a person with the same nationality. Being married to an American increases the employment probability by more than 4 percent. Naturally, these results do not

Table 6.4. Predicted Probability of Employment, Wages, and Market Placement in Select Countries

Country and variable	Probability of employment (percent)	Wage (U.S.$ thousand)	Job placement index
Mexico			
Base	45.77	21.09	11.36
Age + 1	46.27	21.15	11.35
Years in U.S. + 1	46.89	21.49	11.39
Education years +1	48.10	23.83	11.94
Number of children + 1	42.12	20.85	11.34
Grandmother at home	46.25	21.12	11.37
Married to an American	49.62	21.33	11.39
Single	57.92	21.83	11.43
Canada			
Base	58.99	34.33	12.84
Age + 1	59.48	34.43	12.83
Years in U.S. + 1	60.08	34.98	12.87
Education years + 1	61.25	38.77	13.41
Number of children + 1	55.36	33.99	12.82
Grandmother at home	59.46	34.38	12.84
Married to an American	62.70	34.68	12.86
Single	70.31	35.38	12.90
China			
Base	58.76	23.55	12.12
Age + 1	59.25	23.62	12.11
Years in U.S. + 1	59.86	23.99	12.15
Education years + 1	61.03	26.59	12.69
Number of children + 1	55.13	23.31	12.10
Grandmother at home	59.23	23.58	12.12
Married to an American	62.48	23.78	12.14
Single	70.11	24.27	12.18

Source: U.S. 2000 census data.

Note: Base is a woman who was 35 years old in 2000, has been in the United States for six years, was educated at home, has a college degree, is married with no children, is married to the same nationality, and has no grandmother in the house.

imply that migrants should divorce their husband or marry an American man in order to find employment, but they reflect complex relationships and trade-offs between labor market outcomes and family formation decisions. These results might imply a selection effect, as working women are more likely to meet and marry American men. Or women might decide to stay single to pursue a career. This result is consistent with the findings of Meng and Gregory (2005), who find that intermarried immigrants earn higher wages; they attribute these results to faster assimilation.

Labor Market Performance

The next main question is about the labor market performance of migrant women. This is the second stage of our estimation, and, as described earlier, we use two separate measures of performance. The first one, wage, is the standard one used in the labor economics literature and needs no further explanation. It is especially appropriate in this context because most migration decisions are based on the wide wage gap between the source and destination countries' labor market for all skill levels. Thus the wages earned by the migrants become an important measure of their performance and the extent of their assimilation in the destination labor market.

Earnings do not reveal what immigrants actually do, even though they are likely to be highly correlated with occupational choices. The type of jobs a migrant finds, especially highly educated ones, is of interest as well. For this purpose, we use the average education level of the occupation of the migrant. As discussed earlier, we calculate the average education level for each occupation category taking into account all the people employed in each occupation, including native-born Americans and migrant men. This is a measure of the skill level of the occupation. For example, if a migrant with 16 years of education is employed in an occupation where the average education level is only 10 years, then there is significant misallocation of human capital and the migrant is "underplaced" in the labor market. There might be several reasons for this underperformance, and these are explored in detail for male migrants in Mattoo et al. (2005).

The first stage of our estimation is discussed earlier and presented in table 6.3. Now table 6.5 presents the coefficients from the second stage of our estimation controlling for cohort and education and location differences. The only variables in this stage are years of education, age and years in the United States (and their squares), as well as the country dummy variables. Again all of the variables have the expected signs. For example, years of education has a negative sign, but its square has a positive sign. The squared term strongly dominates (after three years), so the net effects for all relevant education levels are positive. When we compare cohorts, we do not see much difference in the effects of education, age, or years in the United States on wages or placement for the home-educated migrants. However, the effects are stronger for the U.S.-educated migrants. Education has a bigger positive impact for the U.S.-educated migrants, especially in terms of

Table 6.5. Second Stage of Heckman Selection Estimation

| | Home educated | | | | U.S. educated | | | |
| | 1990s arrivals | | 1980s arrivals | | 1990s arrivals | | 1980s arrivals | |
Variable	Wage (1)	Placement (2)	Wage (3)	Placement (4)	Wage (5)	Placement (6)	Wage (7)	Placement (8)
Years of education	−0.06 (19.12)***	−0.29 (38.87)***	−0.059 (16.16)***	−0.246 (32.88)***	−0.023 (1.04)	−0.716 (14.29)***	−0.134 (12.68)***	−0.441 (18.11)***
Years of education squared	0.006 (34.29)***	0.029 (69.08)***	0.006 (30.35)***	0.027 (60.58)***	0.004 (4.03)***	0.045 (21.04)***	0.008 (17.88)***	0.034 (31.72)***
Age in 2000	0.021 (9.37)***	−0.018 (3.56)***	−0.004 (0.86)	−0.041 (4.63)***	0.272 (12.42)***	−0.286 (8.55)***	0.08 (12.04)***	−0.121 (9.53)***
Age in 2000 squared	0 (9.55)***	0 (0.48)	0 (0.32)	0 (3.20)***	−0.004 (10.09)***	0.005 (7.60)***	−0.001 (7.89)***	0.002 (8.27)***
Years in the United States	0.014 (2.70)***	−0.058 (5.16)***	0.013 (1.09)	0.022 (0.83)	0.124 (9.20)***	−0.178 (6.69)***	−0.011 (0.71)	0.02 (0.57)
Years in the United States squared	0 (0.32)	0.006 (6.58)***	0 (0.21)	0 (0.21)	−0.007 (7.67)***	0.013 (6.09)***	0 (0.60)	0 (0.42)
Constant	9.155 (40.36)***	12.038 (16.72)***	10.034 (26.33)***	12.149 (36.11)***	4.944 (10.71)***	17.981 (21.29)***	10.672 (33.38)***	15.013 (21.11)***
Number of observations	174,596	174,596	109,679	109,679	50,293	50,293	67,700	67,700

Source: U.S. 2000 census data.

Note: Robust *z* statistics are in parentheses. Country dummies are included.

***Significant at 1 percent.

**Significant at 5 percent.

*Significant at 10 percent.

placement. This indicates that U.S. education is naturally more valued in the labor market.

We now turn to our predicted values for wages and labor market placement in order to compare migrants from different countries. Our artificial migrant is the same one we used earlier: she is 35 years old, has a bachelor's degree, arrived in the United States in 1994, is married to a husband of the same nationality, and has no children. Figure 6.7 presents the predicted wages for these identical migrants from different countries. First, except in the case of Australia and South Africa, U.S.-educated migrants are predicted to earn more than their home-educated counterparts. In some cases, the gap is rather significant. However, we again see large variations in predicted wages based on the country of origin even if migrants completed their education in the United States. This effect might be due to differences in the professions chosen by migrants or to cultural and social explanations that are beyond the scope of this chapter. Another possibility is that there are selection effects based on professional categories. For example, East Asian and Western European women might be choosing careers at the high end of the salary range (such as finance or engineering) where the gap is highest between their home country and the United States. For lower-paying skilled jobs (such as in education or humanities), they might prefer not to migrate or decide to return home after finishing their education in the United States.

The predicted wage gaps are even higher for home-educated migrants, as expected, since the quality and level of human capital acquired in different countries are more likely to differ even if people have the same diploma. As a result, migrants from English-speaking countries, whether these are developed countries such as the United Kingdom, Ireland, or Australia or developing countries such as India and Kenya, have higher predicted wages. The lowest wages are for Latin American and Caribbean countries, which reflect lower levels of educational quality and certain selection effects. Since it is easier for a Mexican migrant to enter the United States, compared to an Indian migrant, whether through legal or informal channels, we expect the Indian migrant to have higher human capital or earning potential, even for people with the same notional education level. This is clearly displayed in figure 6.7.

We also plot the change in the wages of identical migrants from different countries over time for the same artificial migrant we use in figure 6.6, and we only change her years in the United States and her age. The predicted wages are presented in figure 6.8. The Canadian and British migrants have the highest predicted wages, followed by the Indian, Nigerian, Chinese, and Mexican migrants. Nigerian and Chinese migrants have higher predicted probabilities of employment than Canadian and British migrants, but their wages are much lower. Interestingly, the wage gap increases over time in dollar terms but is stable in relative terms. Over a

Figure 6.7. Predicted Wages for an Identical Person

Predicted wage (US$ thousands)-1990s arrival

■ home educated   ■ U.S. educated

Source: U.S. 2000 census data.

Figure 6.8. Predicted Wage for an Identical Person over Time

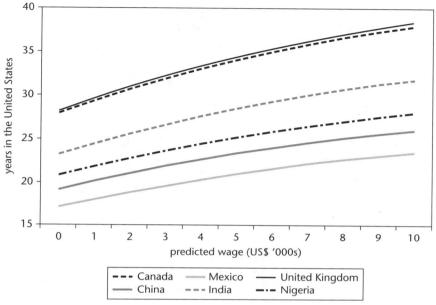

Source: U.S. 2000 census data.

period of 10 years, these migrants are predicted to increase their wages by around 35 percent. This change is due to both the increase in labor market experience and economic and social assimilation effects.

Our final exercise with respect to wages is to estimate the impact of changes in the other variables, as we did with employment probabilities. These are presented in the second column of table 6.4. Our base migrant from Canada is predicted to earn $34,300, whereas the Mexican and the Chinese migrants earn $21,100 and $23,500, respectively. An increase in their age, years in the United States, number of children, or change in their marital status has an expected, but marginal, impact on their wages. These results imply that these variables, especially marital status variables, have an impact on the employment decision of women, but not on their labor market performance. However, an extra year of education increases their predicted wages significantly. The increase is $2,700 for the Mexican, $3,000 for the Chinese, and $4,400 for the Canadian migrant. These numbers can be interpreted as the return to education in the U.S. labor market. When summed over the career of a migrant—say, 20 years—the return to education is rather high.

Our final labor market performance variable—occupational placement and predicted levels according to different countries—is presented in figure 6.9. Recall

Figure 6.9. Employment Placement for an Identical Person: 1990 Arrivals

Source: U.S. 2000 census data.

that our artificial migrant has a college degree, which translates into 14 years of education in the estimation. There is again large variation across countries, and the gaps are larger for the home-educated migrants, as is the case with predicted wages. Home-educated migrants from many Western European countries are placed in higher-skilled jobs. This result might indicate that many European-educated female migrants choose higher-skilled but lower-paying jobs in the United States compared to their fellow citizens who finish their education in the United States. Employment placement is especially low for home-educated migrants from Latin America, indicating that they end up not only with lower wages but also in jobs that are relatively low skilled compared to their nominal education level. Another surprise is the relatively high-skilled placement from the Middle Eastern and African countries. We can argue that labor market participation of Middle Eastern women is rather low and, as a result, only the highly qualified end up working and that this selection bias results in high placement. However, African women have high employment rates so the selection bias is not present. But it is another puzzle why their wages are low given their high-skilled placement. Finally, we observe that the placement levels of Eastern European women are rather low. This might be partially due to the sudden inflow of migrants in the 1990s and the mismatch between their education under the previous communist regime and the demands of the U.S. labor market.

Our final exercise is to examine the impact of changes in other variables on labor market placement, which are presented in the last column of table 6.4. We use the same migrant for our predictions. If she is from Mexico, she is predicted to be placed in an occupation that requires, on average, 11.36 years of education. The level increases to 12.12 if she is from China and to 12.84 if she is from Canada. These results again reflect the varying valuation of their home education in the U.S. market. As is the case with wages, changes in age, years in the United States, number of children, and marital status have only a marginal impact on the migrant's labor market placement regardless of her home country. However, an extra year of education, regardless of the home country, increases the placement level by around 0.6 unit.[6] This again indicates the importance of education in labor market outcomes, especially for migrants, and this is in addition to its impact on employment levels.

Conclusions

Women constitute close to half of all migrants in the United States. Many women migrate together with their family; others migrate alone and send remittances to support their family back home. Some migrate as children with their parents; others go abroad to complete their education and then settle in the host country.

Whatever the patterns and reasons might be, women's labor market participation and performance levels are not properly explored in the migration and development literature. This chapter seeks to contribute to the nexus of gender, development, and migration research agenda.

We use data from the U.S. 2000 census to analyze jointly the labor market participation and performance levels of migrant women. We divide the sample into four groups based on the decade of arrival and location of education and perform the analysis separately for each group. We use two measures of performance: wage and skill level of the occupation of the migrant; the latter is a proxy for the quality of the job that the migrant obtains. The data reveal large variations in education, participation, and performance levels based on the country of origin. Latin American migrants have much lower levels of participation and performance, but this is mostly due to lower education levels. African and Eastern European migrants have higher levels of participation, but lower levels of performance. Asian and Middle Eastern women have low levels of participation and high levels of performance. Women educated in Western Europe and the United States perform much better in every dimension, mainly due to the higher human capital provided by their education. Nevertheless, education levels are the most important variables influencing labor market outcomes, regardless of where they were obtained. An extra year of education, even if obtained in a developing country, increases performance significantly. Other social and demographic variables, such as marital status and number of children, have the expected impact on participation levels, but almost no effect on performances.

Our results have important policy implications. The first is for the design of education policies in developing countries. Significant public and private resources are being spent on those who might make little use of this education because they decide not to enter the labor force or end up being employed in a low-skilled job in the destination country. Having a better sense of what is awaiting them in the destination-country labor market should help individuals and countries to improve their allocation of resources for education. If brain drain and brain waste are a major concern, then it is socially and individually more efficient to use private funds for potential migrants' education. One successful example is the privately financed education of nurses in the Philippines, which uses an American curriculum to train students for the U.S. labor market.

There are also important implications for the design of immigration policies in destination countries. First, there is a need to properly design family unification and employment policies. Under many visa categories in the United States, spouses of migrants (even if the migrants are permanent residents) are prevented from being employed and attending school; this leads to significant waste and erosion of human capital. Such policies disproportionately affect women, who often follow their husband abroad. Second, employment decisions of many migrant women are strongly influenced by personal, cultural, and social preferences. These need to be carefully taken into account in the design of policies.

Endnotes

1. Mattoo et al. (2005) explore the "brain waste" among educated migrant men.

2. This is not necessarily the case with migrant men, as shown in Mattoo et al. (2005). One interpretation is that most migrant men need to work even if they do not face promising prospects in the labor market and end up in lower-paying and lower-ranking jobs even if they are educated. However, women can simply exit the labor force and take care of household responsibilities.

3. Extracts from the census samples were made through the Integrated Public Use Microdata Series (http://www.ipums.org).

4. We consider a migrant to be in the labor force if she is listed as "working" in the census and her wages are reported to be higher than U.S.$5,000.

5. This also has to do with immigration policy, because migrants educated in the United States are eligible for a temporary visa on graduation, which allows them to enter the labor market and apply for permanent residency. This process is more difficult for migrants completing their education abroad.

6. This is a *marginal* effect of an extra year of education for somebody who already has a college degree.

References

Baker, Michael, and Dwayne Benjamin. 1994. "The Performance of Immigrants in the Canadian Labor Market." *Journal of Labor Economics* 12 (3): 369–405.

———. 1997. "The Role of the Family in Immigrants' Labor Market Activity." *American Economic Review* 87 (4): 705–27.

Bhagwati, Jagdish, ed. 1976. *The Brain Drain and Taxation: Theory and Empirical Analysis.* Amsterdam: North-Holland.

Bhagwati, Jagdish, and Koichi Hamada. 1974. "The Brain Drain, International Integration of Markets for Professionals, and Unemployment: A Theoretical Analysis." *Journal of Development Economics* 1 (1): 19–42.

Borjas, George. 1985. "Assimilation, Changes in Cohort Quality, and the Earnings of Immigrants." *Journal of Labor Economics* 3 (4): 463–89.

———. 1987. "Self-Selection and Earnings of Immigrants." *American Economic Review* 77 (4): 531–53.

———. 1994. "The Economics of Immigration." *Journal of Economic Literature* 32 (4): 1667–717.

Chiswick, Barry R. 1978. "The Effect of Americanization of the Earnings of Foreign-Born Men." *Journal of Political Economy* 86 (5): 897–921.

———. 1985. "Is the New Immigration More Unskilled Than the Old?" Working Paper E-85-6. Hoover Institution, Stanford University, Palo Alto, CA.

Cobb-Clark, Deborah. 1993. "Immigrant Selectivity and Wages: The Evidence for Women." *American Economic Review* 83 (4): 986–93.

Commander, Simon, Mari Kangasniemi, and L. Alan Winters. 2003. *The Brain Drain: Curse or Boom?* IZA Discussion Paper 809. Bonn: Institute for the Study of Labor (IZA).

Docquier, Frédéric, and Abdeslam Marfouk. 2006. "International Migration by Educational Attainment, 1990–2000." In *International Migration, Remittances, and the Brain Drain*, ed. Çağlar Özden and Maurice Schiff, 151–200. New York: Palgrave Macmillan.

Duleep, Harriett O., and Seth Sanders. 1993. "The Decision to Work by Married Immigrant Women." *Industrial and Labor Relations Review* 46 (4): 677–90.

————. 1994. "Empirical Regularities across Cultures: The Effect of Children on Woman's Work." *Journal of Human Resources* 29 (2): 328–47.

Friedberg, Rachel M. 2000. "You Can't Take It with You: Immigrant Assimilation and the Portability of Human Capital." *Journal of Labor Economics* 18 (2): 221–51.

Green, David A. 1999. "Immigrant Occupational Attainment: Assimilation and Mobility over Time." *Journal of Labor Economics* 17 (1): 4–79.

Heckman, James J. 1979. "Sample Selection Bias as a Specification Error." *Econometrica* 47 (1): 151–62.

Long, James E. 1980. "The Effect of Americanization on Earnings: Some Evidence for Women." *Journal of Political Economy* 88 (3): 620–29.

Mattoo, Aaditya, Ileana Cristina Neagu, and Çağlar Özden. 2005. "Brain Waste? Educated Immigrants in the U.S. Labor Market." Policy Research Working Paper 3581. World Bank, Washington, DC.

Meng, Xin, and Robert Gregory. 2005. "Intermarriage and the Economic Assimilation of Immigrants." *Journal of Labor Economics* 23 (1): 135–76.

Puri, Shivani, and Tineke Ritzema. 2000. "Migrant Worker Remittances, Micro-Finance, and the Informal Economy: Prospects and Issues." Working Paper 21. International Labour Organisation, Social Finance Unit.

Schoeni, Robert F. 1998. "Labor Market Assimilation of Immigrant Women." *Industrial and Labor Relations Review* 51 (3): 483–504.

Vella, Francis. 1998. "Estimating Models with Sample Selection Bias." *Journal of Human Resources* 33 (1): 127–69.

7

LOOKING AHEAD:
FUTURE DIRECTIONS
FOR RESEARCH
AND POLICY

Andrew R. Morrison and Maurice Schiff

This chapter provides a forward-looking discussion that elaborates on the findings and conclusions from the various chapters in this volume and links those to policies. The chapter is structured around a number of research and policy issues that need to be addressed in the near future in order to enhance our understanding of the nexus of gender, migration, and development and to improve related policies. The chapter is divided into five sections. The first section focuses on issues related to the determinants of women's migration, the second addresses the economic impacts of female migration, the third discusses its noneconomic impacts, and the fourth presents issues related to temporary and circular migration (including mode IV). The final section addresses some methodological issues.

Determinants

As noted in chapter 1, the participation of women in international migration has grown over time; currently, women represent almost half of all international migrants. A growing number of women—married and unmarried—migrate alone or with other migrants outside of their family circle (UNFPA 2006; Piper 2005). As demonstrated in this volume, however, the gender composition of migration stocks varies substantially from country to country.

Many questions remain to be answered regarding the determinants of female and male migration. For instance, do levels of gender equality in sending and receiving nations matter—that is, do women migrate from countries with low levels of gender equality to countries with higher levels of gender equality? Clearly, to the extent that increased gender equality is associated with higher wages for women, we would expect this to be the case. Thus greater gender equality in receiving (sending) countries would result in larger (smaller) flows of female immigration. But does equality matter above and beyond any effect it has on labor market insertion and wages? Anecdotal evidence (see, for example, Ehrenreich and Hochschild 2003) show that women in abusive relationships with their husband or in-laws tend to use migration as a strategy for escaping abuse. Evidence from Massey et al. (2006) shows that women living in patriarchal societies (Mexico and Costa Rica) display lower rates of emigration than their male counterparts, whereas matrifocal countries (Nicaragua and the Dominican Republic) have higher rates of female than male migration. This issue has not been examined systematically, and it warrants more investigation.

Another determinant of female migration is the level of women's empowerment. A significant body of noneconomic literature examines the relationship between international migration and the empowerment of women. As Hugo (2000) notes, "Migration can be both a cause and consequence of female empowerment." The relationship between migration and empowerment is far from linear. According to Hugo (2000), whether or not migration results in increased empowerment hinges on the context in which the migration occurs, the type of movement, and the characteristics of the female migrants.

The relationship between migration and the empowerment of women also hinges on the definition of empowerment used. World Bank (2002) defines empowerment as "the expansion of assets and capabilities of poor people to participate in, negotiate with, influence, control, and hold accountable institutions that affect their lives." Drèze and Sen (2002) define women's empowerment as "altering relations of power . . . which constrain women's options and autonomy and adversely affect health and well-being." While there are multiple definitions—both theoretical and operational—of women's empowerment, a small number of concepts are common to many: options, choice, control, and power. There are frequent references to women's ability to make decisions and influence outcomes that are important to them and their families (Malhotra, Schuler, and Boender 2002).

The fluidity of the notion of empowerment makes it difficult to compare findings across the relatively large body of studies in this area. Both qualitative and quantitative research will be needed to understand the relationship between migration and women's empowerment. Methodological aspects of estimating the determinants of migration are discussed later in this chapter.

Economic Impacts of Migration

Similar to men, many women migrate to increase their income and send remittances that are spent on the household members back home. A number of studies have shown that remittances result in lower levels of household poverty and higher levels of expenditures on education, health, housing, and other investments, and the fact that women's contribution to household expenditures increases after migration may increase their power to influence the allocation of these expenditures.

Female Migrants' Impact on Household Welfare: The Role of Household, Community, and Society

The literature on intra-household expenditures (presented in chapter 5 in this volume) finds that women tend to spend their income in ways that lead to better child development outcomes and more immediate reductions in household poverty than does an equivalent amount of income in the hands of men. Thus if female migration raises women's level of empowerment and income, it might be expected to generate these benefits for the household; it is unclear, however, whether the findings on women's allocation of expenditures generalize to increases in empowerment and income that result from women's migration.

One of the reasons for this uncertainty is that the gender-specific impact of migration on household welfare is likely to depend on a number of household, community, and overall social, cultural, and economic characteristics in source countries and receiving countries as well as on the type of migration, and these may have different implications for male and female migrants. For instance, the existence of older children who can look after the younger ones is likely to be more important when women migrate than when men do. Another issue is that the cost of illegal relative to legal migration is likely to be greater for female than for male migrants because women are more vulnerable to abuse.

Household members in the home country are likely to benefit from women's migration if migration empowers women and gives them greater control over household expenditures. The answer to this question may depend on the counterfactual situation selected. One possibility is to compare the case of women's migration with that of no migration. Another possibility is to compare it to that of migration of a male household member, household head, oldest son, and so forth. It is possible that the migration of a mother has negative impacts on various noneconomic aspects of household welfare, particularly on children's welfare and family stability; however, some existing research documents positive effects on the educational outcomes of children left behind, although this research has not distinguished to date between the impact of absent mothers and absent fathers.[1]

Hence whether the net impact of women's migration on household or children's welfare is positive or negative remains an open question that still needs to be answered.

Sending-Country Wages and Unemployment

An important aspect of migration that is not captured in household surveys is its potential benefit in terms of raising wages and reducing unemployment in migrants' countries of origin. This benefit is potentially very important in reducing poverty. How male and female wages in sending countries are affected by both male and female migration is an important issue where research would most likely have returns.

Fungibility and Agency Problems

The impact of the migration of women on the allocation of household expenditures depends on the degree of control they are able to exercise within the household. This degree of control is constrained by the fact that they live in another country than the rest of the household. Two types of problems exist that limit the increase in women's empowerment: fungibility and agency problems.

Fungibility

Under fungibility, expenditures can be shifted among different types of expenditures so that one cannot identify the source of income used for the various expenditure items. Thus a woman who remits and stipulates that a certain amount must be spent on a certain item—for example, girls' education—cannot be sure that the allocation to this expenditure item will actually increase because household members could reduce the allocation of resources previously spent (that is, spent in the pre-migration situation) on that item in order to spend the freed resources on other items. Ensuring that remittances do result in an increased allocation to the item specified by the female migrant in the presence of fungibility requires that the female migrant stipulate that a *greater* amount be spent on that item than was previously spent.

Agency Problems

Another factor affecting women's control over spending relates to the agency problem, some elements of which are discussed in chapter 5. The woman who migrates (that is, the principal) wants the remittances she sends home to be allocated to specific expenditure items and in specific amounts. The adult in the household who is charged with the allocation of expenditures (that is, the agent) may have a different utility curve than the principal. The problem for the migrant is that she may not have full control over the agent's allocation decisions. As explained below, the agency problem has several causes, including asymmetric information (the migrant may not know how expenditures are allocated at home), lack of overall control, and time-inconsistency associated with reference-dependent preferences.

Second, in addition to the lack of perfect control over the spending of remittances, the migrant has imperfect control over the labor force participation of the remaining adult(s). With the income obtained from remittances, the husband left behind may decide to reduce his hours of work partly or entirely. In male-dominated cultures, the husband's self-esteem may also suffer and may lead him to behavioral patterns that are not in the household's interest, over and above the reduction in labor force participation, including dissipating savings designed for investment such as for improvements to the family house (Ehrenreich and Hochschild 2003).

Third, under asymmetric information, female migrants may not know the precise allocation of expenditures because the agent (the husband, some other member of the household, or someone else such as an uncle or cousin) shares only limited information. Alternatively, the agent may not be entirely truthful about the information provided.

Fourth, even if female migrants have full information and exercise full control over a number of specific items, they may not have full information and control over items that they care about. In that case, female migrants' demands related to the set of items they care about may have limited impact on household (children's) welfare and may even be counterproductive. For instance, the male head of household or other individuals (that is, other agents) taking care of the children may react by threatening to take some action that may not be in the children's interest.

Numerous examples of migrant women exercising limited control over the allocation of household expenditures are provided in Ehrenreich and Hochschild (2003). Various contributors describe cases where women return home after spending several years abroad only to find that their husband did not spend the remittances they sent on additional education for their children or on building a larger house, but instead used them mostly for his own needs. Remittances may also be spent on individuals not specified by the female migrants, especially in cases where her children are taken care of by her siblings or in-laws or where the husband has established a relationship with another woman.

The analysis applies to male migrants as well: their control over women's decisions on the allocation of household expenditures may be limited because of fungibility and agency problems, which increases women's decision-making power over household expenditure allocations and activities. There is, however, a difference between the impact of male and female migration on women's decision-making power due to the relative power of the adult male and female members of the household before migration takes place. Men tend to be dominant in the household in many, if not most, source countries. Because women's initial decision-making power is relatively low, their migration is likely to raise it. However, men's dominance may be sufficiently strong in some cases that they might be able to maintain it following women's migration, in which case the increase in women's decision-making power is likely to be limited. Some of the examples in Ehrenreich and Hochschild (2003) illustrate such a situation.

Assuming, as is claimed in the intra-household expenditure literature, that women spend their income in ways that lead to better child development outcomes and more immediate reductions in household poverty, what policy interventions could be implemented to minimize the agency problem that limits female migrants' control over the allocation of household expenditures? One option would be to develop a system in which the woman pays directly into a bank account from which money can be expended only on the types of goods and services that the woman remitter has selected (for example, for a girl's education). However, this approach would still be subject to the fungibility problem.

Another way to solve the agency problem would be to develop innovative technological solutions. Card-based instruments, such as stored value cards or credit cards, are frequently used to send remittances to locations that have access to card-processing machines. Cellular phones are also increasingly used in Kenya, the Philippines, and other countries as a safe way of transferring remittances. Through other systems such as iKabo.com, remitters can send their money over the Internet (World Bank 2006). All these technologies lower the cost of sending remittances and thus raise household welfare. They might also empower women migrants by reducing the agency problem because of the reduction in information costs and the greater ease of sending money to the intended target.[2] It is important to acknowledge, however, that these solutions may not fully solve the fungibility problem.

Noneconomic Impacts

All of the impacts of female migration tend to have economic implications, whether directly or indirectly. We define here the "noneconomic" impact of female migration as the impact on variables other than education, health, housing, labor force participation, small business formation, and other variables that are typically examined in economic studies of migration. These variables have been examined by sociologists, demographers, and others, although very little, if at all, by economists. However, examining these effects is crucial because they affect the overall impact of migration and may turn a positive economic impact on household welfare into a negative one.

Fertility

A topic that has been of particular interest to migration researchers has been the impact of female migration—both international and internal—on the fertility of migrants. Prior research has looked at the possible effects of adaptation to destination fertility norms, diffusion, and assimilation. The most careful research has corrected for possible selection effects, the impact of spousal separation during the migration process, and income effects (Lindstrom and Saucedo 2002; Brockerhoff and Yang 1994). The remaining challenges in modeling the impact of international migration on migrant women's fertility relate to modeling the proximate determinants of fertility and how these proximate determinants, in turn, are modified by the act of migration. Recent research by Jensen and Ahlburg (2004) on migration in the Philippines notes that the large impact of migration on fertility disappears if migration is not followed by work for pay.

An interesting study by Fargues (2006) examines the impact of migration on fertility of women in *source* countries. This impact is hypothesized to take place through various channels, including information flows and demonstration effects. Fargues finds that fertility declined in Morocco and Turkey, where migration was to Western Europe, a low-fertility region. In contrast, most of Egypt's migration was to high-fertility countries in the Gulf, and its fertility failed to decline. The paper provides strong evidence on correlations over time between the level of migration and remittances, on the one hand, and fertility levels, on the other.

As for the research agenda in this context, one issue that has not been examined is the source-country fertility impact of male migration, female migration, and joint migration. One hypothesis to be tested is that female migration has a greater impact on source-country fertility than male migration. Fargues (2006) considers the reduction in source-country fertility to be beneficial for these countries; if so, female migration would be preferable to male migration from this viewpoint. More empirical work is also needed on the links between migration and gender, bargaining power, labor force participation, and fertility.

Family Cohesion

Another important aspect of migration that seems to have been ignored in the literature is its impact on family cohesion. Women tend to be the center of the household that holds the family together. Hence their migration is more likely to result in a breakdown of the family than the migration of men. In the Philippines, the migration of women is sometimes referred to as a "Philippine divorce" (Parreñas Salazar 2003). However, migration may be women's only way to escape an abusive husband or in-laws. The impact of female and male migration on family structure, divorce rates, and other measures of family cohesion is an area that warrants more research in the future.

Reference-Dependent Preferences

Individuals may have reference-dependent preferences. These may include preferences that are dependent on past consumption. In the case of female migration, the remaining members of the household may have suffered from the departure of the adult female but have become accustomed to living without her over time—that is, they already paid the price of her absence.[3] Moreover, they may also have become accustomed to a higher standard of living and new resource allocation. In other words, their preferences have changed over time. This would not be a problem if households made optimal *household* decisions and foresaw all of these effects.

However, it is likely that some of these effects were not foreseen when the migration of the female took place, and some households might be worse off than in the absence of migration. Nevertheless, once female migration has taken place and new habits have been formed, the new optimum may be for it to continue. Examples are provided in Ehrenreich and Hochschild (2003) of women who return home to face a worse situation than they expected to find and nevertheless return to their job in the host country and continue sending remittances.

Children's Welfare

Another area that deserves more attention is the impact of male and female migration on the welfare and development of children left behind. The first, most basic question to answer is whether these children fare better or worse on a series of developmental measures, such as education and psychological and physical health, than children of nonmigrants, and whether the impact on these developmental measures differs depending on the sex of the migrant.

One might expect poorer outcomes with regard to education, as shown in the voluminous literature on the negative outcomes associated with single-parent families. However, remittances from an absent household member may allow the purchase of higher-quality schooling, which promotes better educational outcomes. In practice, the little research on this topic has tended to show a positive impact in most countries. Acosta (2007) shows for El Salvador and Mansuri (2007) for Pakistan that migration and remittances result in an increase in the level of education for both girls and boys. In fact, in Pakistan, the increase is much larger for girls—for example, migration increases girls' school enrollment by as much as 54 percent compared with just 7 percent for boys. In the case of El Salvador, migration and remittances reduce the level of absenteeism of boys and girls during primary education and prolong the education of girls, but not of boys, beyond age 14.

In the Philippines, recent research finds that, due to the higher incomes associated with remittances, children of migrants are much more likely to attend private schools than children of nonmigrants. Within each school, children of migrants receive slightly higher grades than children of nonmigrants (Scalabrini Migration Center 2004, cited in Piper 2005; Bryant 2005). Another study on the Philippines shows that an increase in remittances results in greater school attendance and a reduction in child labor (Yang and Martínez 2006). Other research, however, shows migrant and nonmigrant Filipino children with essentially identical academic performance and probabilities of attending school (Bryant 2005).

In terms of expenditure patterns in households left behind by migrants, chapter 5 in this volume explores whether expenditure patterns are influenced by the sex of the migrant sending the remittances and the sex of the household head receiving the remittances. The authors find that households receiving remittances from women allocate a larger expenditure share on health and other goods, but a lower share on food, than do households receiving remittances from men.[4] These allocations have implications for the welfare of children living in the receiving households.

In addition to educational outcomes, it is frequently argued that children of absent migrants suffer from psychological problems or problems with interpersonal relations. However, existing research (again from the Philippines) finds no difference between children of migrants and children of nonmigrants along the following dimensions: Social Anxiety Scale for Children, Children's Loneliness Scale, relationship problems, psychological problems, or likelihood of having premarital sex, drinking alcohol, or smoking (Scalabrini Migration Center 2004; Battistella and Conaco 1998; Choe et al. 2004, cited in Bryant 2005). Similar research from Indonesia and Thailand supports these broad findings, with one exception. The presence of both parents in Thailand does seem to lower the risk that an adolescent will smoke, drink, or have premarital sex (Choe et al. 2004).

Although the bulk of the evidence for these three countries points to the fact that children who are left behind do not suffer disproportionately compared to other children, solid research from other parts of the world is warranted in order to explore this issue further. The issue is particularly important given the broader impact that an adverse effect of migration on children's psychological health might have for society. Children who are angry and depressed because of their parent's absence are unlikely to be as good and productive spouses, parents, or members of society as children who have benefited from their parent's presence. Hence they may generate negative externalities for the source country. In other words, even if households maximize household welfare and foresee all of the effects of female migration, their decisions may not be optimal from the viewpoint of society or future generations.

It is particularly important to discern whether the impact of migration on children is influenced by the gender of the absent parent. The existing research on this topic is quite scanty. A 2002 study by the University of the Philippines finds that respondents are more likely to "be sad or worried about their family" if the mother is absent than if the father is absent, while the 2003 study by the Scalabrini Migration Center finds that, on average, children miss an absent mother more than an absent father (University of the Philippines, Tel Aviv University, and KAIBIGAN 2002; Scalabrini Migration Center 2004). Examples are also provided in Ehrenreich and Hochschild (2003) of children who grow up without their mother being severely depressed, particularly if the mother left when they were young. Given the importance of this issue and the dearth of significant evidence, research in this area should have a high rate of return.

As mentioned above, few, if any, of these "noneconomic" effects have been examined by economists. Developing a framework that would allow these effects to be incorporated in the analysis of the impact of female migration should constitute an important element of the research agenda.

In terms of policy options, various types of interventions might help to minimize children's noneconomic costs from women's migration. First, the authorities could launch a targeted information campaign that would raise parents' awareness of these issues so that they can be incorporated in their decision-making process. Second, community arrangements helpful to children might be negotiated, including paying someone they trust to take care of the children on a part-time basis or to help with various tasks within the household. Third, since children obtain an important part of their resources in school, where they have access to education and (often) food and to less tangible resources such as friendship and possibly guidance, schools could be given more responsibility (and resources) in order to monitor the welfare of children with one or more absent parents and take action when needed. A related approach would be to target youth development interventions to children with absent parents, including mentoring programs and after-school programs.

Trafficking of Women

This volume focuses on economic aspects of women's migration in source-countries and on women's labor market performance in the United States; it does not include an analysis of female trafficking. However, this section is included here because of (a) the global importance of trafficking—the International Labour Organisation estimates that at least 2.45 million trafficking victims are currently being exploited and that another 1.2 million are trafficked annually, both across and within national borders; up to 80 percent of these trafficking victims are women and girls (UNFPA 2006); (b) the importance of trafficking for the welfare of the female victims and their households back home; and (c) the impact of trafficking on crime, especially organized crime, in the destination countries. Thus research on how to reduce or prevent trafficking of women is a clear priority, and no volume on the migration of women would be complete without at least a brief discussion of trafficking.

Given the enormous weakness of trafficking data (see, for example, Laczko 2002), it is difficult to set out a research agenda in the area of gender and international trafficking. One urgent need is to develop economic models that can predict emerging trafficking risks in particular areas—a type of early-warning system for trafficking. Current data on trafficked persons, based on data collected in destination areas and with significant biases in terms of origin areas covered, do not allow the estimation of such models, though.

Another priority for the formulation of public policy is to determine whether trafficking prevention programs work or not. The most recent *State of the World Population* (UNFPA 2006) confidently notes, "Effective prevention requires a comprehensive approach. This involves education and includes awareness-raising campaigns, community involvement, poverty reduction initiatives, and the creation of livelihood opportunities. It also involves more equitable income distribution and the rebuilding of societies following conflict. Legal reforms that allow equal rights to own and control property and land will help cut the risks associated with the trafficking of women in rural communities."

Yet these confident policy prescriptions on how to combat trafficking may be premature. While there are many examples of interventions and approaches that aim to reduce the vulnerability of women in poor communities, there is little knowledge about which of these approaches and programs are effective and which are not. A first step in establishing a productive research program would be to take stock of the existing data on trafficking of women and of programs designed to deal with this issue. This would help to determine what sort of research is feasible and relevant. It also would help to establish what data are most urgently needed for evaluating the impact of existing programs and designing other ones. Serious impact evaluation work relying on ex ante experimental design or ex post quasi-experimental evaluations also is needed to determine the effectiveness of trafficking prevention programs. Solid criminological research linking trafficking to the emergence or consolidation of organized crime networks in destination countries would also serve to galvanize political will to combat trafficking of women and children.

Temporary, Return, and Circular Migration, Including Mode IV

All migrants who do not remain permanently or for extended periods in their destination country are temporary migrants. Temporary migrants who return to their country of origin are labeled "return migrants." Of these, a smaller subset, referred to as "circular migrants," may be able to migrate to the host country again.[5]

There is a modest literature on gender and temporary migration (see, for example, Yang and Guo 1999). Early work suggested that the labor force insertion of female temporary migrants to the United States from Mexico may be quite different than that of male circular migrants (Kossoudji and Ranney 1984). More recent research looks at the labor market insertion of female temporary migrants in diverse locations such as China and Germany (Roberts et al. 2004; Dustmann 1997).

Host countries tend to prefer temporary to permanent migration because it entails lower fiscal and social costs. However, an issue of great concern is that temporary migrants may overstay and enter the illegal job market. Since temporary migrants typically migrate without their family, one of the determinants of the decision to return is the degree of attachment to the family. First, single migrants have less of an incentive to return than married ones. As for the gender-specific difference in return migration, the answer may depend on the migrants' cultural background. A large number of cultures tend to give more independence to young men than to young women, suggesting that return migration is more prevalent for the latter. Second, mothers are generally thought to be more attached to their children than fathers, implying that married women, particularly mothers, are more likely to return home at the end of their contract period than married men.

These hypotheses should be tested empirically, as should the issue of whether any of the findings hold in general or vary across countries, time, and skill levels. Regarding the impact of skill levels, a plausible hypothesis is that skilled individuals overstay less because they have more to lose from being caught and may have fewer employment opportunities in the illegal job market. Another hypothesis to be examined is that an increase in skill level reduces overstaying to a greater extent for men than for women, since men are more frequently the principal breadwinner in the family.

It is not clear whether circular migration is more prevalent among married women or men. Single men and women are more likely to engage in circular migration than married ones, and—in many cultures—the same is true of single men more than single women, married men more than married women, and married women with no children more than married women with children.

Permanent migration typically entails simultaneous or subsequent migration by the rest of the family. This tendency reduces the incentive to return migrate, although a share of families or individual family members undoubtedly do return migrate. Whether the desire to return is stronger for the husband or the wife is very hard to assess, as is the influence of each on the family's decision in this area.

As noted, host countries have become increasingly concerned with the surge in the number of immigrants and the perceived social and fiscal costs. Temporary migration, which would enable receiving countries to increase the size of their labor force without increasing the size of their permanent population, would help to resolve this problem. The fact that temporary migrant workers return home at the end of the contract period tends to reduce these perceived costs significantly. At the same time, temporary migration schemes may be only an imperfect solution, because migrants might overstay and enter the illegal job market.

More than one type of temporary migration arrangement exists. Temporary migration contracts have typically been between an individual in a source country and an employer in a receiving country. An alternative arrangement would be for a firm employing source-country labor (in the source country or elsewhere) to sign a contract with an employer in a receiving country for the delivery of a type of service that requires the temporary movement of service providers, a type of trade in services known as Mode IV. This type of arrangement exists, for instance, between firms employing workers from countries in South and Southeast Asia and the Gulf countries.

The fear of rich host countries that migrants might overstay is the reason why negotiations on Mode IV (of the General Agreement on Trade in Services, or GATS) at the Doha Round of the World Trade Organization have not advanced so far. This fear, however, is highly exaggerated. The reason is that host-country governments could impose strict regulations that would dramatically reduce the likelihood of overstaying. One such regulation would be for governments to forbid a foreign firm from ever working in their country if any of its employees fail to leave when their contract expires or, alternatively, to levy large fines on the firm for each such violation. This would provide a strong incentive for the firm's owners and managers to set up a screening process in order to improve the selection of employees and for the owners, managers, and workers' supervisors to monitor their behavior. Perhaps more important, it would provide strong incentives for the firm's employees to monitor one another.[6]

Mode IV, which entails the temporary movement of persons working for a service-exporting company, might constitute a powerful mechanism for the empowerment of women. Developed countries' demand for a number of services that are traditionally intensive in female labor is growing rapidly because of rising incomes, continuing increase in women's labor market participation in rich countries, and population aging. The services include domestic service as nannies or maids, work as nurses in health care centers and in private homes, and more. These are occupations that already employ female migrants and where labor shortages are expected to increase in the future.

There are at least three advantages in exporting female rather than male labor-intensive services through mode IV. First, as discussed in the context of temporary migration, women tend to be more attached to their family and are therefore more likely than men to return home at the end of the contract period. Second, the types of jobs that are intensive in female migrant labor, such as nannies and maids, are likely to enable the more educated native-born women in the destination countries to enter the labor force. The increase in the employment of skilled workers would have a positive impact on the productivity and wages of unskilled labor. In other words, immigration of unskilled female labor might result in higher wages for unskilled labor in general (Kremer and Watt 2004). This is not necessarily the case for male immigrant workers.[7] For instance, male immigrants working in construction or agriculture are unlikely to enable skilled people to enter the labor force. Third, female migrants themselves would benefit from the export of services under mode IV as compared to the standard temporary migration agreements. The reason being that contracts would be between host-country employers (firms or households) and foreign firms employing source-country migrant women, rather than between host-country employers and migrant women. This would tend to reduce the likelihood of abuse of female migrants by their employers.

In conclusion, both sending and host countries would benefit from agreements on the provision of services under Mode IV—whether the agreements are made at the bilateral, regional, or multilateral level—and source-country governments could use the information provided here as an additional argument in advocating for an open-door policy by destination countries regarding the temporary movement of female service providers. An "experiment" in promoting the temporary migration of workers in female-intensive services could also prove to be a useful way to test how well the policy works. Trade in male worker–intensive services under Mode IV might be considered at a later stage.

Methodological Issues

This section presents various methodological concerns related to the empirical study of gender-specific migration.

Joint Decision Making

The use of joint decision (or intra-household) migration models would substantially improve our understanding of the determinants of female and male migration as well as of the sequencing of the migration of various household members.

To date, studies on this topic (including chapter 3 in this volume and other papers presented in the critical review in chapter 2) have estimated the determinants of male and female migration separately. However, household migration decisions for women are unlikely to be independent of those for men. Such interdependence should not be assumed a priori; rather, its existence and characteristics should be determined by the data.

Consequently, an important aspect of the research agenda on female migration would be to formulate joint decision migration models where hypotheses on the conditions for the absence of migration or the presence of male migration, female migration, or male-and-female migration could be derived. The estimation of such models would allow hypotheses to be tested empirically. These models could also capture some migration dynamics. For instance, the male adult might migrate first, with the female adult—and other household members—joining after the male has acquired a decent job or the household has saved enough money to pay for the migration costs of the additional migrant(s). This hypothesis could also be tested empirically.

The issue of joint decision making also applies to the choice of destination—internal or international—and to the sector of employment. Mora and Taylor (2006) contribute to this literature by estimating the determinants of migration from rural Mexico for total migration as well as for four categories of migration: internal and international migration and migration to the agricultural and nonagricultural sectors. By disaggregating migration flows into these four categories, this study provides a significant step forward in the analysis of migration determinants. The next step is to integrate the decisions on the various types of migration, including on male and female migration, into a unified framework.

Policy

Few studies explicitly include policy variables in the estimation of the determinants of international migration. One notable exception has been the voluminous and high-quality research examining the impact on Mexico-U.S. migration of the 1986 Immigration Reform and Control Act (IRCA) in the United States and the North American Free Trade Agreement (NAFTA; see Donato 1993; Orrenius and Zavodny 2005). Some recent research by Donato et al. (2003) looks at the gender-disaggregated impacts of the IRCA and uncovers some differential impacts on men and women. This type of research is the exception rather than the rule, however, and more studies should examine gender-differentiated impacts.

Current policies may affect the incentives to migrate and affect them differentially for men and women. For instance, the migration of men tends to respond more strongly to changes in labor market incentives than that of women. Thus policy changes that affect labor market conditions will affect not only migration in general but also the gender composition of migration, with implications for the impact of migration as well. Moreover, through their impact on migration, past policies would also have an impact on current household structure and migrant networks. Thus current and past policy variables should be included in the analysis of gender and migration.

Remittance Costs

Another improvement in methodology that is warranted is to introduce the remittance costs as a determinant of migration; thus far, this variable seems to be missing from empirical analyses.[8] These costs have declined in recent years, especially in high-volume corridors. World Bank (2006) reports a decline at the global level; for instance, costs declined by more than 60 percent between 1999 and 2005 in the U.S.-Mexico corridor. A decrease in remittance costs implies an increase in the benefit obtained from migration and therefore should lead to an increase in migration flows. These costs may also differ for men and women, possibly because of differences in preferences to remit formally versus informally or because of women's more limited access to financial intermediaries in a large number of countries. Moreover, the increase in migration flows associated with a specific reduction in remittance costs is also likely to differ according to gender.

Change in Household Size

One measure of household welfare is per capita income, which is obtained by dividing household income by the number of members. However, migration changes the size of the household. Thus, even if migration does not affect household income, household welfare increases, since the same income is now shared among fewer individuals. Using data from a household survey on Ghana, Schiff (2006) finds that incorporating the change in household size associated with migration results in an impact on poverty that is between 2.5 and 4.5 times greater than when household size is assumed to remain constant.[9]

Income Earned before Migration

In order to identify the impact of male and female migration on household income, it is essential that income is defined and estimated correctly. Various approaches have been used. A number of studies, for example, have estimated the impact of remittances by comparing the situation where migrants send remittances with that where they do not. This approach implicitly assumes that the migration decision is independent of the remittance decision. This is quite unrealistic because one of the basic motives for migrating is to send remittances to the household members in the home country. In other words, one should examine the impact of the joint decision to migrate and remit. This makes quite a difference because migrants may have earned an income before migrating, and this income is lost to the household. Thus the net change in household income is not equal to the amount of remittances but is equal to the difference between remittances and the income the migrant earned before migrating.

The impact on household income of male migrants is likely to differ from that of female migrants because of likely differences in both remittance levels and income earned before migrating. For instance, women's lower labor force participation rate compared to that of men means that their migration entails a smaller loss of income for the household. Recall, though, that the smaller economic loss associated with female migration has to be weighed against the potentially greater noneconomic cost.

Data Considerations

What is the share of women in migration flows? The answer to even such a basic question may hinge on whether the data used are from source or destination countries. For instance, Ibarraran and Lubotsky (2005) show that the share of women age 16 or older in total migrants who migrated in the previous five years from Mexico to the United States obtained from the 2000 Mexican census is 23 percent, while that obtained from the U.S. 2000 census is 40 percent. This problem is likely to apply more generally.

What are the possible reasons for this large gap? First, we know that surveys or censuses in source countries do not capture those households where all members have migrated, because they cannot be surveyed. Assume for simplicity that on the whole these households consist of the same number of male and female members. Because the absolute number of female migrants from Mexico to the United States is smaller than that of males, the *proportion* of female migrants missed by household surveys or censuses in Mexico is greater than that of male migrants. This is not the case for census data in the United States, which cover the entire population, including the migrant population.

Second, assume that the total number of female and male migrants is identical. If men tend to migrate first and women later, there may still be a gap between the volume of female migration captured by surveys in countries of origin and destination. In households where migration takes place sequentially, a larger share of men will tend to migrate before the women do. Thus women can be interviewed before they leave to a greater extent than men because a smaller share of women tend to migrate first and leave male household members behind who can report on them. In other words, a household where the female adult member has migrated is more likely to be completely absent than a household where the male adult member has migrated, in which case the female adult is more likely to remain in the source country. Hence household surveys or censuses tend to capture male migrants to a greater extent than female migrants.

Third, illegal migration may also have an impact on the gap between the share of women in total migrants obtained from censuses in developing source countries and in developed destination countries. The direction of the impact on the gap is not clear, however. Indications exist (see, for instance, chapter 3 in this volume) that men are more likely than women to migrate illegally, both absolutely and proportionately. This seems to hold in the case of migrants from Mexico to the United States.

In this case, male migrants are likely to be undercounted in source-country censuses to a greater extent than female migrants because illegal migration is underreported. However, underreporting is likely to occur at both ends. The degree of underreporting in source or destination countries may depend on the specific countries involved. The U.S. 2000 census tries to capture all migrants by making an assessment of undocumented migrants. Whether they are able to capture all or most of them is difficult to discern. The U.S. 2000 census is typically more detailed than those in other Organisation for Economic Co-operation and Development (OECD) destination countries, so the latter are unlikely to do a better job of covering illegal migrants. A greater degree of underreporting of illegal migrants in the source country will result in a greater gap between the share of women in total migrants obtained from census data in destination countries and the share obtained from household surveys in source countries. The opposite holds if the degree of underreporting is greater in the destination country.

Not only does the undercounting of female relative to male migrants matter for a large number of issues, but so too does their absolute undercounting. The latter creates a downward bias in migrant flows and is likely to bias the evolution of aggregate and bilateral flows as well as gender-specific ones. Second, it also biases the cross-country distribution of bilateral flows if cross-country differences exist in the share of partial-migration and full-migration households or in the share of illegal migrants. Third, the characteristics of the various types of migrants and households are likely to differ. This will bias the estimation results on the determinants and impact of total migration, gender-specific migration, and results on gender differences. For all these reasons, an effort to improve the accuracy of data on the volume of female migration should be high on the research agenda.

There is also a need to collect data on how migration and remittances affect intra-household bargaining in order to explore the impact of both female and male migration on women's empowerment and on the allocation of household expenditures (one conclusion drawn from chapter 5 in this volume). Moreover, a number of important questions will require that the global brain drain database constructed by Docquier and Marfouk (2006) be extended with gender-disaggregated data. The construction of such a database is currently being done by the World Bank.

Concluding Comments

This chapter has attempted to show that there are a host of interesting issues related to gender and migration about which we know very little and that many of them have important policy implications. There are many opportunities for intellectually stimulating and policy-relevant research. This volume, which provides new evidence and analysis, constitutes a modest step in this direction. It will have served its purpose if it acts as a catalyst for further research on gender and international migration.

Endnotes

1. This research is concentrated disproportionately in the Philippines and Thailand. In addition to research on the impact of absent fathers versus absent mothers, research is urgently needed in other sending countries.

2. Assuming that this new technology is increasingly used over time, data could be collected on the evolution of the volume and share of remittances sent that way, the cost, and its impact on household expenditure allocation, in the case of both male and female migrants.

3. In fact, children may have developed anger against their mother to the point that they do not welcome her presence when she returns after a number of years (see the introduction in Ehrenreich and Hochschild 2003).

4. However, the lower share spent on food might be due to greater food consumption by men than by women, particularly if the men worked in physically demanding occupations (such as agriculture) before migration.

5. The issue of Mode IV migration is a potentially important subset of temporary migration.

6. The impact of reciprocal monitoring by the firms' employees is similar to that obtained under the lending arrangements established by the Grameen Bank, where borrowers in a given community are able to obtain new credit only if *all* the loans to the community are repaid. The Grameen Bank experiment has been considered a success (its founder received the Nobel Peace Prize in 2006), enabling thousands of small entrepreneurs—many, if not most, of them women—to borrow small amounts of money to start a microenterprise. There is no reason why the incentives provided for firms' employees to monitor one another would not be as successful in preventing temporary migrant workers from overstaying. Winters, de Janvry, and Sadoulet (1999) have calculated that the global benefits of temporary South-North migration, which equal 3 percent of the labor force in developed OECD countries, are greater than those obtained from eliminating all trade barriers in the world. Nevertheless, until the authorities of destination governments can be convinced that the risks associated with mode IV are sufficiently small, female migrants and their households back home will not be able to capture these potentially huge benefits.

7. The impact of immigration on unskilled wages is still a debated topic. Most receiving countries fear that that the increase in labor supply that the immigrants constitute will result in a decrease in

wages for unskilled natives. However, Peri (2007) finds that during the period 1960–2004, immigration to the state of California stimulated the demand for and wages of most U.S. native workers. He explains that immigrants were imperfect substitutes for natives with similar education and age. As interesting as this result is, it is not clear that it can be generalized to other regions or countries.

8. The remittance cost is likely to be endogenous because an increase in migration raises the level of remittance flows and thus reduces the cost of remitting.

9. The difference in impact varies, depending on the measure of poverty examined (level, depth, or severity) and on the destination of households' migrants (internal, international, or both).

References

Acosta, Pablo. 2007. "Labor Supply, Human Capital, and International Remittances: Evidence from El Salvador." In *International Migration, Policy, and Economic Development: Studies across the Globe*, ed. Çağlar Özden and Maurice Schiff. New York: Palgrave Macmillan.

Battistella, Graziano, and María Cecilia G. Conaco. 1998. "Impact of Labor Migration on the Children Left Behind: A Study of Elementary School Children in the Philippines." *Sojourn* 13 (2): 220–41.

Brockerhoff, Martin, and Xiushi Yang. 1994. "Impact of Migration on Fertility in Sub-Saharan Africa." *Social Biology* 41 (1-2): 19–43.

Bryant, John. 2005. "Children of International Migrants in Indonesia, Thailand, and the Philippines: A Review of Evidence and Policies." Innocenti Working Paper 2005-05. UNICEF, New York.

Choe, Minja K., Sri H. Hatmadji, Chai Podhisita, Corazon Raymundo, and Shyam Thapa. 2004. "Substance Use and Premarital Sex among Adolescents in Indonesia, Nepal, the Philippines, and Thailand." *Asia-Pacific Population Journal* 19 (1): 5–26.

Docquier, Frédéric, and Abdeslam Marfouk. 2006. "International Migration by Education Attainment, 1990–2000." In *International Migration, Remittances, and the Brain Drain*, ed. Çağlar Özden and Maurice Schiff. New York: Palgrave Macmillan.

Donato, Katharine. 1993. "Current Trends and Patterns of Female Migration: Evidence from Mexico." *International Migration Review* 24 (4): 748–71.

Donato, Katharine, Shawn Malia Kanaiaupuni, and Melissa Stainback. 2003. "Sex Differences in Child Health: Effects of Mexico-U.S. Migration." *Journal of Comparative Family Studies* 34: 455–72.

Drèze, Jean, and Amartya K. Sen. 2002. *India: Development and Participation*. Delhi. Oxford University Press.

Dustmann, Christian. 1997 "Differences in the Labor Market Behavior between Temporary and Permanent Migrant Women." *Labour Economics* 4 (1): 29–46.

Ehrenreich, Barbara, and Arlie R. Hochschild, eds. 2003. *Global Women: Nannies, Maids, and Sex Workers in the New Economy*. London: Granta Books.

Fargues, Philippe. 2006. "The Demographic Benefit of International Migration: Hypothesis and Application to Middle Eastern and North African Contexts." Policy Research Working Paper 4050. World Bank, Washington, DC.

Hugo, Graeme. 2000. "Migration and Women Empowerment." In *Women Empowerment and Demographic Process: Moving Beyond Cairo*, ed. Harriet B. Presser and Gita Sen, 287–317. Oxford, U.K.: Oxford University Press.

Ibarraran, Pablo, and Darren H. Lubotsky. 2005. "Mexican Immigration and Self-Selection: New Evidence from the 2000 Mexican Census." Unpublished mss. University of Urbana, Champaign; Inter-American Development Bank, Washington, DC. May. (https://www.nber.org/books/mexico/ibarraran-lubotsky4-2-06.pdf.)

Jensen, Eric, and Dennis Ahlburg. 2004. "Why Does Migration Decrease Fertility? Evidence from the Philippines." *Population Studies* 58 (2, July): 219–31.

Kossoudji, Sherrie A., and Susan I. Ranney. 1984. "The Labor Market Experience of Female Migrants: The Case of Temporary Mexican Migration to the U.S." *International Migration Review* 18 (4): 1120–43.

Kremer, Michael, and Stanley Watt. 2004. "The Globalization of Household Production." Unpublished mss. Harvard University, Cambridge, MA.

Laczko, Frank. 2002. "Human Trafficking: The Need for Better Data." Data Insight, *Migration Information Source,* Migration Policy Institute. (www.migrationinformation.org/Feature/display.cfm?ID=66.)

Lindstrom, David P., and Silvia Giorguli Saucedo. 2002. "The Short- and Long-Term Effects of U.S. Migration Experience on Mexican Women's Fertility." *Social Forces* 80 (4, June): 1341–68.

Malhotra, Anju, Sidney Ruth Schuler, and Carol Boender. 2002. "Measuring Women's Empowerment as a Variable in International Development." Background paper for the World Bank "Workshop on Poverty and Gender: New Perspectives," June.

Mansuri, Ghazala. 2007. "Temporary Economic Migration and Rural Development in Pakistan." In *International Migration, Policy, and Economic Development: Studies across the Globe,* ed. Çağlar Özden and Maurice Schiff. New York: Palgrave Macmillan.

Massey, Douglas S., Mary J. Fischer, and Chiara Capoferro. 2006. "International Migration and Gender in Latin America: A Comparative Analysis." *International Migration* 44 (5): 63–91.

Mora, Jorge, and J. Edward Taylor. 2006. "Determinants of Migration, Destination, and Sector Choice: Disentengling Individual, Household, and Community Effects." In *International Migration, Remittances, and the Brain Drain,* ed. Çağlar Özden and Maurice Schiff. New York: Palgrave Macmillan.

Orrenius, Pia M., and Madeline Zavodny. 2005. "Self-Selection among Undocumented Immigrants from Mexico." *Journal of Development Economics* 78 (1): 215–40.

Parreñas Salazar, Rhacel. 2003. "The Care Crisis in the Philippines: Children and Transnational Families in the New Global Economy." In *Global Women: Nannies, Maids, and Sex Workers in the New Economy,* ed. Barbara Ehrenreich and Arli Hochschild. London: Granta Books.

Peri, Giovanni. 2007. "Immigrants' Complementarities and Native Wages: Evidence from California." NBER Working Paper 12956. National Bureau of Economic Research, Cambridge, MA, March.

Piper, Nicola. 2005. "Gender and Migration." Paper prepared for the Policy Analysis and Research Programme of the Global Commission on International Migration.

Roberts, Kenneth, Rachel Connelly, Zhenming Xie, and Zhenzhen Zheng. 2004. "Patterns of Temporary Labor Migration of Rural Women from Anhui and Sichuan." *China Journal* 52 (July): 49–70.

Scalabrini Migration Center. 2004. *Hearts Apart: Migration in the Eyes of Filipino Children.* Manila: Scalabrini Migration Center.

Schiff, Maurice. 2006. *Migration's Income and Poverty Impact Has Been Underestimated.* IZA Discussion Paper 2088. Bonn: Institute for the Study of Labor (IZA).

UNFPA (United Nations Population Fund). 2006. *State of the World Population 2006: A Passage to Hope; Women and International Migration.* New York: UNFPA.

University of the Philippines, Tel Aviv University, and KAIBIGAN. 2002. "The Study on the Consequences of International Contract Labour Migration of Filipino Parents on Their Children." Final Scientific Report to the Netherlands-Israel Development Research Programme. Manila.

Winters, Paul, Alain de Janvry, and Elisabeth Sadoulet. 1999. "Family and Community Networks in Mexico-U.S. Migration." ARE Working Paper 99-12. University of New England, Graduate School of Agricultural and Resource Economics.

World Bank. 2002. *Empowerment and Poverty Reduction: A Sourcebook.* Washington, DC: World Bank.

———. 2006. *Global Economic Prospects 2006: Economic Implications of Remittances and Migration.* Washington, DC: World Bank.

Yang, Xiushi, and Fei Guo. 1999. "Gender Differences in Determinants of Temporary Labor Migration in China: A Multilevel Analysis." *International Migration Review* 33 (4): 929–53.

Yang, Dean, and Claudia A. Martínez. 2006. "Remittances and Poverty in Migrants' Home Areas: Evidence from the Philippines." In *International Migration, Remittances, and the Brain Drain,* ed. Çağlar Özden and Maurice Schiff, 81–121. New York: Palgrave Macmillan.

INDEX

Figures, notes, and tables are indicated by f, n, and t, respectively.